Compliments
of
Child Development
Services
of
Wyoming

Ghosts from
the Nursery

Ghosts from the Nursery

TRACING THE ROOTS OF VIOLENCE

Robin Karr-Morse and Meredith S. Wiley

The Atlantic Monthly Press
New York

Published simultaneously in Canada
Printed in the United States of America

Library of Congress Cataloging-in-Publication Data
Karr-Morse, Robin
    Ghosts from the nursery : tracing the roots of violence / Robin
Karr-Morse and Meredith S. Wiley.
       p.   cm.
    Includes bibliographical references and index.
    ISBN 0-87113-734-8 (pbk.)
1. Violence in children—United States. 2. Problem children—
United States. 3. Socially handicapped children—United States.
4. Infants—United States—Development. 5. Child psychopathology—
United States. 6. Juvenile delinquency—United States. 7. Violent
crimes—United States. I. Wiley, Meredith S. II. Title.
HQ784.V55K37 1997
618.92'89—dc21   97-15096

Photograph opposite title page copyright © Robin Karr-Morse
Page 364 is an extension of the copyright page.

Design by Laura Hammond Hough

Atlantic Monthly Press
841 Broadway
New York, NY 10003

01 02   15 14 13 12 11 10

To the people who continue to teach us the most:

Erin, Cameron, Jason, Jordan, Gretchen, Bill, and Caroline

and

to a sweet little boy named Kent

Contents

Preface

"Ghosts from the nursery" is an alteration of a phrase coined by psychoanalyst Selma Fraiberg: "ghosts in the nursery." Fraiberg used this phrase to refer to the tendency of parents to bring to the rearing of their children the unresolved issues of their own childhoods. "Ghosts from the nursery" is used to express the idea that murderers and other violent criminals, who were once infants in our communities, are always accompanied by the spirits of the babies they once were together with the forces that killed their promise.

Each chapter in this book is introduced with pieces of the story of Jeffrey, a young murderer. Told in his own words, his brother's words, and excerpts from his child welfare case records, the story in all important aspects is true. Only names, places, and certain facts not central to the actual crime have been altered to protect his identity. Jeffrey currently sits on death row pending the outcome of his appeal. His story was chosen with the help of lawyers, police, and child welfare and mental health professionals because it typifies the profile of a violent, impulsive, but not premeditated or "cold-blooded" murderer. Psychiatric reports confirm that Jeffrey is not sociopathic. While there were three adolescents involved in the crime, Jeffrey's story is the only one told because of limitations of time, space, and the complexity of conveying his detailed recollections pertinent to each chapter. The authors wish to thank all of the professionals and the extended family of Jeffrey who contributed to this story, as well as "Jeffrey" himself. To a great extent, even though facts and individual circumstances in the lives of violent children vary greatly, Jeffrey's story illustrates key factors in the stories of most children who kill. A note of reassurance to parents: Having received feedback on this manuscript from many experienced parents, we fnd that it is a common response to feel anxious or guilty upon recognizing the potentially powerful impact on babies of treatment over which parents may have had little previous knowledge or control. For example, a mother may have consumed alcohol before she knew she was pregnant or may have suffered a period of postpartum depression.

But we may all be reassured that with the possible exception of certain rare head injuries, no one biological or social factor by itself predisposes a child to violent behavior. The research underscores that it is the interaction of multiple factors (such as fetal alcohol syndrome combined with early neglect due to mothers alcoholism combined with physical abuse of the child) which may set the stage for the child's later violent behavior. No one negative experience predisposes children to violence. The multiple factors which, in interaction with each other have been correlated with later violent behavior are presented in Appendix A.

Everyone makes mistakes with babies. We all have done things as parents that we wish we hadn't done. But the human lapses in essentially constrictive interactions with babies be they due to ignorance or desperation, are not the genesis of violence. If this were the case, all of us would be so disposed. The key to understanding the roots of violence is the number of factors at play in relationship to the number of protective factors available in the child's environment.

Acknowledgments

We are deeply grateful to the many people who contributed to this book and made it possible. In particular, we would like to thank Dr. T. Berry Brazelton, Dr. Penelope Leach, Dr. Bruce Perry, and Irving Harris, not only for their significant contributions to our effort, but also for their passionate work and eloquent voices on behalf of infants and toddlers and their families. We would also like to thank Dr. Allan Schore and Dr. Geraldine Dawson, whose incredible work spans the disciplines and transcends the centuries-old nature-nurture dichotomy. And to Dr. Ronald David, our gratitude for your support from the beginning.

Many other researchers also generously contributed their time, shared their work, and, in many cases, read and commented on the manuscript: Kathryn Barnard, Stella Chess, Craig Ramey, Ed Tronick, Charles Nelson, JoAnn Robinson, David Olds, Harry Chugani, Bob Bradley, Mary Rothbart, Jim Satterfield, Breena Satterfield, Sarnoff Mednick, Adrian Raine, Patricia Brennan, Susan Clark, Mary Schneider, Gary Kraemer, Linda Mayes, John Reid, Gerald Patterson, William Greenough, Robert Cairns, David Chamberlain, Ludwig Janus, Charles Golden, and Matthew Melmed. Friends, both professional and personal including Dave Frohnmayer, Ken Magid, Wade Horn, Barbara Fendeisen, Julian Sturton, Susan Conklin, and Eileen Rossick, contributed information and helped put us in touch with a wide network of people.

We would be remiss not to mention our indebtedness to Ron Kotulak for his Pulitzer Prize–winning series of newspaper articles, "Unlocking the Mind," which was published by the *Chicago Tribune* in 1993 and was the first widely disseminated exploration of the new research on early brain development.

We also wish to thank Jeffrey and his family who shared their private lives and painful experiences with us in order to make a difference in the lives of other children. When the task of synthesizing and translating the brain research became at times overwhelming, it was Jeffrey's courage that spurred us on. Also providing their voices and support to this material were Jeffrey's lawyer, his former child welfare caseworker, and a former district attorney who had known Jeffrey as a victim of abuse and neglect. Our thanks, too, to Tammy, who really wanted to help.

Without our editor, Joan Bingham, and the staff at Grove/Atlantic the embryonic vision of this book would not have been born; it was this group who nurtured a concept into reality. Assisting this process on the other coastline was our research assistant Gretchen Berkey, who juggled her babies and household to spend hours in the library and on the internet finding elusive materials—even when the cites were incomplete. Thanks also to Jan Laird whose remarkable computer skills saved the day on more than one occasion, and to Stephen Dow and Janelle Pierce who gave of their hearts as well as their talents to help Robin put the "face of the baby" on the cover in spite of an impossible timeline.

We give a special thanks to Colin, whose quiet voice and critical thinking contributed more than we can possibly convey. His love and unshakable belief in the value of what we were doing invariably pulled us forward when we became discouraged.

And special appreciation goes to our children and their spouses, our grandchildren, and friends who put up with our frequent and lengthy disappearances to Black Butte Ranch and who loved us anyway—especially Jordy.

Introduction

This book is a call to alarm. It presents data to document what we have long observed: that experiences in infancy which result in the child's inability to regulate strong emotions are too often the over-looked source of violence in children and adults. Story after story points to the importance of intrauterine conditions and early experiences which can lead to future violent behavior. The elegant writing in this book belies its frightening message.

I first met Robin Karr-Morse and Meredith Wiley in 1991 when they asked me to present my research in infancy to the Oregon legislature's Children's Care Team. We became soulmates immediately. Robin and Meredith were shepherding the team which was created to revamp the state's system of services for families with children in response to growing numbers of children who were suffering serious maltreatment.

Having worked in the trenches with children and their families in both private practice and public service, Robin was the consultant to the Care Team. Meredith, with a legal and political background, was the firebrand chief of staff for the speaker of the house. Robin's front line observations of the impact of early maltreatment on children's lives were central in shaping a focus on early and accessible "one-stop" services for families which begin prenatally. But the battle for preventive social services was not, and still is not, easily won.

As Robin and Meredith worked in Oregon to convince legislators of the importance of beginning early, they found that there was too little evidence in the research literature to back up the common-sense understanding that early experience shapes a child's future toward good or evil. They were struggling against huge odds as they attempted to enlist public funds to begin earlier to address child abuse and neglect, welfare, and hunger. There was too little published to convince the American public, let alone legislators and governors, of this necessity. Hence this book.

The authors have done a monumental job of capturing our present knowledge of early development and the influences of the earliest environment on a child's developmental processes. This volume is already a timely classic to add to the present surge of interest in early experience as it relates to the epidemic of violence in our nation. The recent meeting at the White House represented the Clintons' and Gores' sounding of the alarm. Early brain development and its relation to later deviations in impulse control and to the repetition of developmental deprivation and violence was outlined. The nation was alerted to the neglect of our most vulnerable sector-small children. We are the richest, most powerful nation, and yet, we are the least child and family-oriented culture in the civilized world. This volume lays the foundation for a groundswell of public awareness. Hopefully, this alert will lead to solutions. Will they cost a lot? Compared to what!

This book is a call to all of us. It is beautifully written and well documented. If all who care about children and families can use it, maybe we can turn around the tide of our nation's surge toward violence and self-destruction. Otherwise, our children and grandchildren will face a devastating future. We cannot afford any longer to bury our heads in the sand. We do know what to do. This excellent piece of work documents that. Can we create the national will to do it?

—Dr. T. Berry Brazelton

Ghosts from
the Nursery

1

Ghosts from the Nursery

Do Lawd, come down here and walk amongst yo people
And tek 'em by the hand and telt 'em
That yo ain't hex wid 'em
And do Lawd come yoself,
Don't send yo son,
Cause dis ain't no place for chillen.

—PRAYER FOLLOWING EARTHQUAKE OF 1866,
CHARLESTON, SOUTH CAROLINA, COMPOSED BY SLAVES

In the middle of the night, on May 11, 1993, in the rural Northwest,
an eighty-four-year-old man was bludgeoned to death. Three teenag-
ers, high on drugs, had been on a joyride, which by morning included
stealing a car, robbing a convenience store, and murder. The youths
first knocked on the old man's door and then broke inside to use the
bathroom. Jeffrey later confessed to striking the victim on the head with
a flashlight that the man had given them to find their way in the dark.
The man was then kicked by the youths as he lay on the floor. He
was found unconscious the next afternoon by a neighbor, lying near
the front door of the farmhouse where he had lived all of his life and
where he had seen the raising of his children, grandchildren, and great-
grandchildren. He died several months after the attack without ever
regaining consciousness.

The youths were identified by several witnesses as Jeffrey, age six-
teen; Roger, age seventeen; and Roger's girlfriend Crystal, age four-
teen. Both Jeffrey and Roger had juvenile records. Crystal did not.
Crystal was granted immunity and was not prosecuted. Roger was
convicted of robbery and sentenced to twenty years. After the victim
died, Roger was charged with murder and is now awaiting trial on
that charge. Jeffrey pleaded guilty to the robbery and was sentenced to
life imprisonment. After the victim's death, Jeffrey was charged with
murder, tried by a jury, found guilty, and sentenced to death. His case
is currently being appealed.

He looks like the kid next door. Unassuming, he greets you
through the prison visitors' window with a shy but ready smile. He is
nervous, speaks thoughtfully, and clearly appreciates your attention.
His body and his mind move quickly. Anxious for approval, he pours
out complete explanations of what he anticipates you came to ask,
far more than you would comfortably request. You are a stranger to

this boy, but you recognize your own kids' mannerisms, language, interests. He is just days past his eighteenth birthday. He likes to sing and write poetry, which he shares somewhat hesitantly, glancing up often to gauge your reaction. His light brown hair is clean and well kept. His eyes are hazel and clear. Insights unusual for one so young permeate his stories. He chooses to stand apart from his present peer group, hanging out mostly with his cellmate, with whom he shares an interest in self-education and social reform, particularly of the criminal justice system.

Three years ago Jeffrey seemed like just another kid living in the backwash of an unremarkable rural community. A casual observer might have easily overlooked the predictably explosive mixture of life circumstances that heralded disaster for Jeffrey—to say nothing of his victim. Jeffrey's story is one told hundreds of times daily in courtrooms across our nation. It is a story told by events, psychiatric reports, interviews with victims, witnesses, friends, and family. The quest for explanations in the aftermath of violence often delves into adolescence, into grade school and childhood. But the beginning of stories like Jeffrey's goes untold. One chapter is nearly always missing—the first chapter, encompassing gestation, birth, and infancy. And because it goes unseen and unacknowledged, it repeats itself over and over at a rate now growing in geometric proportions.

We overlook this period in our search for the causes of violence because we believe that it is irrelevant, not only to this particular crime, but to later experience generally. The popular belief in the United States is that the baby, let alone the fetus, is exempt from thought and the capacity to record enduring experiences. Nothing could be further from the truth. This overlooked chapter of early growth sees the building of the capacities for focused thinking and for empathy—or the lack of these. From the time of late gestation and birth, we begin to develop a template of expectations about ourselves and other people, anticipating responsiveness or indifference, success or failure. This is when the foundation of who we become and how we relate to others and to the world around us is built.

So Jeffrey's story and others like his become ghost stories. Accompanying this convicted murderer to death row is the ghost of the baby he once was and the echoes of the forces that transformed that baby. As is true of most ghosts, these aspects remain invisible, at least to the naked eye. And in that invisibility lies the power of these forces to continue to haunt us.

Though he was just sixteen at the time of his crime, many would argue that Jeffrey was an accountable adult. When faces like his appear in the news, we see the adult or adolescent criminal and place responsibility with the individual, holding him culpable for his actions. We can readily dismiss the Jeffreys as criminals who now deserve to pay their debt to society. There are procedures and facilities in place to contain and punish adults. That these people are costly to taxpayers, that their contributions are lost to society, and that their numbers are growing at an alarming rate are all issues that concern us.

But the truly terrifying and more complicated addition to this conversation is the wave of new young criminal faces in the news, such as the eighty-pound twelve-year-old whose chin barely rises above the table in a hearing room of the Wenatchee, Washington, courthouse. His thin wrists are cuffed and his ankles are bound with chains. As he sits listening to the prosecutor tell the story of his premeditated murder of a migrant farm worker, his legs barely touch the floor. Using handguns stolen earlier in the afternoon, this boy and several friends had strolled along the Columbia River firing at bottles and logs. When fifty-year-old Emilio Pruneda called from a nearby thicket to "chill out," the boys circled the thicket and fired. Pruneda threw a rock, hitting one boy in the face. The boys fired more shots and then ran to a bank and reloaded the guns. When they found Pruneda lying where he had been hit earlier, one boy emptied the rounds from a .22 caliber semiautomatic pistol and a .22 caliber revolver into Pruneda. There were eighteen bullet holes in his body.

In May of 1995, headline news introduced the country to Robert Sandifer, nicknamed Yummy. Yummy was an eleven-year-old gang member who, having shot a fourteen-year-old girl, brought so much negative attention to his gang that he was executed by them. Yummy was found dead in a highway underpass, shot in the back of the head. His executioners were fourteen and sixteen years old. Yummy captured the nation's attention when he appeared on the cover of *Time* magazine in June 1995. Later that month in an interview with Patrick Murphy, the Cook County public defender, Oprah Winfrey asked whether Yummy and others like him had "slipped through the cracks." Murphy responded emphatically:

> There was no crack here. We knew—we should have known exactly what was going on. . . . What you saw in Sandifer wasn't a kid who fell between the cracks. You saw a kid that was born to a mom who had her first child when she was fifteen, who was welfare-dependent, who came from a family who is welfare dependent. . . . The grandmother was in her younger thirties when Mom had the kid at fifteen. Robert's father . . . was in and out of the picture at best. When he [Robert] came into the system at two years and ten months, he had cigarette burns on his arm, his neck, his butt. . . . The sister was brought into the system when she was ten months old, about three months before Robert. . . . She had second-degree burns in her vagina, and the mother said that she dropped her on the radiator.[1]

Very young and generally undetected victims of trauma or chronic maltreatment who become very young perpetrators of violence are no longer rare news stories. And the growing percentage of the crimes being committed by these children are shocking in their cruelty and aggression: a ten year old who killed a nine-month-old baby by kicking and hitting her with shoes and a basketball until she stopped crying; a four year old who climbed into a crib in his grandmother's day care center and stomped an eight-week-old baby to death; a ten year old who killed an eighty-four-year-old neighbor by beating her with her cane and then slashing her throat with a knife from her kitchen; four second-grade boys who pinned a seven-year-old girl to the ground during recess and tried to kill her for "breaking up" with their eight-year-old gang leader.

As in Jeffrey's case, we don't see the ghosts from the nursery in these stories. Because of the tender age of these criminals, however, as we look for explanations, we may look more in depth at the childhoods they have not yet left behind. It is this group of offenders, children twelve and under with a history of chronic aggression, who are forcing us to look earlier. For the majority of these early offenders, the records are clear: By age four they show consistent patterns of aggression, bullying, tantrums, and coercive interactions with others.[2]

The headline of a *New York Times* article on November 19, 1995, which reported a decline in the rate of adult crime also warned of "coming storms of juvenile crime." Professor John DiIulio of Princeton University said that we are experiencing "a lull before the crime storm." He cited the "40 million kids 10 years old and younger" who are about to become teenagers, the largest group of adolescents in a generation. He believes that there are more children now than ever before who are growing up without guidance, responsibility, or internalized social values.

The Uniform Crime Report issued by the FBI in October 1997 shows that for the last two years there has been a decrease in violent crimes by juveniles. The report also shows that given this decrease, the juvenile arrest rate for violent crime far exceeds the adult rate (464.7 per thousand compared to 318.3 per thousand among adults.) James Alan Fox, Dean of Criminal Justice at Northeastern University responded that the new numbers are "reason to be hopeful, but not reason to be overconfident." In a press conference following the release of the data Fox pointed out that the population of teen-agers will grow by fifteen percent by 2005. "If we become complacent and think that all of our problems are over, we will be blind-sided by another crime wave," he responded. In spite of the recent drop, the violent crime rate among juveniles has quadrupled over the last twenty-five years and the last decade has seen a doubling of weapons offenses for children 10 to 17. Internalized or self-directed violence has also soared, with the suicide rate for children ten to fourteen years of age tripling in the same period. Aggravated assault by teenagers has jumped by 64 percent in the last decade. And forty American children have been killed in schools each year for the last five years.

Reported nationwide trends on the magnitude and the projected magnitude of juvenile crime vary depending on the source. Many, if not most, knowledgeable individuals at local, state, and national levels remain concerned about the rates of aggression and violence among young people. School resources for dealing with delinquent children at the junior and senior high school level, particularly in city schools, are increasingly overwhelmed beyond their capacities. The juvenile justice system is similarly besieged. And the building of prisons is a major growth industry in the nation.

On March 9, 1997, the U.S. Department of Justice released the results of a new study that showed that if our present rates of incarceration continue, one out of every twenty babies born in the United States today will spend some part of their adult lives in state or federal prison. An African-American male has a greater than one in four chance of going to prison in his lifetime, while a Hispanic male has a one in six chance of serving time.[3] A quarter of all households in the United States are victimized by crime each year. Homicide is a leading cause of death among our young people.[4] And our prison population has exploded. California, for example, is now spending more on its criminal justice system than on higher education.[5] Though we have been greatly concerned about government spending on the U.S. health care system, which many deem to be in crisis, we have not noticed that the cost of the criminal justice system is three times the cost of the nation's entire health care budget.

While we have more than doubled our rate of incarceration in the last decade, people still do not feel safe. The inmate population is expected to expand further as politicians of all stripes try to outdo each other in being "tough on crime." If the current rate continues, according to the *New York Times,* the number of people incarcerated will soon overtake the number of people attending colleges and universities in our country. Already one in three African-American men in this country are under the supervision of the criminal justice system.[5] Even community policing—our most effective crime prevention effort to date—has resulted in warnings from the officers that they can already see a wave of children who in numbers and in depth of rage far exceed our current levels of concern.

Media coverage of violence—murder and rape, gang violence, serial killings, the murder of parents, children, and coworkers—treats violent behavior as if it suddenly emerges from a developmental void. It is a rare story that looks for the sources of this behavior even in preadolescence or grade school. And this is far from the real root in most cases. In order to understand the tide of violent behavior in which America is now submerged, we must look before preadolescence, before grade school, before preschool to the cradle of human formation in the first thirty-three months of life. Those months, including nine months of prenatal development and the first two years after birth (33 months), harbor the seeds of violence for a growing percentage of American children. In the violence equation, in the stories of Jeffrey and each of the children described earlier, this is chapter one, the missing chapter.

The ghosts of children lost to rage and despair, overlooked or abused by a community unaware of their existence, do retaliate. These children—like all children—"do unto others." It may be easy and politically expedient to ignore them or to close our eyes to the appalling circumstances of their lives while they are voiceless and powerless—little bodies tucked away where no one is looking. But these children—grown larger and angrier—are swelling the rising tide of violent young offenders in our communities. Rage-filled adolescents only seem to come out of nowhere. They come, too often, from the nursery.

We yearn for simple answers. When horrific details reel from television or newspaper stories, we grasp for quick explanations. We want to believe that we can separate ourselves from the infection. Poverty and race become easy scapegoats. But neither adequately explains the increase in violence, particularly not among younger and younger children. The answers are complex but no longer unknowable.

Historically, theories have abounded regarding the source of criminal behavior. Much of this discussion has been polarized by a pervasive and very human effort to reduce this quest to a single factor. The "nature-nurture" argument has raged for hundreds of years and has crossed many fields, including science, religion, and philosophy. The effort to account for criminal behavior—especially violent criminal behavior—is confounded by the complexity of human nature, to say nothing of cultural variables.

But we have made progress. We know, for example, that in spite of a clear role for genetics in explaining some antisocial behavior, there is no "crime gene." Several studies point to the possible role of heritable genes in explaining chronic property crimes such as stealing, but no links have been found for inherited tendencies toward violent crimes.[6] On the other hand, genetic deficits stemming from environmental causes such as prenatal exposure to alcohol or drugs do play a strong role in setting up violent behavior.[7] By causing subtle changes in the organization of the genes of the fetus, the baby's brain may be damaged, causing, for example, difficulty with focusing on learning or controlling impulsive behavior. These vulnerabilities in turn render the child even more vulnerable to negative environmental conditions such as child abuse or neglect. Genes may have a role in shaping later violent behavior, but environmentally altered rather than inherited genes are implicated. And in order for even those altered genes to have an adverse role in later behavior, they must interact with negative factors in the child's environment. For example, during the early critical period of maturation of the brain, prolonged periods of intense stress may actually alter DNA, the building material of the genes.[8]

The understanding of the interaction between internal vulnerabilities and external risk factors is essential to understanding the story of Jeffrey and the plethora of young criminals surfacing in the following pages. This interactive process is even more crucial as we seek to understand adult violence. In a hallmark study of the genesis of violent behavior in 1989, noted criminologist Dorothy Lewis found that neither exposure to early violence nor internal factors alone predicts adult violence. She also found that the combination of one vulnerability with an abusive family was not predictive of adult violence. While each of these factors is a clear warning signal that a child may be on a course toward violence, Lewis found that adult criminal violence resulted from the interaction of two or more internal factors (i.e., cognitive and/or neuropsychiatric deficits) with early negative family circumstances. Lewis's theory amplifies the new emphasis on the interaction between these internal vulnerabilities and negative environmental factors. In reviewing the medical histories of violent juvenile delinquents, Lewis found a significantly higher incidence of neuropsychiatric and cognitive impairments among the most aggressive offenders, including hyperactivity, impulsivity, attention deficits, and learning disabilities. Both prenatal complications and serious accidents or injuries appeared often in their histories. The parts of the brain responsible for judgment, impulse control, and reality testing are disproportionately impaired in this population, along with the capacity for empathy and the ability to accurately interpret the actions and intent of other people.[9]

This analysis of the biological and social variables that go into the making of adult violence places a whole new emphasis on the human brain, where all of the variables meet and where central control is generated for all of our behaviors. Dr. Bruce Perry of Baylor University succinctly summarizes this concept by saying: "It's not the finger that pulls the trigger, it's the brain; it's not the penis that rapes, it's the brain."[10] As the brain and its functions emerge as the mediator of human experience, we begin to appreciate the crucial nature of physical, emotional, and cognitive care during the first thirty-three months of human life. As we begin to discover the previously unimaginable impact of the smallest insult to the brain at crucial times in development, we are beginning to see that much of what we have formerly written off as unknowable in origin and therefore unchangeable, can and must be prevented. The current upswing in violent behavior is a clear sign of systemic distress. If human life is to continue, our entire species needs to attend differently to our young.

Thirty years ago, Rachel Carson penned her classic *Silent Spring*. That book was an urgent warning by a field biologist who was distressed by the plight of eagles, peregrine falcons, and many songbirds

11

that were quietly disappearing from the American landscape. Carson revealed an unseen and insidious threat to the entire chain of life. Through the use of DDT and other chemicals routinely applied in farming, forestry, and mosquito abatement, our nation was leading the world into destruction of the natural environment. Not only were pesticides poisoning our air, earth, rivers, and seas, they threatened the survival of our own species.

In spite of considerable controversy and an ongoing debate, *Silent Spring* penetrated the national consciousness. A spring without songbirds was a chilling image, and, in contemplating that grim prospect, we finally began to understand the true price of insecticides. Carson confronted us with our own passive participation in the destruction of the natural world. We now understand the intricate linkages that exist and the cumulative devastation that occurs when poisons are introduced at the front of the ecosystem.

More than thirty years after *Silent Spring,* however, we have yet to understand that the same dynamic is at work in the human system. Toxic experiences—family violence, abuse, and chronic neglect, along with toxic substances such as nicotine, alcohol, and illegal drugs—are being physically and emotionally absorbed by our babies in record numbers. As a result of this systemic degradation at the beginning of human life, our nation faces a threat that is potentially as lethal as the effects of DDT.

As in the natural world, there are complex links between the quality of individual human development and the status of the human community. Infancy, a time to which our nation is blindsided, is a crucial developmental stage when an individual forms the core of conscience, develops the ability to trust and relate to others, and lays down the foundation for lifelong learning and thinking. The quality of the human environment is directly tied to each individual's ability to love, to empathize with others, and to engage in complex thinking. By failing to understand the cumulative effects of the poisons assaulting our babies in the form of abuse, neglect, and toxic substances, we are participating in our own destruction.

Our ignorance of and indifference to the complex nature of infancy has significantly contributed to one sign of systemic distress that we can no longer ignore. Violence is now epidemic in American society. It dominates our media, permeates our play, steals our loved ones, implodes our families, and claims a growing percentage of our young. Our response is to deploy the most rapid rate of incarceration in the world.

While it appears that the overall crime rate has decreased slightly, over the last three years (the last data available are for 1995), crime remains a source of great concern in the United States, particularly as compared to other industrialized nations. In April 1997, *Parade* magazine reported an Interpol census that analyzed America's status in relation to the rest of the world on a number of indicators.[11] The census reported that in spite of recent decreases, we have the second highest murder rate of all industrialized nations, after Russia. In addition, compared to all nations in the world, including developing third world nations, we have the second highest rape rate, the eleventh highest rate of serious assault, and the third highest violent rate of theft.

Each year the Children's Defense Fund publishes a yearbook entitled *The State of America's Children*. According to their 1996 and 1997 issues:

- A baby is born every minute to a teen mother.
- The mortality rate for American babies under the age of one is higher than that of any other western industrialized nation; African-American babies are more than twice as likely to die in their first year of life as white babies.
- Twenty-five percent of our preschool children live below the poverty level.
- One in four foster children in five states sampled entered foster care before his or her first birthday. Newborns make up the largest share of those infants.
- One in three victims of physical abuse is a baby less than twelve months old. Every day a baby dies of abuse or neglect at the hands of his or her caregivers.

- Three of every four children murdered in the twenty-six top industrialized nations *combined* were American.
- Only 8.4 percent of infant and toddler care in U.S. child care centers is considered developmentally appropriate care; 51.1 percent was judged mediocre quality care, and 40.4 percent poor quality care.

In reviewing this data, the Carnegie Corporation called this the "quiet crisis."[12] The grim reality is that a growing percentage of our babies are now gestating in and being born into an environment perfectly designed to breed rage and despair. Violence takes many forms—physical, emotional, social, verbal—to name but a few. It has many definitions and is to some degree a concept that varies with time and culture. For example, killing for God or country or ideological affiliations may be considered a noble and highly valued behavior. Killing as random vengeance is generally not. For the purposes of this discussion, violence is defined as behavior not condoned by law, which is intended to inflict harm on others, behavior that actively victimizes another person by an aggressive act. Perpetrators of unlawful violence fall roughly into one of two types: impulsive or premeditated. The great majority of violent crime committed in this country is of the impulsive type. Most of the research in this area is based on the study of "hot-blooded" impulsive violence. While premeditated, or "cold-blooded," violent behavior has some roots in common with impulsive violence, it also develops from some unique causes. Whenever relevant, these two distinct paths of development are distinguished in the following chapters.[13]

While the causes of violence are highly complex and multifaceted, a growing body of scientific knowledge demonstrates that maltreatment during the nine months of fetal growth and the first twenty-four months after birth often leads to violent older children and adults. The poisons accumulating in the human community from widespread maltreatment of babies are only in part the toxins we already recognize—drugs, alcohol, and tobacco. The last three decades have provided us with research that brings to light a range of more subtle toxins profoundly influencing our children's earliest development: chronic stress or neglect, which affects the development of the fetal or early infant brain; early child abuse and neglect, which undermine focused learning; chronic parental depression; neglect or lack of the stimulation necessary for normal brain development; early loss of primary relationships or breaks in caregiving. These are the precursors of the growing epidemic of violence now coming to light in childhood and adolescence.

We must broaden the scope of our conversation about violence. Infancy and toddlerhood are times of enormous complexity when potentials for favorable adult outcomes can be maximized, diminished, or lost. Through the interplay of the developing brain with the environment during the nine months of gestation and the first two years after birth, the core of an individual's ability to think, feel, and relate to others is formed. Violent behavior often begins to take root during those thirty-three months as the result of chronic stress, such as domestic or child abuse, or through neglect, including the prenatal ingestion of toxins. Even where violent behavior does not occur as a direct result of these stressors, maltreatment of a baby may lead to the permanent loss or impairment of key protective factors—such as intelligence, trust, and empathy—that enable many children to survive and even overcome difficult family circumstances and later traumas.

And so we return to Jeffrey. Through his story we can see that there are many kinds of ghosts from the nursery. Some result from biological factors such as head injuries or learning disabilities. Others emerge from familial experiences such as child abuse, domestic violence, or the impact of maternal depression or rejection. As children grow older, larger societal factors, such as chronic community violence, may compound the damage from earlier experiences. One factor by itself rarely creates antisocial outcomes in human development.[15] As in Jeffrey's case, several factors combine to produce those outcomes. But a majority take root in the nursery, where few people are looking.

2

Grand Central:

EARLY BRAIN ANATOMY AND VIOLENCE

"But, I don't understand you," said Dorothy, in bewilderment. "How was it that you appeared to me as a great head?"

"That was one of my tricks," answered Oz. "Step this way and I will tell you all about it."

He led the way to a small chamber in the rear of the Throne Room, and they all followed him. He pointed to one corner, in which lay the Great Head, made out of many thicknesses of paper, and with a carefully painted face.

"This I hung from the ceiling by a wire," said Oz; "I stood behind the screen and pulled a thread, to make the eyes move and the mouth open."

—L. FRANK BAUM
The Wizard of Oz

Psychiatric testing shows that he is neither psychopathic or socio-pathic. He has a problem controlling his impulses. Sometimes he does things without being able to stop what he is doing. He can know it is very wrong when he starts and still keep doing it or he can know that something he is doing is right and then do it excessively. He constantly seeks attention as if he has been deprived of it. He has social skills that are sufficient to interact with other people but his relationships, for the most part, are superficial. . . . He comes from an extremely chaotic, tense, and abusive home environment which is characterized by harsh and inconsistent discipline. Not surprisingly, given his early home en-vironment, he has significant interpersonal difficulties. This is to be expected. If you don't know how to act and you are not taught this at home, you will act inappropriately elsewhere. As this pattern of inter-personal difficulties continues, anger or violent behavior may result. To cope with his frightening and unpredictable home environment, Jeffrey learned to think of himself first and others later. . . . He func-tions within the normal range in his intellectual capacities and out-side the normal range in his ability to control some of his impulses. At the time of this evaluation, he showed extreme anxiety and was ex-tremely depressed. He had alcohol and substance abuse problems from a relatively early age. . . . He was introduced to serious drugs before the age of five. This is significant in that many of the drugs he reports ingesting are mood intensifiers that affect the limbic region of the brain.

—TESTIMONY OF FORENSIC PSYCHOLOGIST
FROM JEFFREY'S LEGAL DEFENSE FILE

THE HUMPTY DUMPTY YEARS

Like the Wizard of Oz manipulating the show of sounds and lights for Dorothy, the human brain lies at the seat of control of all human behavior. Until very recently we had limited opportunities to look inside at this mysterious three-pound wizard nestled inside the human skull. Because of ethical considerations the primary research methodologies have historically been limited to studies on animals and the rare human specimens available through autopsy. But with new technologies like the Positron Emission Topography (PET) scan and Magnetic Resonance Imaging (MRI), we can now look inside the living human brain with noninvasive techniques that produce graphic images of what is going on. The "wizard", while becoming less mysterious, is inspiring even more awe as we begin to comprehend the complex machinations that take place to produce even the simplest behaviors.

Seemingly normal at birth, Chelsea was born more than forty years ago in a small coastal town in the Pacific Northwest. But unknown to her parents—and to a host of doctors who by school age evaluated her as retarded—Chelsea was deaf. She was isolated in school, where she was classified as being of low intelligence. It wasn't until she was thirty-one years old that a neurologist recognized her real disability and had her fitted with a hearing aid. Now Chelsea is an active member of her community. She works in a veterinary clinic. The only problem is that after fifteen years of therapy and with normal intelligence, she still cannot speak intelligibly. Chelsea is living testimony to the lesson that in human brain development, there is a critical period for spoken language. Because her brain was deprived of the sounds she needed to hear at a crucial time, the physical connections necessary for organizing speech in coherent sentences have forever been lost to her. Chelsea will never master normal sentence construction.[1]

Ryan was born to an unmarried college student who decided that the best future for her baby would be secured by placing him with married parents through adoption. However, the adoption agency, unaware at that time of the importance of earliest attachment, was concerned about Ryan's irregular heartbeat. A response to anesthesia his mother had received for her cesarean delivery, the arrhythmia disappeared fairly quickly. But since medical assurances were paramount to the agency, it placed Ryan in a private foster home where, without the social worker's knowledge, the foster mother was taking care of nine other children under age three.

Ryan lay in a crib day after day. He drank cold milk from bottles that were propped to feed him. He heard the sounds of the other children, but he rarely saw an adult face. He was handled infrequently; his diapers went unchanged for most of the day. He developed a full-body rash, a bleeding diaper rash, cradle cap, ear infections in both ears, and, most fearsome, an unwillingness to be held or to look at an adult face. At nine weeks, when Ryan was finally placed in his adoptive home, he would turn away from efforts to engage him, staring instead at a bright light or a shining object. He had gained weight normally and, in spite of his rash, was a handsome, red-haired baby. But he did not want to be touched. If he cried, he preferred to lie on a flat space, where he would comfort himself. Ryan was not autistic. He was twice separated from major caregivers and severely neglected. What his brain had missed was touch, trust, and reciprocal contact with a parent. Now twenty-five years old, Ryan looks normal. He is a college student and works full-time. But he is still somewhat withdrawn, and his relationships with people, while improving each year, are superficial and lack spontaneity. Trust is still precarious for Ryan. Touch is still measured.

Neither Chelsea nor Ryan is a violent individual in spite of early losses. Both were raised in loving homes and environments that were protective and prosocial. But Chelsea and Ryan remind us that there are "critical periods" and sensitive periods for several key aspects of human development, including the ability to trust or to feel connected to other people. While we might like to believe that given sufficient opportunity we can reverse any damage done to children, the research tells us that the effects of some early experiences cannot be undone.

Scientists use two terms to describe these specifically timed processes. "Critical periods" is a phrase used to describe a window of time in which a specific part of the brain is open to stimulation, after which it closes forever. In human development, neurobiological researchers have confirmed two functions that develop in such critical periods—vision and spoken language. Both fall into a very specific "use it or lose it" opportunity in early life. "Sensitive periods" is a phrase used primarily by psychologists to describe a less precise period of time when it appears that key functions are strongly affected but may not be lost forever. Examples of these functions include the acquisition of a second language and math and logic development.

The enormous power of human experience in shaping the brain has only been gradually accepted following the pioneering work of Dr. David Hubel and Dr. Torsten Wiesel done nearly forty years ago. The doctors sewed shut one eye of newborn kittens to test the effects of sensory deprivation. When the sewn eyes were opened a few weeks later, they were permanently blinded. But the eyes that had remained open could see better than normal eyes. No amount of visual stimulation following this experience could restore sight in the blind eyes. The same procedures performed in adult cats did not result in this rewiring. The doctors received a Nobel Prize for their landmark finding that sensory experience is essential to teach developing brain cells their jobs and that there is a short and early critical period for connecting the retina to the visual cortex, beyond which the opportunity is forever lost.

Babies born with cataracts have taught us that this dependence on environmental input is also true for humans in the development of vision. Babies with cataracts who did not receive surgery in the earliest months grew up blind because the brain cells that would normally process vision died or were called to work elsewhere. By four months of age, babies totally deprived of vision from birth are blind. Children who grow up alone or in the wild without exposure to language until age ten cannot ever learn to speak. In addition, when a baby is deprived of hearing human voices, the connections that allow brain cells to process sound, and consequently language, can become ineffectual. Instead of the neat columns of cells that are characteristic of normal brain structure, the cells are scrambled. The resulting aberrant formation of the cells that provide the biological underpinnings of speech may cause language disorders and in some cases may result in childhood seizures and epilepsy.[2]

Capacities acquired during critical periods have been confirmed by new graphic imaging techniques that actually illustrate the growth of connections between brain cells going on inside the brain at specific sites such as the visual cortex during the critical period. Sensitive periods have been delineated primarily through the longitudinal study of human behavior. Some scientists speculate that growth and changes occurring during sensitive periods involve the integration of several rather than one key system of the developing brain. As knowledge of the human brain and its development becomes more sophisticated, it is possible that scientists will develop techniques to document the neural components of the now much more ephemeral behavioral changes, such as the development of trust, with graphic images of corresponding changes in brain physiology or chemistry.

While the last decade has shown that the developing brain retains great "plasticity," including the ability to offset damages in most areas, there are exceptions. And the exceptions primarily occur with key systems developing in earliest childhood. We used to believe that the brain and its activity were set on course and developed on a path controlled entirely by heritable genetic programming. From this perspective, we believed that the brain like any other organ grew to its genetically predestined size and function uninterrupted from the outside world except by injury or disease or the influence of drugs. A burst of new research in the last decade has shown us conclusively that this is far from reality. To the surprise of no one who has specialized in observing the rapid pace of fetal and newborn development, the new technologies show the rest of us some previously unimaginable truths about human brain growth.

The most amazing result of all has been the portrait that emerges of the brain itself. Far from the preset, isolated, and independently functioning organ pictured in our biology texts of a decade ago, the brain is, in fact, a dynamic organism that is constantly reflecting and adjusting to the environment the individual is experiencing. While genetics do set the broad parameters, actual matter in the brain is built—or not—by sound, sight, smell, touch, and movement from the outside environment. By the eighteenth week of gestation, when the brain is still primitive, the fetus has developed all of the one hundred to two hundred billion basic brain cells or neurons that it will ever have in a lifetime. But by birth, connecting structures (dendrites and synapses) between those nerve cells have just started to form. Those connections now depend on the outside environment for completion. Stimulation from the baby's world actually generates the building of the corresponding systems to process that stimulation in the baby's brain. Seeing people and objects, for example, generates the building of dendritic and synaptic growth in the visual cortex; hearing sounds builds the auditory cortex; and so forth.

Both the matter of the brain and to some degree the function this matter performs are generated by exposure to stimulation. Because we are each different genetically and because each of our environments is different, no two brains are exactly alike. Babies who are talked to and read to or who are exposed to more than one language are building a different set of connections than those who are receiving primarily large-muscle stimulation—patty-cake, prewalking games, etc. While there are scientists such as Dr. Frank Kiel of Cornell University who believe that the brain comes prewired with some concepts, such as a preference for a human face over inanimate objects, there is general agreement in the scientific community that even before birth the brain is shaped by stimulation from the environment. After birth, development is an interactive process between the baby's physiology and his or her environment.

The dependence of the human brain on the environment for its growth begins to make sense when one considers the purpose of the brain in all organisms. The primary goal of the brain is to enable the organism to survive. The key to survival and to human dominance on the planet is our ability to adapt to the kind of environment in which we find ourselves. Live video photographs can now show us that both the organic matter and the chemistry of the human brain change in response to our environments to allow us to cope with variables in our worlds. The parts of the brain that grow and the parts that don't depend on the baby's experience. Dr. Bruce Perry calls this phenomenon "use-dependent development."

So the genes provide the blueprints and lay down the basic framework of the brain. But the shaping and finishing within that framework is facilitated by the environment. As Ronald Kotulak said in his Pulitzer Prize–winning series on brain development published in 1993 in the *Chicago Tribune:*

> They work in tandem, with genes providing the building blocks, and the environment acting like an on-the-job foreman, providing instructions for final construction. . . . Sounds, sights, smells, touch— like little carpenters—all can quickly change the architecture of the brain, and sometimes they can turn into vandals. . . . The discovery that the outside world is indeed the brain's real food is truly intriguing. The brain gobbles up its external environment in bits and chunks through its sensory system: vision, hearing, smell, touch and taste. . . . The digested world is reassembled in the form of trillions of cells that are constantly growing or dying, or becoming stronger or weaker, depending on the richness of the banquet.

Our familiar global measures of children's systematic development, like head circumference and behavioral milestones such as crawling, walking, and talking, are now validated and enhanced by new graphic, computer-generated techniques that enable us to view precise functions in the developing brain. What we are now able to see is the physiology that accompanies and shapes these behavioral milestones. The newly achieved behaviors in turn catalyze the next round of physiological development. Behavior and neurobiological activity are inextricably linked and are, in a sense, two aspects of the same happening.

Perhaps the greatest advantage of the neurophysiological research is its potential to predict or anticipate corresponding behavioral changes. Dr. Harry Chugani of the University of Michigan uses PET scans to measure the metabolism of glucose by the developing brain. He has learned that high rates of glucose use in regions of the brain correspond with periods of rapid overproduction of synapses and nerve terminals. When glucose metabolism declines, this signals the selective elimination, or "pruning," of excess connections and marks a decline in developmental plasticity. This pattern of proliferation and pruning is then followed by a period of reorganization, when newly formed connections are integrated into existing systems. Dr. Geraldine Dawson of the University of Washington and Dr. Kurt Fischer of Harvard University describe at least thirteen of these levels or stages of brain development. They believe that one stage builds directly on the last, so that later infancy skills are built on those established in early infancy and so on. More than half of these levels occur in the first twenty-four months of life.[3]

The implications of this new understanding are both promising and discomforting. While the human baby is born with literally trillions of unprogrammed circuits just waiting to be stimulated into great poetry or science or music, there is the reality that for many key capacities, circuits not used may die. The experiences of a child will determine the circuits connected. In an article published in February 1996 in *Newsweek,* Sharon Begley, having interviewed several prominent neurobiologists, wrote, "They suggest that, with the right input at the right time, almost anything is possible. But they imply that if you miss the window, you're playing with a handicap."

WHEN WHAT YOU SEE IS WHAT YOU GET

Like a tapestry constantly being woven, the brain responds to the world around it. While this adaptability is clearly an evolutionary asset, the brain's dependence on the environment can also have dev-astating results. When the stimulation is nonexistent or aberrant, op-portunities can be lost or muted. While there presently are only a few known critical periods for the development of key capacities, research is showing that the first thirty-three months is the most profound time of opportunities. Scientists are now measuring and documenting these opportunities—or the lack of them—not just in discernible behav-ioral differences but also in concrete terms such as brain weight.

Several years ago, Dr. William Greenough at the University of Illinois at Champaign-Urbana exposed young rats to enriched envi-ronments full of toys, exercise equipment, food, and playmates. On autopsy he found that the enriched rats had 25 percent more con-nections between brain cells than those rats raised in standard labo-ratory cages. The brains were actually larger and weighed more. Dr. Craig Ramey at the University of Alabama found that he could produce similar results with studies done on children. Beginning with babies as young as six weeks of age, he exposed a group of impover-ished inner-city children to a daily environment that included learn-ing, toys, playmates, and good nutrition. The enriched children were found to have higher IQs than the control group of children from a similar background. The study also found a lower rate of mental retardation and developmental difficulties in the enriched group.

In an interview with the authors, Ramey stated:

> In at least eleven separate studies [comparing high risk children with those who do not receive intervention], we have data to show that, if you do not intervene before twenty-four months, these children will be seriously developmentally delayed.[4] And we have no data to show that we can reverse the majority of these delays.[5]

In three related studies spanning thirty years of research, Ramey has demonstrated that the timing and targeting of early intervention makes all the difference. Concerned about the lack of sustained gains in follow-up studies on children in Head Start, where gains in IQ tend to fade after about three years, Ramey makes a strong case for beginning earlier, in the first months of life, when the neurological circuits for learning words and sound are being built. He began his Abecedarian project in 1972 as an experiment to test whether mental retardation coming from inadequate environments could be prevented. The interventions included intensive high-quality preschool programs combined with medical and nutritional supports beginning shortly after birth and continuing until children entered kindergarten. The researchers assigned children from 120 impoverished families into one of four groups: intensive early education in a day care center from age four months to eight years; from four months to five years; from five to eight years; and none (control group).

Among these families, all of whom were poor, the researchers discovered that the factors that most placed children at risk of cognitive delays or mental retardation had to do with the parents' educational histories and their intellectual and language abilities. The single strongest predictor of all is the mother's tested level of intelligence. In the Abecedarian project, of the control-group children, all of whom had mothers with IQs less than seventy, all but one child emerged in grade school retarded or of borderline intelligence. In the intervention groups, children who, beginning at four months, participated in the program five days a week, fifty weeks a year, all tested within the normal range by age three—an average of twenty points higher than children in the control group. When children did not receive intervention until after age five, 86 percent tested below an IQ of eighty-five. Ramey's research has conclusively shown that interventions that begin at birth and are provided during the preschool years, but not later, have a measurable impact on children's development, which is sustained to age fifteen. In a recent follow-up study with Dr. Frances Campbell, Ramey reported that children who were enrolled early in the Abecedarian project still scored higher in reading and in math by five points at age fifteen than did children who did not receive intervention. Ramey believes that early enrollment in the enriched day care is key to these enduring gains. Children enrolled after the age of five showed no sustained gains in IQ or academic performance. In an interview reported by Ronald Kotulak in his *Chicago Tribune* brain development series, Ramey stated:

> The quality of the environment and the kind of experiences children have may affect brain structure and function so profoundly that they may not be correctable after age five. If we had a comparable level of knowledge with respect to a particular form of cancer or hypertension or some other illness that affected adults, you can be sure we would be in action with great vigor.

Neurobiologists studying how the brain develops give us insight into how Ramey's observations occur biologically. Dr. Charles Nelson of the University of Minnesota studies how the brain changes from experience. As mentioned earlier dendritic and synaptic nerve connections are overproduced and the brain "prunes" those not properly reinforced by stimulation. Nelson refers to this process of overproduction, selective stimulation, and pruning as an "information capture mechanism." This learning process allows the organism to shape itself in accordance with the variables consistently occurring in the environment and to specialize its responses accordingly. If the information is distorted, so is the development.

Dr. Greenough explains critical periods—such as that for vision—in terms of Nelson's information capture mechanisms. The critical period occurs because the cells for capturing certain information are there on a time-limited basis before they are pruned or used elsewhere. Greenough postulates that information capture mechanisms may also be set in place neurologically to allow the animal to adapt and incorporate the responses appropriate to specific social environments. He believes that if inappropriate experiences (e.g. abuse) occur or if appropriate experiences do not occur—especially when these are combined with biological factors such as attention-deficit/hyperactivity disorder—later behavior is likely to reflect this early programmed distortion on a sustained basis. Dr. H. F. Harlow's classic work with monkeys is one example of the information capture process at work in the arena of social development. Baby monkeys separated from their mothers at birth, nursing from a cloth-covered wire substitute mother, were deprived of mutual emotional exchanges with a live, nursing, mother monkey. Although the little monkeys received adequate nutrition, the neurons available for reciprocal social communication were not stimulated. As a result, wire-mothered baby monkeys became agitated and withdrawn and had difficulties relating to other monkeys. This pattern of social incompetence continued throughout their lives.

Building upon the work of Dr. Nelson, Dr. Greenough postulates that the brain not only adapts but also orchestrates a pattern of changes throughout the organism in response to repetitive stimulation. Learning a new athletic skill is an example of this process; a series of changes occur beyond physical conditioning. Greenough's studies on rats show that when something new is learned, there is a synaptic reorganization of the brain. In the motor cortex, nerve cells begin to form additional connections that encode the general skill. Tissue and blood cells are added, making the whole brain better equipped for new skills. The changes that occur are not limited to the brain; they also affect the spinal column and muscles. The brain adapts to the specific changes by orchestrating a cascading pattern of changes.

The size of a toddler's vocabulary is a more concrete example of the early developmental opportunities afforded by the information capture process. Dr. Janellin Huttenlocher of the University of Chicago has demonstrated that when socioeconomic factors are equal, babies whose mothers talk to them more have a bigger vocabulary. At twenty months, babies of talkative mothers knew 131 more words than the infants of less talkative mothers. At twenty-four months the difference was 295 words. Regardless of the words used, exposure to the sounds of human speech builds the circuitry in the infant brain that creates the path for more words to be absorbed. Repeated exposure actually builds the physiological capacity. The more words the child hears by age one, the larger the vocabulary at age two.[6]

The cognitive advantages of early intellectual stimulation carry forward as a child reaches school age. From the earliest months of life, babies who are encouraged by caregivers to take an interest in their environments and to explore their world through vision, touch, and hearing, score higher on cognitive and language tests both at preschool and at grade school. Dr. Peter Huttenlocher, also at the University of Chicago, has shown that the power of a brain grows in direct relationship to the number of neurons and the number of connections between the cells it contains. The linkages between neurons (synapses) are the connections that make the brain work. Huttenlocher counted these connections during autopsies and found that a tissue sample the size of the head of a pin from a twenty-eight-week-old fetus contains 124 million connections. A newborn sample has 253 million connections, while a sample from an eight month old has 572 million. Connections are the most prolific in the beginning of life and start to slow down in production at the end of the first year, tapering off at 354 million connections per sample at age twelve.[7]

The fetal stage and the first two years of life are the period of most rapid brain growth. During early development the brain produces many more cells and connections than it can use. Which cells survive and what a brain can or cannot do are determined by what a child learns in the first decade of life. Proceeding cumulatively from the beginning, the opportunity to nurture synaptic growth and retention is at its greatest during this early time. It is at this time that we have the greatest possible potential to directly enhance the quality of brain power ultimately applied to language or music or social, emotional, math, or logic skills. Yet the educational system in this country begins at age five. The fundamental wiring of the brains of our future workforce occurs—or not—before we are paying attention.

The last decade of brain research has clearly demonstrated that the best time for children to learn a second language is in early grade school, not high school. As we learn about brain systems and their maturation, there is growing evidence that preschool rather than higher education ought to be the focus of our most creative educational strategies, including interventions to stem emotional and cognitive disabilities that can undermine learning from the time of birth.

In a recent television interview on *Prime Time Live,* Diane Sawyer discussed the subject of critical periods in brain development with Dr. Michael Phelps, who co-invented the brain-imaging technique called the PET scan. Phelps was quoted by Sawyer as saying: "The development years are not just a chance to educate, they're actually your obligation to form a brain and if you miss these opportunities then, you've missed them—forever." The program concluded with poignant images of caged songbirds while in voiceover Sawyer said: "At Rockefeller University there is a birdcage and it's quiet. The scientists tell us that they've learned that when baby songbirds like these don't hear a parent singing, when they grow up, they will never learn to sing."[8]

FROM THE BOTTOM UP

Anatomically, the brain can be divided into four basic parts: the brainstem, the midbrain, the limbic brain, and the cortex. These parts develop in a hierarchical progression starting with simple and gradually moving to more complex functions. This development begins with the brain stem, which controls the basic and most essential functions necessary to sustain life, including involuntary functions like blood pressure, heart rate, and body temperature. Next to develop is the midbrain, which controls appetite and sleep, among other things. Then comes the limbic brain, which is the seat of emotion and impulse. And, finally, the cortex, where logic, planning, and cognition—the executive functions—take place, is developed. Each of these parts of the brain is responsive to the environment, or use-dependent, according to Dr. Perry, and will be shaped by the individual's unique experience of his or her surroundings.

When we seek to understand violent behavior from the perspective of brain anatomy, we find some surprising realities. First of all, violent impulses are generated in the lower parts of the brain, particularly the limbic system. Under conditions of extreme threat or rage, when the brain is flooded with stress hormones, the "fight or flight" human is not under the governance of the analytical cortex, the seat of rationality and wisdom. Under those extreme conditions, it is the limbic brain and midbrain which are quickest to respond to mobilize the individual. This biological process is well understood by the army. The constant drill and practice in boot camp to prepare for combat is deliberately directed at the limbic brain. The training of new recruits for war conditions, where instantaneous and precise action is called for must bypass the analytical and time-consuming cortical functions. Even those of us who have never served in the military have our own experiences with the body's response to emergency or threat and can recall moments of freezing or running when normal rational thoughts were totally unavailable to us until fear or fury subsided. Dr. Perry succinctly explains that our ability to think before we act is related to the ratio between the excitatory activity of the primitive areas of the brain and the moderating efforts of the cortical or higher areas:

> Any factors which increase the activity or reactivity of the brainstem (e.g. chronic stress) or decrease the moderating capacity of the limbic or cortical areas (e.g. neglect) will increase an individual's aggressivity, impulsivity and capacity to display violence.[9]

This understanding of the stress response system and its impact on brain development has huge implications for working with people with attentional or impulsive disabilities. For children with developmental disabilities or damage (e.g., attention-deficit/hyperactivity disorder or post-traumatic stress disorder), cognitively based therapies may be an exercise in futility. To be effective, interventions need to be directed at the limbic and midbrain levels.

Violent behavior is most likely to occur when a young child's experiences result in lack of adequate stimulation to the cortex—the system for modulation and control—together with overstimulation of the alarm system. The check-and-balance system in the brain may be thrown off. According to Perry, if those experiences are chronic and occur early enough, a state of hyperarousal or of numbing may become a permanent trait in a child, setting the stage for a host of learning and behavioral problems. This is when we build the blueprint. These months are the time of greatest access and potential—and vulnerability—for creating competent and balanced responses to the stressors all children to one degree or another will face in our society.

ALARM CENTRAL: THE LIMBIC SYSTEM

The limbic system lies wrapped at the center of the protective layers of the cortex. The cortex, with its more advanced rational and uniquely human capacities, sits above the limbic brain ready to edit, adapt, and analyze the impulsive behavior originating from this ancient source of fight-or-flight mobilization. Central to the limbic system is the amygdala, from the Greek word for almond. This structure generates strong emotional signals, acting, according to neurophysiologist Joseph LeDoux, as an "emotional guardian." LeDoux's research on the role of the amygdala has clarified how impulsive behavior can occur without rational processing or even awareness. According to LeDoux, under conditions of great emotional excitement, signals from the amygdala may, by design, bypass the neocortex, the rational and strategic part of the brain. This seems to be nature's insurance in case of a need for immediate action in the face of serious threat. In a description of this process in his book *Emotional Intelligence,* Daniel Goleman writes: "In the brain's architecture, the amygdala is poised something like an alarm company where operators stand ready to send out emergency calls to the fire department, police, and a neighbor whenever a home security system signals trouble."[10]

When a sight or a sound signals a strong negative or painful association such as Dad's entry into the bedroom at night followed by sexual violation, the amygdala won't necessarily wait for analysis by the thoughtful neocortex before, upon again hearing Dad's footsteps in the room, it floods the brain with neurochemicals for fight or flight. The more the painful connection is experienced, the more quickly the limbic alarm response will be triggered. The entry of any man into the bedroom at any time may come to trigger the response. If stimulated intensely or often enough, this alerting system may not subside. Hypervigilance may be the result, so that the individual becomes extremely sensitive to associated cues—such as the sound of heavy footsteps—that warn of oncoming threat. Dr. Perry believes that this kind of trauma occurring often enough or intensely enough can rob a very young child of the ability to learn normally by pulling circuitry meant for other tasks to monitoring for threatening cues in the environment. Initially, these occurrences induce chronically fearful states of hyperarousal in children. If the child is too young to be able to run or resist, she or he will develop a "surrender" or dissociative response. Neurochemical and hormonal responses enable children to go numb or freeze and remove themselves emotionally. Over time, such states may become integrated as traits in the developing child. These can be difficult neurological patterns to change and may inflict permanent damage depending on the age of the child and the type, intensity, frequency, and duration of the trauma.[11]

Impairment or injury may also affect the activity of the limbic system. In normal individuals, the emergency response generated by the amygdala is held in check by the neocortical process, specifically the left prefrontal lobe. Goleman refers to the role played by this area of the brain as a "neural thermostat." Impairment or injury may result in an inability to modulate the signals from the amygdala and related limbic structures. The consequence is highly impulsive behavior, unchecked momentarily by reason. People whose behavior is affected by this neurobiological abnormality are at great risk for school failure, drug abuse, and criminality—not because they lack intelligence, but because they have a limited ability to control their behavior. Strong negative emotions like rage or jealousy can suddenly heat up and overrun the entire system—emotion can overtake rationality.

Researchers, including Dr. Frank Wood of Wake Forest University in Chapel Hill, North Carolina, and Dr. Adrian Raine of the University of Southern California, assert that they can see a characteristic pattern of underactivation of the prefrontal lobe together with excessive activity in the region of the limbic system in the brains of impulsive killers. Emotionally charged memories may be stored in the limbic system and may be restimulated—often years later. The neural alarm system is often imprecise or out of date, and, since it acts without rational (cortical) screening, behavior may appear totally out of context in the present circumstances.

There is a great deal of speculation about the possible causes of this kind of brain abnormality. The hypotheses range from injury to the prefrontal lobes to genetic causes. What we know is that children with early discernible impulse-control problems, such as attention-deficit/hyperactivity disorder (ADHD), are at considerably higher risk of later violent behavior when the problem is left untreated, or is treated only by stimulant medication. Negative outcomes for these children are greatly increased when ADHD is exacerbated by familial or environmental factors such as maternal rejection, child abuse, or the modeling of violent solutions to everyday problems.

THE MIND BODY SYNTHESIZER:
THE ORBITOFRONTAL CORTEX

An area of the brain that is receiving increasing attention in relation to infant development is the orbitofrontal cortex. This part of the brain connects the cortex to the limbic system and is critically involved in the regulation of emotions. Here sensory input of all kinds—vision, hearing, touch, taste, and smell—is connected with our visceral body sensations. This is the area responsible for our "gut reactions" to people and events—our earliest associations between experiences in the outside world and our internal physical responses. Dr. Allan Schore, of the Department of Psychiatry and Biobehavioral Sciences at the UCLA School of Medicine, views the orbitofrontal cortex as the key area involved in both infant attachment and emotional regulation, the failure of which can result in impulsive violence.

The orbitofrontal cortex (so called because it sits just above the orbit of the eyes) is positioned at the undersurface and between the two cerebral hemispheres.[12] This area represents a central point of convergence of the cortex and subcortex. Because of its unique anatomical location, it receives both sensory stimulation (vision, touch, sound, smell) from the external social environment, and visceral information concerning the body's internal environment, so that interpersonal experiences can be associated with emotional and motivational states.

According to Schore, all of the connections between the cortex and the subcortex are regulated by this particular area. As a result, sensory information from the environment, such as the expression on the mother's face and the tone of her voice, is associated in the baby's experience with the physical sensations the baby is simultaneously experiencing, such as intense pleasure and excitement or fear and discomfort. When this goes awry, for example, when a baby "fails to thrive" or fails to gain weight, stops growing, and seems to lose interest in living, this is the area of the brain responsible for the linkages between sensual and emotional deprivation and the physical symptoms that result.

The orbitofrontal areas contain neurons that are especially sensitive to the emotional expressions on the human face, which is a primary source of information sent and received in social situations. The orbitofrontal cortex is particularly expanded in the right hemisphere, which connects deeply into the limbic system, where positive and negative emotions are generated. In fact, this part of the cortex sends direct connections to all the lower limbic areas, including the amygdala. Because it is the only part of the cortex that projects directly to the hypothalamus and autonomic centers deep in the brain stem, the orbital frontal cortex acts as a central control center over both the sympathetic and the parasympathetic nervous systems, which generate the bodily components of emotional behavior.

Schore points out that the critical period for the development of this system exactly coincides with the time period extensively investigated by attachment researchers. He emphasizes that the maturation of the orbitofrontal system is experience dependent: it is directly influenced by the nature of the attachment relationship. The child's first relationship, typically with the mother, acts as a template for the imprinting of circuits in the child's developing, emotion-processing right brain. Schore believes that this is the biological root of the shaping of the individual's adaptive or maladaptive capacities to enter into all later emotional relationships. If Schore is right, an early relationship with an emotionally attuned primary caregiver who regulates the baby's physical and emotional states provides a growth-promoting environment for the infant's developing orbitofrontal cortex. Conversely, early experiences with an emotionally unresponsive or abusive caregiver can inhibit the maturation of this system. Schore concludes that a negative early relationship can lead to a lifelong limited ability, especially under stress, to regulate the intensity, frequency, and duration of primitive negative states such as rage, terror, and shame. Schore states:

> There is now evidence that the orbitofrontal areas show a preferential vulnerability to a spectrum of later forming psychiatric disorders, including sociopathic and character disorders that display antisocial behaviors and problems with impulse control.[13]

We did not understand the significance of the orbitofrontal cortex until the 1940s, when lobotomies were performed experimentally for a time to control extremely emotional individuals. A lobotomy essentially amounts to the disconnection of the orbitofrontal area and results in the total loss of emotionality. While intelligence is unaffected by a lobotomy, the individual loses his or her "personality"—and the ability to relate emotionally. Normal emotional responses are flattened or absent.

Recently this area of the brain has been highlighted in studies of Vietnam veterans who suffer from post-traumatic stress disorder (PTSD). Dr. J. Douglas Bremner, a psychiatrist at Yale, showed slides of Vietnam battle scenes to two groups of veterans, one group of whom suffered from PTSD and one of whom did not. Computerized x-rays (PET scans) that measure the rate of glucose metabolized in different areas of the brain were used to indicate which parts of the brain were functioning during the viewing of the slides. By contrast to those with PTSD, the orbitofrontal area in non-traumatized veterans was highly active, enabling them to distinguish "real" from re-enacted scenes. Dr. Bremner explained this process in a recent article published in *The New Yorker*.

> The orbitofrontal region is the part of your brain that evaluates the primal feelings of fear and anxiety which come up from the brain's deeper recesses. It's the part that tells you that you're in a hospital watching a slide show of the Vietnam War, not in Vietnam living through the real thing. The vets with PTSD weren't using that part of their brain. That's why every time a truck backfires or they see a war picture in a major magazine they are forced to relive their wartime experiences: they can't tell the difference.[14]

GONE BUT NOT FORGOTTEN:
THE AMYGDALA AND MEMORY

Since babies have neither language nor reason and since most of us have no conscious memories of our lives before age two, it would seem to make sense that this time has little influence on our present functioning. This is the logic we have traditionally used to dismiss the role of our earliest experiences. But neuroscientist Dr. Joseph LeDoux points out that the amygdala, together with the hippocampus in the limbic brain, may explain what analysts have been telling us for years: that the events in early life, particularly those experienced with strong emotion, can and do remain an influence throughout our lives. Memory, as it turns out, is not just a matter of rational or even verbal recall. We also have a nonverbal, essentially emotional memory, particularly for experiences, events, and people that carry a strong emotional valence.

Sensual experience (auditory, visual, tactile, and olfactory) typically travels first to the neocortex for analysis. But when perceptions are accompanied by strong emotional impact, particularly those perceived as life threatening, they may bypass the neocortex and send a message directly to the amygdala, which mobilizes the organism for fight or flight. All of this can happen in an instant—and without input from rational processing by the neocortex.

Studies done by Dr. LeDoux in 1989 that exposed rats to fear-inducing visual stimuli provide strong evidence that the amygdala matures very early in life, so that emotional messages can be processed before cognition. In addition, LeDoux found that these fear-based associations experienced early were difficult to erase, even when the sensory cortex was later completely severed. According to LeDoux, early experienced precognitive emotions continue to play out in later life even though the individual may have no conscious memory of the association.[15]

Dr. George Engel documented this process at work in a thirty-year longitudinal study of "Monica."[16] Monica was a child born with congenital atresia of the esophagus, a condition that precluded her being fed by mouth. For the first two days after birth she choked and regurgitated her feedings. On the third day a feeding tube was inserted into her stomach. For two years she was fed through the tube while lying flat on her back without holding or contact of any kind. She was in fact frequently fed "while crying, fussing or playing" and did not participate in the process. A tube placed in her neck to continuously drain the saliva limited how Monica could be held. Her mother subsequently became depressed and withdrew from her baby. Monica became unresponsive and for a while showed a failure to thrive.

At age two, Monica was hospitalized for nine months while her esophagus was reconstructed. She began to receive oral feedings either lying flat on her back or propped in her crib. Her mother and the nurses still rarely held her. After she returned home, she was able to eat normally. She grew up with no conscious memories of her early tube feedings; she was told by her mother much later that she had been fed by a tube in her abdomen as a baby.

Engel and his associates continued to observe Monica as she grew. As a little girl she fed her dolls in the exact position she herself had experienced, flat on their backs without holding or contact of any kind. Engel also noted that her conversations with the dolls indicated preconscious memories of her earlier experiences. She would place the dolls down on the bed and stand at their side. At four years of age she said to one, "Poor baby, you ain't got a mouth." She also talked about the dolls "leaking at the neck," where she herself had experienced the early drainage tube.

When Monica babysat as a teenager, she fed her charges in the same strange way. When she had children of her own, in spite of having observed her mother feeding her younger siblings normally, Monica seldom, if ever, held their bottles during their feedings. Her mother, husband, and a sister all coached her to hold her babies enfolded in a face-to-face position. Although she was generally compliant with requests from others, she consistently refused close body or face-to-face contact with her babies while feeding them. Instead, clearly acting from early and enduring preverbal memory, she lay them flat across her lap and replicated her own experience.

Infant memory is the subject of much current research at several universities, including the University of Massachusetts. Drs. Rachel Clifton and Nancy Myers, both psychologists, have successfully documented the capacity of two-and-a-half-year-old children to exhibit learning they experienced at age six months.[17] Originally researching motor and hearing skills, Dr. Clifton placed sixteen six-month-old babies in a pitch dark room with objects that made different sounds and used infrared cameras to capture how and when infants reached

41

for the objects. After the initial experience, the stimuli were not repeated until follow-up testing two years later. At that time, the original children were paired with a control group of thirty-month-old toddlers who had not had the original experience. "All of the children were again placed in a dark room with the same objects making the same sounds. The children who had the prior experience reached for the objects without signs of fear." Fewer of the control group reached for the objects, and many cried. Clifton and Myers believe that the babies, when put into a situation similar to their earlier experience, were able to access memories of a time when they were six months old and the task appeared less frightening.

A growing number of scientists believe that the limbic memory does not wait until birth to begin. Dr. David Chamberlain, a psychologist who was one of the founders of the Association for Pre- and Perinatal Psychology and Health, finds increasing evidence of a primitive memory stored at the sensory level beginning during late gestation. Chamberlain refers to these memories as "cellular" because they are unconscious and preverbal and are often held and expressed in specific parts of the body.[18]

Dr. Lenore Terr, a child psychiatrist at the University of California Medical Center in San Francisco, studied children under the age of five who had experienced serious trauma from birth to thirty-four months. Verifiable proof of the trauma the children experienced was recorded in photos, police reports, statements from eyewitnesses, confessions, or corroborating injuries. This is presumed to be a time when little or no verbal memory exists. Yet these children clearly showed that they had retained behavioral memories of their trauma, which Terr found to be reenacted in part or in entirety in their play. Terr believes that traumatic events—especially those experienced early—create "burned-in" images that last a lifetime.

PEASE PORRIDGE HOT, PEASE PORRIDGE COLD

It was only a game. Even though it was for science—it was only a game. The first person who hit the button after the light flashed got to zap his partner with an electric current. The winner could pick a charge ranging from one, a light twinge, to eight, a jolt of pain. These were college students at McGill University in Montreal. They usually picked low dosages of electricity, giving what they got, exchanging only the level of pain they received. That was before the drink. Scientists deliberately raised the aggression level of participants by giving them a dose of amino acids that lowered their levels of the brain chemical serotonin. Soon the game changed. Volunteers began zapping their partners with higher and higher numbers in spite of receiving lower charges themselves. Next, the students were given another snack, this time a dose of tryptophan, an essential ingredient for the brain to produce serotonin. As the serotonin levels rose, the choice of painful jolts diminished. An Orwellian experiment, perhaps, but proof positive that the manipulation of neurochemicals can alter levels of aggression.[19]

Serotonin reducing chemicals such as certain amino acids lower the threshold for aggressive tendencies. In rodents, serotonin-reducing drugs were first viewed as aphrodisiacs because the rats became very sexually active under their influence. But aggression soon followed. Handlers were bitten and other rats were attacked just for coming close—behaviors previously unseen in the animals.[20]

The role of the neurotransmitter serotonin in aggressive behavior has been under study since the mid 1970s when Marie Asberg, at the Karolinska Hospital in Stockholm, observed the linkage between low serotonin and violent suicides, suicides involving guns, knives, ropes, or jumping from high places. Soon criminals with a history of violence were discovered to also have low levels of serotonin. But the effect of serotonin can only be understood in relation to a counterbalancing neurotransmitter, noradrenaline.

While serotonin is known to be key to modulating impulsive behaviors at the neocortical level of the brain, noradrenaline is the alarm hormone designed to alert the system to respond to danger. Together they have a teeter-totter type of relationship: in normal people, serotonin is higher during sleep and decreases during wakefulness, while noradrenaline is higher during wakefulness and lower during sleep. The balance between the two is the key to normal function. For most of us, there is a balance, enabling us to react in reasonable ways. But, as with the McGill students, our functional levels can be altered, at least temporarily. Alcohol and extremely stressful environments can have similar effects to the students' initial drink of amino acids. When these exposures occur to a developing fetus or infant, the levels of serotonin and noradrenaline are just being built, shaping lifetime patterns.

Violent behavior is roughly of two types: impulsive and premeditated. Most acts of violence are impulsive. "Cold-blooded" or premeditated acts are far less common and are typically enacted by a very different personality than the "hot-blooded" crime. When environmental experiences early in life cause noradrenaline levels to be too high and serotonin levels too low, the result, in the presence of later emotional triggers, may be impulsive violence. Conversely, very low levels of noradrenaline together with low levels of serotonin result in underarousal, which may generate an appetite for high-risk behaviors to achieve arousal, setting the stage for predatory violence or premeditated crimes. Interestingly, very high levels of serotonin are not a means of counteracting this effect. Excessively high serotonin levels result not in well-being, but in rigidity or obsessive-compulsive behavior, like Lady MacBeth's repetitive hand washing. The balance of neurochemicals in either scenario is thought to be set primarily by early experience.[21] When babies develop in an atmosphere of terror or trauma, these neurochemicals can be called upon to enable them to survive. But that which enables survival may also create permanent and lethal imbalances.

Low levels of serotonin may be the result of a genetic error. A single gene inherited by some people from their fathers results in an inability to adequately convert tryptophan from common foods into serotonin. The individual inheriting this gene may have no problem unless there is an additional stressor, primarily alcohol. In affected individuals, alcohol briefly raises, then drastically lowers, serotonin levels. At the latter point, the individual is prone to acting out aggressively. This gene is common—affecting 40 percent of the Swedish population tested at random.[22] With 48 percent of the homicides in the United States committed under the influence of alcohol, the role of this interaction is clearly of concern.

Normal serotonin and noradrenaline levels are extremely important to balanced functioning. Without realizing it, our culture is creating more and more individuals with an imbalance in this delicate equation in the brain. Alcohol, drugs, and other toxic exposures such as lead are being implicated in damage to the genes responsible for these neurochemicals. So are conditions after birth such as abusive, terrifying, or war-torn environments, in which impulsive or reactive behaviors are essential to survival. Researchers suspect that conditions of child neglect, child abuse, gang warfare, and domestic violence are—without our awareness—biologically, as well as socially, feeding the cycle of violent crime. As Ron Kotulak stated in his series on the brain:

> Underlying the scientific quest, which has revealed genetic and environmental links to abnormal brain chemistry, is the growing suspicion that society may unwittingly be feeding the nation's epidemic of murder, rape and other criminal acts by making childhood more dangerous than ever.[23]

Abuse and neglect in the first years of life have a particularly pervasive impact. Prenatal development and the first two years are the time when the genetic, organic, and neurochemical foundations for impulse control are being created. It is also the time when the capacities for rational thinking and sensitivity to other people are being rooted—or not—in the child's personality.

3

Before We Know It:

PRENATAL EXPOSURE

TO DRUGS AND MALNUTRITION

It was all very well to say "Drink me," but the wise little Alice was not going to do that in a hurry, "No, I'll look first," she said, "and see whether it's marked '*poison*' or not"; for she had read several nice little stories about children who had got burnt, and eaten up by wild beasts, and other unpleasant things, all because they *would* not remember the simple rules their friends had taught them: Such as, that a red-hot poker will burn you if you hold it too long, and that, if you cut your finger very deeply with a knife, it usually bleeds; and she had never forgotten that, if you drink much from a bottle marked "poison," it is almost certain to disagree with you, sooner or later.

—LEWIS CARROLL
Alice in Wonderland

My grandma grew dope in the basement, and everybody used to go down there on the weekends and clip buds off the dope plants and get high. And they loved to make love not war. She kind of brought the sixties into the seventies and the sixties into the eighties and then into the nineties. Outrageous! She had glaucoma, so she had a prescription for medicinal purposes to smoke marijuana . . . plus she could say she had a license to possess and grow marijuana for medicinal purposes. . . . My grandma got involved in drugs right after her first child was born. . . . She was fifteen. . . . My mom was smoking marijuana at age eleven. Alcohol and marijuana, a little heroin, a lot of prescription drugs. . . . Mom was fourteen when she got pregnant with my brother. My mom and dad knew each other because he was part of my grandma's circle of friends. But they really met for the first time officially in church. He picked up my mother pregnant and took care of the baby even though it wasn't his. I came along just a year and a month and a few days later. They never did get married. My dad started hitting my mom pretty early, especially when he was drinking. My mom was pretty depressed. She just laid on the couch some days and wouldn't get up. She didn't know what to do.

JEFFREY, AUGUST 1996

Mom smoked cigarettes all the way through all her pregnancies. She smoked since she was a little kid and to this day. She probably did alcohol and marijuana—maybe white dope, too, I don't know. She said she stopped as soon as she knew [she was pregnant], but I saw her with Julie [while pregnant]. They were all doing it, and maybe she stopped some time after she really knew. . . . They always fought and stuff— always fought. They fought all the time—screaming, yelling, grabbing stuff and throwing it. Always drugs. Always alcohol. I'm sure Mom was doing all of it during her pregnancy, including white dope—crack or cocaine.

JOHN, BROTHER OF JEFFREY, AUGUST 1996

49

The incubation of violence happens quietly, subtly, out of sight and awareness. We don't see it. We don't expect it. It creeps up on little cat feet and catches us unaware, seeming to come out of nowhere. We look for its sources in all the obvious places. Fear drives our search. We are moved to think quickly, often narrowly—taking aim at the symptoms as they appear. As we move to contain one layer of problems, a new one unfolds. Old solutions don't fit. Metal detectors replace jungle gyms as essential equipment in schools. But the tide keeps coming, it's genesis unrecognized.

Ironically, babies in our culture are still commonly viewed as living in a twilight zone of unfinished wetness. Viewed as dewey-eyed and unseeing, moving only reflexively and preoccupied with little beyond eating, sleeping, and eliminating, infants have been routinely viewed as irrelevant to policy discussions concerning education, let alone the prevention of crime. But with new technology an amazing picture is emerging of the human infant. Far from the *tabula rasa* of John Locke's view of the human baby, new graphic imaging reveals a riveting portrait of unmistakable complexity taking shape before we know it.

In America, we seem to think that intelligence, learning, and emotional responses suddenly kick in at birth or sometime after we are born. Graphic-imaging technology and the study of cognition and emotion in the fetus are so new that in-depth studies on fetal behavior and prebirth capacities are still sketchy chapters in the education of today's physicians and psychologists. Most of us have taken the period of gestation for granted as an unconscious and insensitive time of purely physical development. That assumption, based on an absence of information, has kept us believing that, beyond physical development, little about us is happening before birth. In Asian cultures, a child is considered one year old at birth, and the parent-child relationship begins nine months earlier. In contrast to most ancient cultures and many contemporary Eastern cultures, pregnancy in our country is seen as a time when only the physical structure of the brain is created. After birth, we assume that very slowly babies develop the hardware and gradually begin to develop the software for a system that has never before functioned. Even Western developmental psychologists generally refer to birth as marking the beginning of learning and feeling. Chapters in developmental textbooks on "the first year of life" begin with birth and continue to the child's twelfth-month birthday. This belief that fetuses and babies are not sentient is a fundamental reason that we have not been successful in stemming the roots of violence.

JACK IN THE BOX

The wall of the female belly has historically provided an effective shield against intrusive visual scrutiny of the developing fetus. But the advent of ultrasound gives us a new perspective through a relatively noninvasive window. As this technology has advanced, the clarity and precision of our observations have produced new information. Beginning at approximately two and a half weeks after the sperm has fused with the egg, neurons begin multiplying in the embryo at an unimaginable rate. Dr. Richard Restak, a neuroscientist and author of *The Infant Mind,* says:

> Assuming that the adult human brain contains on the order of a hundred billion neurons and that no new neurons are added after birth, we can calculate that neurons must be generated in the developing brain at an average rate of more than two hundred and fifty thousand per minute. . . . An electrician delegated the task of wiring up a circuit as complex as that of the human brain and capable of soldering connections at a rate of one per second would take over thirty million years to complete the job.[1]

All of our senses are fully installed and are being test driven prenatally. The first to develop is touch. But all will be employed before birth—which is why, to anyone paying attention, the infant is so capable of his or her incredible menu of skills and emotions upon arrival. Long before we are born, we are experiencing. Our early brain is hard at work recording sensual input, beginning with:[2]

Touch: By seventeen weeks of gestation, the infant can feel touch all over the body except for the back and top of the head, which have feeling by twenty weeks. At just two months the fetus will kick and jerk if poked, and by the fourth month will make facial expressions such as frowning, squinting, or grimacing if its scalp is tickled. He or she will kick violently if the mother drinks cold water.[3]

Taste: By fifteen weeks, taste buds are beginning to detect taste differences in the amniotic fluid due to the presence of varying chemicals.[4]

Hearing: By the twenty-fourth week, a baby hears the mother's voice and the father's, if he is close during gestation, and will distinguish them from others at birth.[5] Several researchers have found that a fetus will quiet to Mozart, Vivaldi, and Bach.[6] Dr. Anthony de Casper has recently demonstrated that French babies whose mothers repeated the same nursery rhyme while pregnant recognized it after birth. The mothers read the rhyme three times a day for a four-week period from the thirty-third to the thirty-seventh week of gestation. After birth the babies responded to the rhyme with rhythmic sucking and showed no sign of recognition of other rhymes.[7]

Vision: Dr. T. Berry Brazelton, of Boston Children's Hospital, has shown that fetuses are light sensitive from the sixteenth week. A direct light held to the mothers abdomen will startle the fetus and cause it to move away. Some cover their eyes in response to light and their ears in response to ultrasound. By thirty-two weeks of gestation a fetus has the same capacity to see as that which is present at birth.[8]

In addition to development of the senses, the fetus is busy with:

Motor Development: Between ten and fifteen weeks, a cough from the mother will cause the fetus to move rapidly within seconds.[9] Normal fetal functioning seems to include the practicing of reflexive movements that are necessary for later survival. New brain research indicates that the reflexive movements create sensations that provide early stimulation for the developing brain.[10]

Primitive Emotions and Memory: In 1994 researchers measured the impact on the fetus of a mother watching short clips of a violent movie. The fetus became agitated along with the mother as measured by heart rate and movement. And in another test, in 1981, using ultrasound, researchers observed fetuses who were experiencing amniocentesis. The fetuses responded fearfully—pulling away from the needle, defensively covering themselves—and sometimes aggressively by attempting to hit or kick at the needle.[11] In light of the fact that their eyelids were still fused at the time of the testing, this is startling information. In reviewing all the evidence of the learning a baby engages in while still in the womb, Dr. David Chamberlain wrote in an article published in the *British Journal of Psychotherapy* in 1987:

> There is mounting evidence for a theory of "cellular" memory which reaches back into the prenatal period. These memories are called cellular because they are usually behavioral rather than verbal memories and because specific parts of the body seem to hold and express these memory patterns.[12]

The reality is that there is no time in human development that equals fetal growth in the speed and complexity—and therefore vulnerability—of development. Long before birth, we have each developed all of the basic brain cells (neurons) that we will ever have: The period of neuron proliferation begins within the first four weeks of development and is complete by twenty-four weeks. The process of neuronal migration to their intended location in the brain begins at about the same time and tapers off by about the thirtieth week. The process by which neurons differentiate to their specific functions begins at approximately fourteen weeks of gestation and continues through the first year of life. Before we know it, harmful agents or maternal experiences can have a huge impact at these crucial times, evidence of which may not appear until an affected system matures and begins to perform behaviorally. For example, early signs of an attention disorder may not become apparent until sometime after the child is walking and talking.

In summarizing the consequences of prenatal injuries to the brain, many of which may not be detectable until later development, Dr. Restak says:

> If this complex process of migration is disturbed by genetic factors or toxins, the cells may not reach the proper position. If it is extreme, the fetus will be aborted. If it is milder, the pathologist would detect this malformation. However, if it is even milder, it will not come to the pathologist but to the psychiatrist.[13]

More likely in the nineties, depending on the environment of the child, psychiatrists will share this role with judges. New research provides convincing evidence that violent criminals have poorly functioning brains. Low verbal IQs, attentional problems, impulsivity, poor school performance, inadequate processing of information, inflexibility, restlessness, agitation, and difficulty processing social cues are all characteristics commonly associated with criminal behavior. Adverse conditions during pregnancy are the seeds of significant distortions found in the brains of many violent criminals. The growing number of children who are surfacing at school age with attention deficits and other learning problems is compelling evidence that prenatal neurological damage is an escalating problem, a problem that may become more severe given the recent rise in drug use by children under eighteen.

While prenatal exposure to drugs in and of itself is probably not as strong a factor in producing violent children as later negative circumstances and experiences, the prenatal environment is a crucial protective opportunity. The quality of the prenatal environment can either maximize healthy development or create biological and behavioral vulnerabilities in a child's brain. Children born already impaired are more likely to be the brunt of destructive parenting behaviors and abuse. They are less likely to do well with those consequences than a child with greater emotional and cognitive resources, such as an ability to recover quickly from frustration and to sort out relevant information from irrelevant distractions while learning a skill.

Witness the story of Eric Smith. Different from the beginning, Eric was born with protruding ears that curled inward, a minor physical anomaly that we now know often signals subtle neurological irregularities. As a toddler he was slow to walk and talk, and his mother enrolled him in an early intervention program for stimulation and therapy. Until he was four, Eric had frequent violent tantrums during which he would bang his head on the floor and hold his breath. Due to developmental delays, by school age he stood out from other children, who made fun of him. He had learning problems and was held back for two years in his grade school. By his mother's accounts, given in court, he complained often that he was stupid and "never going to be anybody." When he was nine, Eric tried to choke a neighbor's cat. He set fire to paper on the stove in the middle of the night. The mother of another child recommended to Eric's mother that she get counseling for Eric concerning his school, behavioral, and self-image problems. Eric's stepfather, Ted, who had adopted Eric, argued frequently with Eric's mother, Tammy. He physically disciplined the children, including Eric's older and younger sisters. According to Ted, by early adolescence, Eric was afraid of his own temper and had confided that "he wanted to hurt somebody." He soon acted on his desire.

On a summer morning in 1993, when Eric was thirteen, a neighbor living adjacent to a park said she heard what she thought was "a child's scream." When she went to check, her dog was barking at two cats, and she assumed they had made the noise. Before she left for work ten minutes later, she saw Eric ride by on his bike. Later that morning, a sudden rainstorm hastened the mother of four-year-old Derrick to the park to pick her son up from a summer recreation program. A counselor told her that Derrick had never arrived. Terrified, Derrick's mother searched the school yard next door, checked neighbors' houses and the church where her son went for day care. Soon a police search was underway. Neighbors joined with helicopters in looking for Derrick. Eric's dad was one of the volunteers.

They found Derrick's body that afternoon among the weeds on the property of the woman who had heard a child scream. The injuries inflicted on his small body were shocking in their brutality. Derrick had been bludgeoned repeatedly in the head and chest, choked, and sodomized with a stick. That night Eric stayed overnight at the home of the woman who had urged Tammy to get counseling for Eric. She recalled that he seemed frightened. What she didn't know was that during the night Eric burned the nose of her teenage son with a cigarette while he slept. The following day the police still had not identified a suspect for Derrick's savage death. Eric asked the neighbor what might happen if the killer "turned out to be a kid." The neighbor once again went to Tammy out of concern for Eric, and at this point, Tammy took Eric to speak to the police who were investigating the crime. Under pressure from his mother, grandfather, and great-grandfather when his story proved to be inconsistent, Eric finally confessed.

Eric's account to the police of what happened was straightforward. He told them he "wanted to take [Derrick] someplace and hurt him." According to Eric's account, on seeing the four year old walking alone the short distance to the park, Eric lured him into the weeds, choked him, stuffed a napkin and plastic bag from Derrick's lunch into the little boy's mouth and struck him repeatedly with rocks, one weighing twenty-four pounds. He stuck a sharp twig up Derrick's anus and poured Kool-Aid from Derrick's lunchbox into his wounds. He then pulled the little boy's body into the weeds and rode away on his bike. But as he thought about what he had done, he worried that Derrick might still be alive and would tell someone, and so he went back to make sure that Derrick was dead.

At the trial, Eric appeared emotionless. Two psychiatrists testified as to the numerous social and biological factors contributing to Eric's violent behavior. The complex recipe resulting in Eric's impaired brain and antisocial behavior began with a family history of alcoholism and depression. The doctors testified that his strange ears and slow development were likely caused by his mother's ingestion of trimethadione, which she took for epilepsy during the crucial first months of Eric's gestation. Changes in Eric's living situation and harsh physical discipline by his stepfather added to the problem. The medical testimony established that Eric had a mild attention deficit and hyperactivity disorder. One psychiatrist diagnosed Eric as having an "intermittent explosive disorder." In an account of Eric's story published in the *Ladies' Home Journal,* author Ronny Frishman wrote:

> The psychiatrist cited other factors contributing to Eric's mental illness: a family history of alcoholism and depression, his loneliness and the physical punishments he endured. He attributed Eric's low self-esteem in part to his slow development and odd physical features, particularly his protruding ears. Physicians concluded that both abnormalities were caused by the anticonvulsant drug, trimethadione. . . .[14]

Eric was the youngest person in the country ever to be tried for murder as an adult. He was tried and found guilty of second-degree murder. He was sentenced at age fourteen and is currently serving nine years to life, the first few years to be spent in a juvenile facility.

There are two areas of very recent research that shed some light on the story of Eric Smith. The first of these focuses on teratogens, which are implicated in Eric's mother's testimony about the prescription drugs she took while pregnant with Eric. The second area, which we are just beginning to recognize, is the effect of prenatal stress. Particularly when such stress occurs simultaneously with exposure to teratogens, the effect on the developing brain may be profound.

PASSIVE POISONS

Until the 1950s, the development of the human fetus was commonly viewed as a genetically controlled operation. Sealed in the safety of the womb, fetal life seemed inviolate to outside influences. That was before thalidomide, a drug widely tested and commonly prescribed for anxiety and nausea, the bane of many pregnant women. In West Germany thalidomide was so widely used that it was released to nonregulated, "over-the-counter" consumption. Less known in the United States, it became a household word when it was linked with a wave of babies born with serious deformities, particularly in the limbs.

So for more than three decades science has warned us of the risks posed by a wide array of drugs, both legal and illegal, to the physical development of the unborn. It is only in the last decade, however, that we have begun to make the link between those drugs and behavioral risks, including later aggression and violence. Chemical or physical agents that cause fetal malformation are known as teratogens. The root of this term is the Greek word *teraton*, "monster." Teratogens tend to selectively damage certain organs. The type and extent of the damage depends on the timing of the exposure, the quantity consumed, and the sensitivity of the developing organ to the teratogen. The exact processes whereby teratogens take their toll on the developing brain is still being researched. Fetal brain development may be directly affected by a particular toxin that kills developing cells. Or the damage may happen indirectly by the alteration of neurochemicals or impairment of the placental function.

Alcohol, nicotine, lead, and cocaine are teratogens, each of which has been associated with an array of later behavioral problems. Lead, in particular, has been directly linked in some children to violent behavioral patterns such as impulsive rage, aggression, and paranoia. Other teratogens, such as nicotine, while not directly linked to violent behavior, are linked to negative physiological and behavioral changes that can be the precursors of aggression. For example, nicotine is a cause of low birth weight and prematurity, which may later unfold into increased risks of learning disabilities, difficulty in connecting emotionally with others, and neurological impairments such as attention deficit disorder. These characteristics may render children at greater risk for school failure, lowered self-esteem, and alienation, which in combination with environmental factors may place them at a higher risk of becoming violent. Any teratogen that renders a child relatively more vulnerable to subsequent environmental risks by weakening his or her basic physical, emotional, or cognitive capacities may be viewed as indirectly contributing to antisocial behavior. The vast majority of these precursors to aggression are preventable.

The bridge between prenatal exposure to teratogens and later violent behavior occurs quietly in the recesses of the fetal brain. It is difficult to establish whether or not an individual fetus is affected and, if so, how and when the damage occurred. Scientists are just beginning to understand these complex processes. Generally speaking, that which enters the mother's bloodstream also enters the baby's. There is a "blood brain" barrier that serves to protect the central nervous system so that many toxins that easily enter into the cells of other soft tissues, such as muscle, do not enter the brain. The integrity of this barrier, however, varies with the age of the fetus or infant. An immature brain allows many more substances through. When a toxin crosses the barrier, not all areas of the brain are affected equally. There are considerable variations in the adverse consequences of a given toxin, which are based on the impact of neurochemistry on different vascular patterns and differing cell types.[15]

At the time of birth, approximately 5 percent of infants in the United States have observable physical defects. By age one, this figure doubles to 10 percent as problems not detectable in newborns begin to emerge.[16] The subtle effects of toxins on certain regions of the brain may not be picked up until even later when the development of the child, reveals impairments. Babies exposed to alcohol or cocaine may appear normal at birth. But tiny time bombs may be ticking away—waiting for the maturation of the affected system.

While the nature of the teratogen, factors in the mother, and perhaps even the fetus's constitution may play a role, by far the greatest determinant of fetal damage is the timing of the developmental processes that are underway at the time of exposure. For example, thalidomide had an affect only on the babies of women who took the drug between the thirty-fourth and fiftieth days after their last menstrual period. The window of vulnerability was very specific. And the effects were even more so. If the drug was taken between the thirty-ninth and forty-fourth days, the baby's arms were stunted or missing at birth. If the exposure was between the forty-second and forty-eighth days, the baby's legs were shortened or absent. Exposure on days forty-one to forty-three affected the hands as well as the limbs of babies at birth. Babies of mothers who took thalidomide less than thirty-four or more than fifty days after the last menses showed no malformations.[17]

The same rule applies to other drugs that affect the fetus by interfering with and minutely altering brain development. The impact on the baby's brain of drugs such as alcohol, nicotine, and cocaine depends on the specific neurological process underway at the time of exposure. There are similarities in the impact of several teratogens that are due to timing of the insult. It appears that there is a period of great vulnerability to many types of drugs and to alcohol during the embryonic period, which is defined as the first eight weeks of pregnancy. This period, which precedes the period of fetal growth (eight weeks to delivery), is the time of *organogenesis,* when cells are first dividing, proliferating, specializing, and then migrating to their permanent locations.

Unfortunately, this is a time when many women are unaware that they are pregnant. The subsequent detection of damage due to early drug consumption is often confounded by a mother's pain in confronting her fears and guilt about the impact on her baby of her early, sometimes unwitting, use of drugs or alcohol. Her denial may reduce the likelihood of clear, early diagnosis. Fetal alcohol syndrome and its effects, for example, are often undetected in their earliest manifestations in infancy both because they are difficult to recognize and because physicians and mothers are uncomfortable with this conversation.

The impact of drugs on the fetus is now widely publicized. In the 1990s, most of us are aware of the potentially destructive effects of harmful substances like cocaine and alcohol. It is interesting to note, however, that in our culture when we think about "drug-affected babies," it is crack babies who come immediately to mind. These are the babies who in the mid-eighties had all the media and the American public on red alert—a wave of cocaine-exposed newborns would soon overrun the schools. Television news footage poignantly featured tiny newborns, small for the months of gestation or born prematurely. We watched their little bodies shake and startle with tremors and seizures as they endured the agony of withdrawal from the substances their mothers had taken to avoid their own pain. Apprehension approaching panic permeated our observations of these children, particularly among the child-focused professions.

But the wave of brain-damaged crack babies never materialized—at least not in the form ominously predicted. Some of the cocaine-exposed children did appear and are still surfacing with attention deficits, an increased rate of learning problems, and distractibility. But most crack babies who were placed in nurturing and stimulating foster care or adoptive homes now perform normally and are generally indistinguishable from their peers.[18]

While the role of cocaine continues to capture our attention, the reality is that alcohol is far more pervasively used and appears to be more damaging to babies. In January of 1994, *Alcohol Health and Research World* revealed in a survey of drug use by women during their childbearing years that among women ages 18 to 25 and 26 to 34, 84.7 percent and 89.8 percent respectively reported lifetime alcohol use. Approximately 55 percent of the women reported use within the previous month. By contrast, only 9 percent of the women reported ever using cocaine, and less than .5 percent reported using it during the previous year. Less than 1 percent (.8 percent) of the women reported ever using crack cocaine. Alcohol use by women is highest among young, unmarried Caucasian women who are better educated, with higher incomes, and who work outside the home.[19]

Crack use was highest among African-American women. And most women who use crack also use alcohol and nicotine.[20]

From all that we currently understand, drawing on multiple studies, about the relative effects of cocaine versus alcohol, alcohol appears to have more enduring effects on the brains of far more children. Clear conclusions as to the long-term impact of cocaine are confounded by the fact that cocaine-abusing mothers may also be using alcohol and nicotine. But we do know without a doubt that fetal alcohol syndrome from alcohol use alone is a major cause of retardation. Given the documented impact of alcohol versus cocaine, and the huge disparities between the numbers of women abusing alcohol or abusing cocaine, we appear to be pointing to the wrong drug and the wrong people in our concern about drug-exposed children. Many experts believe that fetal alcohol exposure, particularly because it may occur undetected and go untreated, may well be the single largest factor setting up physical and neurological conditions that predispose American babies to aggressive and violent behavior.[21]

TEETER TOTTER, FIRE AND WATER

The ways in which teratogens affect the fetus, in addition to the current data on the scope of the problem, are summarized below. Each of these drugs is the subject of numerous studies. They appear in the order of their popularity and use among childbearing women. This summary is limited to variables that are linked to aggressive behavior.

Alcohol: Exposure to alcohol during fetal development causes a continuum of effects, the most extreme of which is fetal alcohol syndrome (FAS). Fetal alcohol effects (FAE) is a term used to describe a range of effects that are not as severe as FAS. Because the effects are subtler than those of FAS, they often go undiagnosed in early development. Alcohol (ethanol) ingested by the mother crosses the placenta and can alter the development of the fetal nervous system by interfering with cell migration, the production of neurotransmitters, and brain growth. Even before the mother is aware of her pregnancy, alcohol may have caused significant damage. Immature neurons first appear around the eleventh day after conception, when the embryo is no larger than a grain of rice. If at this time a mother is drinking to the point of intoxication, alcohol may affect the growth and differentiation of the neural cells. Early and excessive alcohol consumption causes chromosomal aberrations, impedes the transfer of essential nutrients through the placenta, and impairs the baby's immune system. The possible damage to a fetus associated with intrauterine exposure covers a wide range of systems such as heart, kidneys, limbs, lungs, skin, and connective tissue. But the effects of alcohol that play the greatest role in setting up later violent behavior are those that affect the brain. Cognitive deficits, learning disabilities, and behavior problems, including attention deficits, hyperactivity, and high distractibility, are all strongly associated with fetal alcohol syndrome and fetal alcohol effects.

Many studies confirm the long-term teratogenic effects of prenatal alcohol exposure on infants, children, adolescents, and adults. The symptoms evolve with maturation. At birth FAS babies may be below the tenth percentile for normal birth weight, arrive prematurely, and have small head circumferences. They may have visible distortions of the face, but these may be hard to recognize in the newborn. As the baby progresses through the first months, damage to the central nervous system may gradually become detectable when he or she is slow to walk and talk and has difficulty learning and remembering new skills.

One study done in 1993 followed 382 inner-city mothers and their babies prenatally and throughout the child's first year. Based on twice-monthly prenatal interviews of the mothers, the researchers calculated the amount of alcohol consumed during pregnancy. At birth, the infants were divided into groups reflecting the timing and amount of the mother's alcohol consumption. The infants were followed at regular intervals for a year to assess their cognitive development. The study found that there were clinically significant effects on mental performance even in infants prenatally exposed to as little as .5 ounce of alcohol per day, the amount in a single drink. The number of children with discernible mental handicaps more than doubled with exposure to one drink per day. Another study of fifty-three eighteen- to nineteen-month-old toddlers corroborated these findings. The children exposed to alcohol during the first two trimesters or throughout pregnancy scored significantly lower on later assessments of language and other cognitive tasks. Continuous exposure to alcohol throughout gestation resulted in impairments to both gross- and fine-motor skills such as walking and self-feeding.[22]

As with thalidomide, specific birth defects from alcohol exposure are related to the quantity and timing of the mother's consumption relative to the specific developmental processes underway in the fetus, irrespective of other factors such as family history or the nutrition of the mother. Pregnant women who consume between one and two drinks per day are twice as likely as nondrinkers to have low-birth-weight babies and are at increased risk of miscarrying during the second trimester of pregnancy.[23] Chronic heavy alcohol consumption, which is defined as three or more drinks a day, throughout pregnancy usually results in retarded physical growth and impaired brain functioning together with the classical facial indications of fetal alcohol syndrome: small head, small eyes, short openings between the eyelids, flattening of the jawbone region, thin upper lip, and poorly developed vertical ridges between the nose and mouth. Facial malformations are linked to alcohol exposure during the first eight weeks. The effects on head circumference and brain growth appear to be linked to exposure in both the first and the third trimesters. One study has connected minor physical anomalies in children to heavy drinking (defined as one drink per day) at or around the time of conception. Defects in learning and motor skills are associated with exposure in the third trimester.[24]

Episodic binge drinking, which is defined as six or more drinks in one day, or regular consumption in just the first and second trimesters increases the probability of general developmental deficits, delayed speech acquisition, and skeletal abnormalities. Alcohol abuse limited to the third trimester can have a negative impact on future cognitive and behavioral functioning. Moderate social drinking anytime during pregnancy, especially in the first eight weeks, may result in more subtle neurological deficits such as attention difficulties or memory problems.[25]

A 1997 report of alcohol use among pregnant women revealed that more than 16 percent admitted to at least one alcoholic drink in the previous month.[26] Of the 1,313 women surveyed, 3.5 percent admitted to seven or more drinks a week or binge drinking of five or more drinks at one time within the previous month. This represents an increase in alcohol use by pregnant women of more than 300 percent since the same survey was conducted in 1991, when only .8 percent admitted these practices.

Perhaps the most damaging combination of all to a baby is prenatal alcohol exposure in conjunction with maternal stress. Dr. Mary Schneider, of the Harlow Primate Laboratories at the University of Wisconsin in Madison, believes that this is the worst possible combination for producing aggression in offspring, particularly when it occurs early in the pregnancy. In discussing her research on long-term impact on rhesus monkeys of prenatal exposure to alcohol combined with maternal stress, Dr. Schneider says:

> These animals look sort of ADD [attention deficit disordered] when they're younger. Later, they are the most aggressive in their peer groups, especially when those groups are just forming. It appears that early gestational stress is more harmful than mid- or later-term stress.[27]

When the same monkeys were tested for learning and memory tasks at twelve to eighteen months, which is equivalent to about five years of age in humans, they were highly destructible, were delayed in their motor development, and had lower than average muscle tone and activity levels. But then they would unpredictably flip into high intensity and become very impulsive in their learning tasks.

Taken together, the studies indicate that there is no safe time or safe level for fetal exposure to alcohol. In a recent study, Dr. Paul LeMoine, the French physician who first discovered FAS twenty-five years ago, found that it appears that tobacco further facilitates the damaging effect of alcohol on the fetus. LeMoine says that in even "moderately alcoholic" mothers, heavy smoking greatly increases the chance of FAS.[28]

Alcohol consumption by the father may also be a factor affecting fetal intellectual development. While the researchers theorize that there may be a genetic link, none has yet been confirmed.[29] There is general agreement, however, that the sons of alcoholics, regardless of how they were raised (e.g., adoption by nonalcoholic parents), have a higher incidence of alcoholism. The heritability of alcoholism is currently being studied. It also appears that alcohol abuse by a male may affect his ability to produce normal offspring. Studies done on rodents show that delayed sexual maturation and onset of puberty are consistent outcomes of paternal alcoholism.[30] Researchers postulate that alcohol and other drugs may impair the sperm directly, or that the chemical composition of semen is altered so that the ejaculated sperm may be affected, or that certain sperm may be selected for survival following prolonged exposure to alcohol. Questions have also been raised as to the impact on the ovum or embryo of semen that has been negatively affected by alcohol. Further research on these theories is currently underway.[31]

Fetal alcohol syndrome is the leading cause of mental retardation in the Western world, surpassing even Down's syndrome, cerebral palsy, and spina bifida. There are 2.2 diagnosed FAS babies out of every 1,000 live births, with related expenditures estimated at approximately $250 million annually.[32] The incidence of FAE children is three times that of FAS. In addition, there may be an even more subtle impact from alcohol that does not show up in either the FAS or the FAE diagnosis. A recent study that examined the behavioral patterns of sixty-eight five year olds prenatally exposed to alcohol but not diagnosed with either FAS or FAE found that they showed higher rates of aggressive, highly reactive, and acting-out behavior.[33]

In the children adversely affected by prenatal exposure to alcohol, we see the entire spectrum of educational, social, and behavioral problems that compromise their future. With measurable deficits in IQ ranging from profoundly retarded to low normal, these children perform very differently in school than their nonexposed peers. They have problems with short-term memory on both verbal and visual tasks, difficulty in processing information, very low comprehension in mathematics, and inflexibility when solving everyday problems. In addition to these cognitive impairments, 85 percent of FAS children have attention deficits combined with hyperactivity (ADHD). Because the ADHD percentage holds true regardless of wide environmental differences among these children, this outcome provides clear evidence of the permanent damage alcohol wreaks on the central nervous system during fetal development.

FAS children also show a variety of social deficits. One longitudinal study found that parent ratings of 158 of these children placed them at the ninety-first percentile on a mean ranking of social problems.[34] They were stubborn and hard to discipline and had extreme difficulty in respecting their own and other people's boundaries. The FAS children inappropriately sought affection and demanded attention and were overly tactile with other people. Other children avoided them.[35]

The tragedy of FAS children and their parents is poignantly told by Michael Dorris in his book *The Broken Cord*. Dorris describes the anguish of learning that his adopted son, Adam, is permanently "learning disabled" at the time Adam is in kindergarten:

My son, however, was not destined to follow in my musical or medicine ball footsteps, nor was he likely to become, according to his WPPSI scores, a star in any other field. The psychologist's summation of Adam's performance was less than encouraging. His overall

IQ fell into the "borderline" category, and his skills ranged from approximately a year below his age level in some visual tasks to considerably greater disparities from the norm in "areas requiring attention to auditory input." This translated to mean that Adam had trouble concentrating, particularly when dealing with abstractions. Furthermore, he was found to be more active than expected for his age level, impulsive in his approach to tasks, and highly destructible ("both auditorily and visually").

I listened, stunned with disappointment and worry, as she outlined a recommended educational program for "children like Adam." If he were to be in a regular school, he would require lots of external structure and would have to avoid "overstimulation." A teacher might want to provide him with a "study booth" set apart from his classmates to ensure a distraction-free environment. The main body of the psychologist's eventual written report concluded with the sentence: "In the same sense, monitoring of TV programs and movies would be even more important to a child like Adam, as he is highly stimuable and unable to inhibit the excitement once the wheels are set in motion."[36]

As FAS children mature, these characteristics may become more pronounced. Long-term follow-up typically shows an increase in attention deficit and hyperactive behaviors when children's scores in grade school are compared to their earlier preschool scores. As the children become adolescents, they often show an increase in distractibility, impulsivity, inattentiveness, disorganization, restlessness, and agitation, and they become less cooperative.[37] Lack of judgment, poor decision making, high frustration, impulsivity, and difficulty in perceiving social cues render these children at high risk for aggressive behavior and of being co-opted by negative role models during adolescence. When LeMoine went back to find 124 of the 127 FAS patients who first brought the FAS diagnosis to public knowledge, he found 106 of them in institutions.

Michael Dorris's account of his personal journey with Adam is testimony to the fact that, even with loving parents and exceptional resources, the damage is not reversible. In the foreword, Dorris's wife, noted author Louise Erdrich, writes:

> Yet, in loving Adam, we bow to fate. Few of his problems can be solved or ultimately changed. So instead, Michael and I concentrate on only what we can control—our own reactions. If we can muster grace, joy, or happiness in helping him confront and conquer the difficulties life presents . . . then we have received gifts. Adam has been deprived of giving so much else. . . . Everyone agrees that the best answer is not to lock up pregnant women, but to treat them. However, this problem is now generations in the making. Women who themselves suffer from Fetal Alcohol Syndrome or Effect are extremely difficult to counsel because one of the most damaging aspects of FAS is the inability to make cause-effect connections, or to "think ahead."[38]

Tobacco/Nicotine: Among women of childbearing age, cigarette use occurs as frequently as alcohol use. But women are less likely to decrease tobacco use than the use of other drugs while pregnant. Women who smoke are most likely to be Caucasian, married, less educated, and users of alcohol and illicit drugs. Tobacco exposure correlates with low birth weight, prematurity, lung disorders, and sudden infant death syndrome.[39] Nicotine-exposed children may experience delays and difficulties in performing the basic tasks of infancy such as eye contact, sucking, and head turning. Dr. David Olds and his colleagues found that by ages four and eight, children born to mothers who smoked had IQs that were four to five points lower than the comparison group of children born to nonsmoking mothers. At school age, children of mothers who smoke may be at risk of poor reading skills, attention deficits, and hyperactivity.[40]

Prenatal exposure to nicotine may also directly affect the developing brain.[41] Data from the Ottawa Prenatal Prospective done in

Canada in 1992 show that prenatal exposure to nicotine, as to alcohol, is related to impulsiveness and attention deficits in six year olds.[42] Another report, using a national sample in the United States, found that prenatal exposure to tobacco predicted an increased rate of behavior problems in children ages four through eleven.[43] Numerous studies have found small deficits in intellectual development and higher rates of hyperactivity attributable to smoking during pregnancy.[44]

Smoking seems to do the most damage during the last four months of pregnancy. Birth weight does not appear to be affected by smoking before the end of the fifth month. The implication of these findings is that reduction in smoking even as late as mid-gestation may be enough to effectively protect the developing fetal brain. By supplying the fetus with greater nutrients and oxygen and by reducing the cerebral cortex's exposure to nicotine, many potential problems can be averted.[45] In 1995 Brigham and Women's Hospital in Boston reported that smoking by pregnant women was linked to the deaths of 5,600 babies, 115,000 miscarriages, 53,000 low-birth-weight babies, and 22,000 babies who needed intensive care at birth each year in the United States. The study stated that 18 percent to 19 percent of all pregnant women smoke. Another 3,700 children die each year by the age of one month from complications caused by tobacco smoke during the mother's pregnancy, many because they were too tiny to survive. Also attributed to smoking by pregnant women are 1,900 cases of SIDS (sudden infant death syndrome) annually. Tobacco has been implicated as an exacerbating factor in increased impairments to the fetuses of women who drink alcohol.

Lead: Lead has long been linked with a capacity to induce abortion, a use to which it was commonly put at the turn of the century to terminate unwanted pregnancies. In high doses, lead will cross the placenta and accumulate in the fetal bones and liver. Contaminating pregnant women through water from old pipes, old paint, improperly glazed dishes, and gasoline emissions, this toxin appears to be showing up more, particularly in the blood of urban children.[46] Lead's most invasive impact is on the nervous system, whether prenatally or postnatally absorbed. Studies show that lead absorption by children can lead to a lowering of IQ and a significant increase of impulsivity, distractibility, and learning disabilities.

A 1996 study by Dr. Herbert Niedleman, professor of psychiatry and pediatrics at the University of Pittsburgh Medical School, found that even when race, poverty, and family stability are taken into account, low levels of lead significantly increase the rate of attention problems, aggression, and delinquency. Children who had been exposed to lead showed no external physical differences from normal children; the effects were entirely behavioral. Niedleman believes that lead acts on the neocortex in such a way as to block its ability to limit impulsive behavior. He estimates that one in twelve children are affected, primarily boys growing up in urban communities where old pipes, old paint, and auto emissions are concentrated. In February 1996 during an interview on National Public Radio, Niedleman stated that 5 percent to 20 percent of criminality could be prevented by "removing lead from old housing stock before it gets into children rather than removing it from children once it gets into their bodies."

The connection between later criminality and the early poisoning of brain tissue has triggered a recent study by Deborah Denno, a law professor at Fordham University in New York. Denno looked at a group of nearly five hundred boys ages birth to twenty-three. To her surprise, rather than the family factors, which she expected to be the largest contributing factor to delinquency, she found that lead poisoning is the single best predictor of boys' disciplinary problems in school. These problems are in turn associated with later adult crime.[47]

Cocaine: Cocaine-exposed babies show clear signs of addiction at birth. Researchers have found that babies exposed prenatally to cocaine, as to alcohol, have a lower weight at birth, are shorter, and have a smaller head. They cry, often piercingly, shake, show erratic sleep-wake cycles, have trouble feeding, and are difficult to comfort. Due to its effect of raising blood pressure and restricting blood flow to the placenta, cocaine increases complications during pregnancy, including prematurity, preterm labor, precipitous labor, and premature detachment of the placenta.[48]

Despite the initial press and public hysteria, the long-term impact of prenatal exposure to cocaine is not yet clear. During the late 1980s and early 1990s a series of studies measuring intelligence and motor skills failed to find significant differences between cocaine-exposed babies and nonexposed babies. The tests used in these studies, however, did not directly measure the babies' abilities to regulate emotional states or their attentional capabilities. More recent research, on both other animals and infants, suggests that cocaine may damage the areas of the brain that regulate the capacities for arousal and attention—areas that may not show up except on more finely tuned assessments, which are typically not performed until later in life when some affected children show attentional or emotional differences in a classroom setting. Cocaine-affected children are frequently more reactive to stimuli, have a reduced ability to modulate their level of arousal, and have more difficulty focusing and attending to specific stimuli. Researchers believe that the most serious damage occurs during the first trimester of gestation. Cocaine exposure at that time may irreversibly alter the development and function of neurotransmitters that are key to assuring that the embryonic brain cells migrate to their proper place in the cortex. This process, which is completed during the first 120–125 days of life, has a profound impact on synaptic development, which begins during the third trimester of gestation and continues for the first few years after birth. These interruptions of cell migration due to cocaine exposure may result in minute differences in brain wiring, later causing children to become more agitated in the face of novelty or stress, and more destructible and less persistent in completing structured tasks.[49]

In one study done recently at Yale University by Dr. Linda Mayes, three-month-old infants who had been exposed to cocaine in utero had a more difficult time processing novel information than nonexposed babies. For example, rather than becoming alert and showing interest in a picture of a new face, they became overaroused and irritable more quickly, showed more negative facial expressions, and cried for longer periods of time. Researchers have also reported significant differences between cocaine exposed and nonexposed preschool children in individual developmental domains such as speech and language.[50] Mayes warns, however, that most cocaine-abusing mothers may use one or more additional drugs and that not all babies are affected: "It's very hard to separate out these effects in a human study. Most of these children are also growing up in complicated and tragic worlds where many of the effects of prenatal drug exposure, including cocaine, are combined with environmental neglect due to the mother's illness."[51]

While the worst of the anticipated effects of prenatal cocaine exposure have failed to appear, children who have had such exposure remain at high risk. During the initial withdrawal from cocaine dependency following birth, they are difficult babies to care for, even in supportive and loving environments. But when these infants are entrusted to parents who are themselves addicted to drugs, child neglect and abuse rather than prenatal toxicity may be the real threat to the developing child. Addicted parents leave their babies with multiple, often unskilled caregivers; the children are often malnourished, poorly housed, and deprived of the experiences and opportunities for play necessary for normal cognitive development.[52] Cocaine-abusing parents also tend to be agitated and inconsistent in their responses to their babies. Capacities for trust, self-esteem, focused learning, and problem-solving skills may be diminished by lack of competent adult attention. In addition, parents who use illegal drugs are also frequently involved in the criminal justice system. As a result, cocaine-exposed children often grow up without a consistent adult to teach prosocial values. In an environment where antisocial behaviors may be the norm, aggressive, even violent behavior, may be an everyday response to minor irritations.

Dr. Mayes, who has spent much of her career studying the long-range impact of teratogens on children, believes that the real poverty such children face goes well beyond a lack of dollars. Rather, it is a deeper emotional impoverishment caused by such factors as the absence of adult time and consistent loving attention, or the presence of parental depression or chronic medical problems that push the child's needs into the background. "Too often with these children there is a poverty of attention, consistency, safety, health, stimulation, and basic attention to the child's needs," Dr. Mayes says. "And, when we lose one generation, we really lose several."[53]

The number of children born exposed to cocaine in utero has not significantly changed in the last decade; it exceeds 100,000 children annually.[54] While hundreds of thousands of such children remain in the care of drug-addicted parents, the number in foster care continues to rise. Because children in foster care are often moved from one home to another and not provided with the therapy necessary for children to deal with the loss of parents, placing the children of drug-abusing parents in foster care does not generally offset the early risks associated with later violent behavior.

Marijuana: Marijuana seems to have its strongest impact on the verbal and memory domains of learning. Children who were prenatally exposed to marijuana were tested at age four as part of the Ottawa Prenatal Prospective Study. On cognitive tests, marijuana-exposed children showed lower scores on both the verbal and the memory tasks. Another study focusing on six year olds exposed to marijuana found that they performed poorly on tasks requiring attention. The mothers of these children described them as being impulsive and hyperactive.[55] While these studies are far less numerous and less conclusive than those done on alcohol, tobacco, and cocaine, they are of interest due to their relevance to both cognitive and behavioral problems that may place children at relatively greater risk of aggression. To date, there are no studies reported that examine the correlation between prenatal exposure to marijuana and behaviors identified as antecedents to later aggressive behavior.

Heroin: Studies consistently link prenatal heroin exposure to a relatively low incidence of brain damage (6 percent) that includes microcephaly and cerebral palsy.[56] As with the other drugs, decreased head circumference, increased prematurity, and decreased birth weight are associated with parental heroin addiction. Like the cocaine babies, infants born to a mother addicted to heroin go through withdrawal and there is an increased risk of infant death. It is interesting to note that children born to heroin-addicted fathers (7.9 percent) showed higher rates of neurological impairment than children born to heroin-addicted mothers (6 percent).[57] It is uncertain whether this is due to a genetic effect or to environmental neglect.

A study of eighty-three Israeli children born to heroin-addicted mothers showed that the environment after birth exerts a strong influence on developmental outcomes. Twenty percent of the heroin-exposed children who were adopted at a young age had attentional problems at ages five and six compared to 75 percent of children raised by a biological parent or parents. The conclusion of this 1995 study was that when one or both parents are addicted, severe environmental deprivation is the key factor influencing children's performance, rather than the earlier biological vulnerabilities, which appear to diminish in a nurturing home.[58]

The long-term studies on the impact of prenatal exposure to heroin suggest that by adolescence heroin-exposed children show more behavioral and conduct problems, including impulsivity, criminal activity, early substance abuse, antisocial behavior, and school dropout. Here again, it is not clear how much these problems stem from prenatal heroin exposure and how much they stem from the cumulative effect of the discord and dysfunction that is typical of substance-abusing households.[59] There also appears to be a relatively high correlation between attention-deficit/hyperactivity disorder and later opiate use. As is true of cocaine users, ADHD is often seen in heroin addicts.

Prescribed Legal Drugs: Legal drugs are another category of toxins that bear watching for adverse effects on fetal development. Thalidomide, DES, and Bendectin are examples of prescription drugs once widely prescribed and thought safe that, in fact, proved drastically harmful to fetal development, though none of these were linked either directly or indirectly to damage to the central nervous system or to the variables associated with later violent behavior. As the sensitive processes underway in the embryonic brain are only recently coming to light and their functions still are being discovered, the best policy for pregnant women is "when in doubt, don't."

As we become more conscious of the sensitivity of the baby during and immediately following birth, the routine administration of drugs during labor and delivery, once unquestioned, is being examined in relationship to later behavioral outcomes. Several studies indicate that the use of obstetrical anesthesia during delivery may cause subtle alterations in the formation of neurons, synapses, and neural transmitters that are undetectable at birth. One seven-year study of over three thousand babies showed long-lasting effects of anesthesia on behavior and motor development. These babies were more likely to be slow to sit, stand, and walk. By age seven they lagged in language skills; their capacities for memory and judgment were also affected.[60] Dr. Bertel Jacobson, a Swedish researcher, found a connection between adult addiction to opium and the use of opiates, barbiturates, and nitrous oxide at birth.[61]

Malnutrition: While teratogens such as alcohol and tobacco may cross the placenta to disrupt development in the fetal brain, the absence of essential nutrients during pregnancy may generate similar repercussions. Sensitivity to malnutrition is particularly profound during the period of most rapid brain growth, which occurs from the third prenatal trimester through the second year after birth. The brain is one of the most metabolically active organs, utilizing 20 percent of the body's total oxygen in a resting state. A steady supply of glucose is essential for brain cells to grow and to communicate with each other. In addition, diet, especially amino acids, appears to play a role in the synthesis and balance of neurotransmitters, which are implicated in neurological and psychiatric disorders. Iron is of particular importance to brain development. Iron deficiency in utero or during the first twenty-four months after birth may cause permanent damage to the brain. Anemia (iron shortage) is associated with short attention spans, impaired memory, and disruptive behavior in preschoolers.[62] Low levels of iron also have been linked to lower scores on learning and school achievement tests.[63]

Protein deficiencies can lead to shortages of tryptophan or tyrosine, amino acids essential to production of serotonin and dopamine, which are linked to reactive behavior. A shortage in either of these neurotransmitters may cause already aggressive children to perceive hostile intentions where none exist. When presented with an ambiguous situation, tryptophan-/and tyrosine-deprived boys will read it as threatening and are more inclined to behave impulsively.[64]

Similar to the effects of alcohol and other drugs, malnutrition during gestation may result in a series of cognitive, social, and behavioral deficits with long-term consequences. Due to obvious ethical considerations, most of our information on malnutrition comes from animal studies or studies of naturally occurring conditions for children in underdeveloped countries. These studies provide information with serious implications. The impact of malnutrition on cognitive skills appears to be less invasive than the impact on social and emotional behaviors. Animals malnourished prenatally may perform essential tasks as quickly and as well as normal animals. But they are less able to learn nonessential skills that demand flexible or adaptive responses, or to perform as well under stress. They show little interest in new environments, are shy or aggressive with cage mates, and tend to withdraw from social situations. And animals malnourished both before and after birth are unpredictable, apprehensive, and aggressive as adults. They do not engage in normal play and are often aggressive toward humans and other animals.[65] Studies on humans have shown that children born small for their gestational age later showed lower IQs than normal children. Early and continuing malnutrition combined with extreme deprivation may lead to mental retardation.[66]

Most researchers agree that it is difficult to separate the purely biological impact of malnutrition from other environmental influ-

ences. For the last twenty years, malnutrition has been seen as inseparable from its environmental context, where a host of conditions such
as poverty, illness, and competition for resources are typically inter-
twined in their impact. The ongoing interactive nature of these variables is poignantly illustrated in a 1979 study by Dr. Barry Lester that
examines the relationship between newborn nutritional status and the
responsiveness of parents to their child's cry. As is typical, the "small-
for-date" babies studied generally showed poor organization of their
physical responses. They were easily startled, had tremors, and showed
abnormal skin color changes compared to babies who were adequately
nourished. Their cries, which were acoustically evaluated by the researchers, were higher, of shorter duration, and had longer gaps between them. Instead of engendering loving and protective feelings
from parents, these cries often caused parents to feel irritated or
alarmed and anxious. In responding to their babies, the parents were
often upset and agitated rather than calm and soothing. Malnutrition inhibited the babies' development of the skills that typically elicit
sympathetic emotional responses from caregivers, responses that are
particularly essential to future gains by malnourished babies.[67]

While the cognitive performances of malnourished children are
clearly compromised, particularly in impoverished environments, a
greater threat for these babies is in the area of emotional and social
behaviors. Malnourished babies appear to have difficulty attending
to directions, persisting in a difficult task, and screening out irrelevant
details. Attentiveness in general is compromised, as are persistence,
curiosity, interest in exploration, and demonstration of initiative. They
become more agitated, especially under stress. These qualities persist
over time and take their toll in cognitive tasks as the children move
into adolescence. Even when nutritional problems are remediated after
the first two years, malnourished children may have temperamental
characteristics such as hyperalertness and distractibility. The caregiver
reacts negatively to those characteristics, and the child's learning then
suffers.[68] A growing body of evidence suggests that the damage done

by prenatal malnutrition is greatly exacerbated in deprived social environments.

The behaviors of prenatally malnourished children bear a similarity to those of children who are alcohol or drug affected. It appears that either toxins or the absence of essential nutrients at this crucial time causes children to be distracted and inattentive and reduces their ability to relate to other people. It is also likely that neglectful emotional environments commonly contribute to these similarities in the lives of both malnourished and drug-affected children. For many children, this may pave a path to later antisocial behavior. Because there is a high correlation between poverty and malnutrition, this information, though mostly from animal subjects, has important policy implications, especially when we realize that more than a quarter of American children under four now live below the poverty level. Americans have long been familiar with the extreme cases of malnourished children in faraway places like Somalia, India, and Rwanda. We read the statistics or see footage of American Red Cross rescue efforts elsewhere in the world and fail to recognize that in any month in the United States we have more children malnourished than the total number of children in Angola, Haiti, Zimbabwe, El Salvador, or Cambodia.[69]

Genetic Influences: It is important in any discussion of the term *genetics* to understand that great confusion often results from the imprecise way in which this term is used. Many people assume that genetic means an unalterable condition or trait that is inherited from parents or ancestors. In fact, it means only that the trait or condition in question came through the genes and is part of the biological makeup of the organism. Genes do carry hereditary information, but this can be at least partially altered by environmental factors in the womb. For example, ADHD is considered a genetic condition, but it is not clear whether it comes through the genes because it is inherited from a biological relative or because of damage to the baby's genes (e.g., from prenatal exposure to alcohol or cocaine). A child's genes may be shaped by either nature (inherited factors) or nurture (the chemical or hormonal environment during gestation).

In his recent book *The Psychopathology of Crime,* which attempts to redefine violent crime as a form of mental illness, Dr. Adrian Raine summarizes the role of heritability in criminal behavior by reviewing all known studies in this area.[70] Much of the data is from studies of twins reared apart or of children adopted from or by criminal parents. Studies originating from several different countries seem to conclude that there is no heritability for either juvenile delinquency or violent crime. Interestingly, fourteen out of fifteen of these studies point to heritability for petty property crimes.

There does appear to be some evidence that people with certain biological vulnerabilities born into high-risk environments are more likely to act in violent ways. For example, scientists hypothesize that people who are born with relatively "low arousal" or nervous systems that are slow to reach a point of emotional excitement are more able to face risky situations with minimal stress. A child with such qualities might in one environment develop into a race car driver or a stockbroker, and in another, turn to robbing convenience stores. Research on this variable, known as serotonin (5HT) system function, has linked this low-arousal pattern with aggressive disorders and suicide in humans and with aggressive and self-injuring behavior in animals.[71] Emotional problems, particularly major depression, is linked to the serotonin-norepinephrine systems as well as to imbalances of other brain chemicals such as dopamines.[72] These factors, while environmentally influenced, are also partially genetically controlled and may be heritable.[73] Alcohol and other toxins may cause the mutation of the genes that control the production or set points (established levels) of these neurotransmitters.[74]

A controversial but respected figure in the study of the potential role of genetics is Dr. Sarnoff Mednick at the University of California. Dr. Mednick's work focuses on schizophrenia, which he believes is caused by prenatal exposure to the flu virus during the second trimester of pregnancy. He also believes that this environmentally induced genetic alteration produces an increased risk of violent behavior in subsequent generations. In a study of forty-seven children of schizophrenic mothers, Dr. Mednick found that 55 percent of the children developed a serious psychiatric disorder that included violent behavior. Of the forty-seven, five became schizophrenic, eleven are in prison for violent offenses, and nine have been diagnosed as sociopaths. Dr. Mednick attributes these outcomes to a combination of altered genetics and environmental neglect due to the mothers' mental illness.

Another researcher, Dr. David Lykken, at the University of Minnesota's Twin Research Center, has found that the traits of aggressiveness and impulsivity correlate as strongly in twins who have been raised apart as in twins who have been raised together.[75] But like the research on malnutrition, the research on genetics leads to the conclusion that none of these factors in isolation cause negative outcomes. Rather, it is the interaction of biological variables with environmental variables that results in prosocial or antisocial outcomes. The linchpin in this relationship is consistently the baby's developing brain. While such genetic vulnerabilities may not be preventable, their presence can be ameliorated with nurturing care from the first years of life.

Minor Physical Anomalies: Eric Smith's strange ears are a classic example of minor physical anomalies (MPAs)—external physical signs that correlate highly with central nervous system damage during gestation. A growing body of research links MPAs with aggression, attentional problems, and hyperactivity. Researchers specializing in hyperactivity suspect that the same prenatal insults that cause MPAs inflict minor damage to the central nervous system, often resulting in a predisposition toward impulsive behavior. This impulsivity, particularly in combination with negative familial or environmental factors, may lead to antisocial behavior later in life.[76]

A longitudinal study of 129 twelve-year-old boys with minor physical anomalies found that they had significantly higher rates of arrest through the age of twenty-one than normal boys matched for other variables. This relationship was statistically related to violent crime and was also strongly linked to recidivistic violent arrests.[77] While the number of studies linking minor physical anomalies with violence is not large enough to be conclusive, the existing evidence warrants further inquiry and may provide us with an overt physical signal that neurological assessments are warranted when unusual physical features are detected at birth. Focused health and educational interventions on Eric and his family from the beginning of his life could have made a great difference for Eric and for his little victim, Derrick.

4

Love's Labor Lost:

ADVERSE EXPERIENCES

IN THE WOMB AND AT BIRTH

. . . Sancho Fergus,
my boy child, had such great shoulders,
when he was born his head
came out, the rest of him stuck. And he opened
his eyes: his head out there all alone
in the room, he squinted with pained,
barely unglued eyes at the ninth-month's
blood splashing beneath him
on the floor. And almost
smiled, I thought, almost forgave it all in advance.

When he came wholly forth
I took him up in my hands and bent
over and smelled the black glistening fur
of his head, as empty space
must have bent over the newborn planet
and smelled the grasslands and the ferns.

—GALWAY KINNELL
The Book of Nightmares

My grandma told me that when I was first born I didn't breathe for seventy-nine seconds. Everybody was freaking out. The umbilical cord was wrapped around my neck, and I was blue. So they rushed me away, and I wasn't crying and I wasn't breathing and I wasn't doing nothing. I was totally blue. Finally, my grandpa had to take one of the doctors and slam him up against a brick wall before they would tell him anything. And they said that I hadn't breathed for seventy-nine seconds and right now they were going to do some tests to make sure that I was okay. And the whole time my mom was screaming, "I want my baby. I want my baby." And they wouldn't let her see me. So for the whole time she was in the hospital, I think it might have been about six days or so, the whole time she was in there she didn't get to see me until the day they finally released us. She was freaking out and screaming. The nurses wouldn't tell her nothing. By the time she was healthy enough to get up and walk—she was really weak after I was born—she was throwing things around. She was going into that manic depressive thing where one minute she was depressed and the next minute she was just like totally anxious and totally just real aggressive to everybody and spouting off at the mouth and acting like they was doing wrong to me. . . . At first my grandma and grandpa thought it was post-partum depression. . . . They figured it would be anywhere from like a week after I was released from the hospital up to a month. And after that is when they began to start worrying really. . . .

My mom and dad were living in a house behind my grandparents. . . . My grandmother thought maybe I cried so much because of the gas leak. My mom left for the day, and [Grandma] took me over to the house to make sure everything was okay, and there wasn't nothing burning and she said that I was fine the whole time I was in the house that my mom wasn't there. . . . She was there eight hours or so cleaning up my mom's house because my mom wouldn't clean. There was dirty diapers from my brother everywhere, and the whole time I was there I was fine. And she said she didn't think it was the gas. It was my mom being so stressed out and so uptight it was causing me to maybe sense it. [Mom] was freaking out the whole time, real depressed, bouts of screaming and crying and outrageous fits. Then she'd clam up and wouldn't talk to anybody. My grandma said she was acting like a little ten-year-old kid that was throwing a fit.

JEFFREY, AUGUST 1996

He was born blue. He had yellow jaundice. He had a lot of medical problems. It wasn't anything he had to have surgery for. He was just always sick. There was always some sort of an illness that he was in the hospital for. I was upset, you know, 'cause my little brother that they kept on talking about all this time that he was comin', that he was comin', that he was comin'! Then he comes and it's like I can't be there with him. Why can't he be there with me, you know? All I know is that he was always sick. He was just sick. That's all my mother would tell me. I really don't think my mother could have taken care of him, anyway.

JOHN, AUGUST 1996

While she is still wet from the womb, as she breathes her first breath, cries her first cry, feels her first gusts of cool air, her brain is building itself at a rate never to be repeated. She already knows the sound of her mother's voice and turns to it. She gazes at her mother's face with great concentration. Synapses in her tiny brain are sprouting in response to each sensation. The most powerful computer in the world has been waiting for these moments of light, and smell, and touch, and sound, and taste—the carpenters of the human brain.

She will turn toward her mother's voice to keep it coming. She knows her mother's smell and her father's voice if he has been close to her mother in the last two months. She may already recognize and prefer a familiar nursery rhyme, or song, or concerto. Her limbs may move spontaneously toward her mother's voice in a dance that mirrors the rhythms of the words. Within a few weeks her own sounds will replicate those rhythms. She can imitate facial expressions. She can follow a bright object moving slowly across her field of vision. She sees the world in color and contrasts. She is fully equipped to engage her people, to learn, to connect. Everything is new. And every system is poised to take in information—for the first and perhaps most incisive impressions of a lifetime.

Most of us remember our first date, or our first airplane ride, or our first loss of a pet. Those memories are now long ago perceived, processed, and stored in the cortex of our brains where they have been at least somewhat gentled by time and reason. But for the newborn, while conscious memories of the day will be lost, the first somatic sense of what this world is like begins with the tugs and touches of emerging from the womb. Our first experience of this life begins here on the first day. This won't be recorded in language or be retrievable into rational thought. But the limbic brain remembers, and our body remembers. Here is when we begin to build our model of what to expect, of who will be there, of how we will be received, of how safe it is out there, of how we can make ourselves known and be comforted.

This scene, the birth of a competent and complex organism learning at an unimaginable rate, occurs thousands of times every day in our nation. But it occurs too often with little appreciation, let alone celebration of the potential that has just arrived in our midst. We are just beginning to lift the veil on the reality of the competent newborn. Many Americans still view babies as inattentive and unaware. Infants are routinely brokered to whomever will abide the anticipated boredom of physical baby tending, perceived essentially in our culture as a routine and nonskilled series of feedings and diaper changings. In spite of a growing group of educated and very involved fathers, most American men regard their newborns like newly birthed kangaroos that need several months to ripen in mother's pouch. Personhood seems to go hand in hand with a hearty size, and control over one's mouth, limbs, and elimination. Says Dr. Richard Restak, author of

The Infant Mind: "If you start off assuming that infants know nothing, then by a kind of self-fulfilling prophecy, the infant's competence escapes attention."[1]

Until very recently, the notion of connected interactive communication between an adult and a newborn, let alone a fetus, would have been viewed by most parents as foolish. Just three generations ago, the *Atlantic Monthly* described as "a godsend to parents" the following advice from Dr. John B. Watson, who was at that time America's leading child care authority and author of *The Psychological Care of the Infant and Child*, published in 1928:

> The sensible way to bring up children is to treat them as young adults. Dress them, bathe them with care and circumspection. Let your behavior always be objective and kindly firm. Never hug and kiss them. Never let them sit in your lap. If you must, kiss them once on the forehead when they say goodnight. Shake hands with them in the morning. . . . Put the child out in the back yard a large part of the time. Build a fence round the yard, so that it can come to no harm. Do this from the time it is born . . . let it learn to overcome difficulties almost from the moment of birth . . . away from your watchful eye. If your heart is too tender, and you must watch the child, make yourself a peephole, so that you can see without being seen, or use a periscope.[2]

But parents and those who advised them weren't alone in overlooking the capacities of their infants at birth. Until about ten years ago, doctors considered babies to be unseeing and unfeeling at birth. Newborns were routinely held by their feet upside down and slapped at delivery. Routine welcoming for most of us born before the last two decades included immediate removal from our mothers to a table where we were wiped off, weighed, and received stinging drops into our new eyes. Then we were swaddled and laid in a sterile and portable plastic rectangle aptly named the "isolette," where we were wheeled to a brightly lit room full of medical equipment, antiseptic smells, hospital noises, and other distressed newborns. For premature babies, expectations of sentience have been even lower; thought, feeling—even the capacity for pain—was dismissed in the baby born early. Since the advent of neonatal intensive care units in the late 1960s through the late 1980s, breathing tubes, suction tubes, feeding tubes, and shunts were routinely installed without any anesthesia. Shrieks of pain and terror were discounted by medical professionals as being reflexive and without meaning.

Dr. David Chamberlain, president of the Association for Pre and Perinatal Psychology and Health, recounts that one routine procedure necessary for 50 percent of infants weighing less than 1,500 grams involved cutting a hole in the chest and in both sides of the neck, making an incision from the breastbone to the backbone, prying the ribs apart, retracting the left lung, and tying off an artery near the heart. This operation took an average of an hour and a half, during which the baby was flooded with pain and terror. Many died from pain and shock. Yet until 1986, anesthesia was routinely withheld.[3]

A 1993 survey showed that 12 percent of doctors performing circumcisions believed that babies do not feel pain; 35 percent believe they will not remember it even if they do; and only half used any form of anesthesia.[4] The newborn has simply not been seen as whole, as perceiving, as sensitive or thinking in any meaningful way. "It" is the typical pronoun of choice referring to the fetus and as often as not to the newborn. Practices at birth have reflected this objectification. For babies born to loving, welcoming, nurturing families, these early rituals have been a rude shock but have been ameliorated by parental handling and family support. But for babies born into negative or compromised family circumstances where stress has been and will continue, this awakening to life as a painful and discounting experience provides the first factors in the violence equation.

The dismissal of the sentience of the baby is a major obstacle to the curtailment of violence. As long as sensitive attention is denied to the fetus, the newborn, and the toddler, we need not look very far to observe rage in the making. For infants whose birth is compromised by physical difficulties coming into the world, such as struggling with a breech birth or threatened with suffocation from a cord wrapped around the neck, there is exceptional vulnerability and need for reassurance and comfort. When a traumatized baby is instead rejected by his mother, the stage is set for rage and often for violent criminality in adulthood.

Dr. Patricia Brennan at the University of Southern California at Los Angeles, has studied a group of 4,269 males born in Denmark between 1959 and 1961. Birth complications had been recorded at the time of delivery. Demographic, family, and psychosocial factors were recorded during pregnancy and when the child was one year of age. Information collected included whether the pregnancy was wanted or unwanted, whether there had been an attempt to abort the fetus, and whether there was placement of the infant into an institution for more than four months during the child's first year. When the boys were seventeen to nineteen years of age, their criminal status was assessed through a search of the Danish National Criminal Register. Violent crimes were defined as crimes that intentionally threatened, attempted, or inflicted harm on others. These included murder, attempted murder, assault including domestic assault, rape, armed robbery, illegal possession of a weapon, and threats of violence.[5]

Children who suffered birth complications together with maternal rejection in their first year of life were far more likely than others to become violent offenders as adults. Only 4.5 percent of the number of boys had both risk factors. Yet this relatively small number accounted for 18 percent of the total crimes committed by the entire group. Most people would assume that poor social circumstances—especially poverty—would exert an impact at least as strong as maternal rejection, but poor social circumstances combined with birth complications did not produce violent outcomes. The effect was specific to the interaction of maternal rejection with birth complications in this study. Drs. Patricia Brennan, Adrian Raine, and Sarnoff Mednick, also of USC, found a significant correlation between delivery complications (e.g., ruptured uterus, eclampsia, or prolapsed cord), parental mental illness, and violent crime during adolescence and adulthood. In this 1993 study, the highest rates of violent crime occurred when subjects had experienced both a high number of delivery complications and a mentally ill parent. Of those subjects who experienced both parental mental illness and high delivery complications, 32.3 percent were violent as adults compared to 5 percent for mental illness only and 0 percent for high delivery complications only.[6]

When mental illness results in the institutionalization of a parent, the chances of violent outcomes for the children are further increased. The disruption of the mother-infant attachment process due to institutionalization of a child or mother has been associated with affectionless psychopathic criminal behavior.[7] This breaking of the web of trust between primary caregiver and vulnerable infant is often the first step in reducing a child's capacity for empathic connections within other later relationships. It appears that maternal deprivation or separation, especially when combined with a biological factor due to birth complications, greatly increases the likelihood of violent behavior. The influence of birth complications in this equation may be indirect (e.g., cognitive deficits that lead to school failure, then to occupational failure, and ultimately to violence) or direct (e.g., explosive and impulsive behavior due to neuropsychiatric deficits). In either case, a negative familial environment is an exacerbating factor.[8]

This equation doesn't wait for birth. The first environment actively shaping the human brain is the womb. Even before first smiles or tantrums, the womb is host to an interactive biological and neurobiological dance between the mother and the fetus. For more than half a century we have known that what affects mothers emotionally also affects babies. In 1934, Drs. Sontag and Wallace, using very primitive measures of heart and respiratory activity of the mother and fetus, found that when a pregnant patient was pursued by a psychotic husband, the baby was alarmed right along with the mother.[9]

In the same way that the external environment after birth can shape positive infant neurological responses such as curiosity and normal exploratory behavior, and negative responses such as fear of exploration and extreme emotionality in response to stress, researchers suspect that the mother's experience, which is conveyed through the chemistry of the womb, exerts a clear and pervasive influence on the fetus, both emotionally and cognitively. Drs. Susan Clarke and Mary Schneider, of the Wisconsin Psychiatric Research Institute at the University of Wisconsin, have studied this phenomenon in juvenile rhesus monkeys.[10] Dr. Clarke and her colleagues removed six pregnant monkeys from their home cages once a day and exposed them to three brief, unpredictable bursts of sound from an alarm horn over a ten-minute period. This was done beginning in mid-gestation for ninety days. The sound produced a startle response (a stress symptom) and raised the mother monkeys' blood levels of brain chemicals associated with stress. Six undisturbed monkeys, matched for age, weight, and time of gestation served as controls. On four occasions, blood samples were collected from all of the fetal monkeys under anesthesia and were assessed for the level of brain chemicals associated with stress (cortisol and ACTH). The fetuses whose mothers were stressed during pregnancy reflected their mothers' emotional states.

After birth, the babies of the stressed mothers and the control mothers were subjected to a series of stressors, including change of cage, change of cage plus noise, separation, and separation plus noise. When the monkeys were assessed at fifteen and eighteen months of age, the baby monkeys stressed both during gestation and after birth were more likely to experience extreme stress and extreme emotional responses to later stressful events. Monkeys stressed only after birth showed some difficulty as well, but not to the extent of those stressed before birth. The researchers are unsure of exactly how this experience is transferred from mother to baby biologically but theorize that the mother's production of stress hormones has a negative effect on the hippocampus of the baby's brain, which affects the baby's later stress responses. Permanently set on high, the stress response systems of such babies may have a domino effect on their developing brains. Other systems in the brain attempt to counterbalance the high levels of stress hormones produced by such experiences and move to establish normalcy. Researchers hypothesize that prenatal stress sets off a series of reactions in the brain that may ultimately result in depression, premature aging, Cushing's disease, and post-traumatic stress disorder.[11]

Studies on this same group of prenatally stressed infant monkeys as youngsters showed increased and unpredictable defensive behavior and reduced interest in exploring a new environment as compared to the nonstressed control group.[12] Additional studies comparing the two groups show six times more play behavior in the nonstressed group; stressed baby monkeys showed more clinging behavior and less grooming, less approaching, and less sitting with peers. The lack of normal social behaviors among prenatally stressed babies resulted in less adaptive social relationships and ultimately a much higher risk of aggressive behavior to the point that four abnormally stressed animals attempted to kill or actually killed their cage mates. This violent behavior came as a surprise to the researchers; it was not a predicted outcome for the studies. For ethical as well as economic reasons these researchers do not deliberately undertake studies in which aggression is a likely outcome.

Evidence of the long-term impact of prenatal stress on monkeys raises troubling questions about human babies. The abnormal behaviors of rhesus babies resemble that of children described in human temperament research as "inhibited." These children explore their worlds less, are less playful, and become more extremely upset in unfamiliar situations. Their later behavior under stress is more rigid and often self-defeating. The research on primates seems to indicate that prenatal stress is very likely a factor that predisposes children to a "difficult" temperament.[13]

A new generation of researchers at the Harlow Primate Laboratory at the University of Wisconsin have found that prenatal stress induces attentional disorders, diminished cognitive abilities, and neuromotor problems in rhesus monkeys. The earlier the stress is experienced in gestation, the more intense the symptoms. In addition, stress experienced early in rhesus pregnancies produces offspring that weigh less at birth and spend more time in sleep and in a drowsy state. These early stressed babies show greatly increased stress responses by comparison to nonstressed monkeys when they are separated from their mothers.[14]

Rodent studies provide even more troubling evidence of the damage that prenatal stress may cause. In one study, pregnant mice were exposed to unfamiliar laboratory mice, which physically attacked them. High levels of prenatal attacks during late gestation—not early—consistently produced offspring that were aggressive in adulthood. These behavioral differences were accompanied by measurable increases in plasma corticosteroid levels,[15] indicating high stress. This team of researchers hypothesize that antisocial behavior in children may include the fetuses' experience of domestic violence before birth.

During his annual address to the Association for Pre and Perinatal Psychology and Health in 1995, Dr. David Chamberlain illustrated how this prenatal adaptation to stress can play out in a human life. He told the early story of Robert Harris, who had been recently executed in the state of California's gas chamber:

> Harris was born three months early after his mother was kicked brutally in the abdomen by her angry husband and began hemorrhaging. This was only the first of many violent experiences this murderer-in-the-making suffered at the hands of his mother and father, a violence he later turned on innocent animals and people. At age twenty-five, he shot two teenagers point blank, laughed at them after he pulled the trigger, and calmly ate the hamburgers they had just bought for lunch. We could not find a more dramatic example of a life that began and ended in violence.[16]

In humans, stressful life events during pregnancy obviously include unwanted pregnancies and unwanted babies. In Europe several studies have documented links between being prenatally unwanted and increased rates of both suicide and juvenile criminality.[17] Several large groups of babies were followed in Finland, Sweden, and Czechoslovakia over a period of thirty years. Mothers denied abortions were forced to raise children they did not want. As those lives unfolded in comparison with groups of wanted children, the unwanted children were at much greater risk of psychiatric and social problems.[18] The study done in Sweden showed that juvenile criminality among unwanted youths was double that of those who had been wanted. In a Prague study, unwanted children had almost three times the risk of appearing in the criminal register. There is little doubt that later environmental and biological factors contributed to those outcomes. But there is now strong evidence that the womb does in fact provide powerful early environmental forces that interact with genetic factors to create the biological roots of these behaviors.

An interesting small study of a handful of boys by Andrew Feldmar in 1974 followed four suicidal boys. Through extensive interviews of the families of these adolescents, Feldmar found that in all cases the suicide attempts were taking place at the same time of the year as their mothers had tried to abort them, a fact that none of the adolescents had consciously known.[19] Another study of eight thousand pregnant women provides strong evidence of the impact of prenatal maternal rejection. The women were divided into those who wanted their babies and those who did not. The unwanted babies were 2.4 times more likely to die in the first month of life.[20]

While correlative information is not to be confused with proof of causality, the preponderance of new data from so-called hard science on the human brain and brain chemistry increases the interest in such correlative information. As studies and their implications accumulate, we can turn for hope to empirically tested program models that focus on prenatal education, parental attachment to the fetus, and prenatal stimulation. Enhanced knowledge, support, and communication can turn the fetal experience from one of rejection to one of acceptance and security.

Many adults in our culture find it difficult to acknowledge that the child they once were continues to live at the core of the adult they have become. It may be an even greater leap, therefore, to

95

acknowledge that the experiences of the maturing fetus and the baby who preceded the child exert a powerful influence. Even among childhood-focused professionals, there is a view that life really only begins after birth. It is ironic that it takes the cumulative effects of irrational behaviors to bring people to therapy, where the relationship between earliest experiences and later behavior can be unlocked.

Historically in our society there is a denial of any connection between the earliest stages of life and those that follow. At the beginning of this century, following the work of Sigmund Freud and his followers, there was a shift toward recognizing the significance of early childhood. But even Freud was affected by the criticism of his detractors, who accused him of exaggerating the capacities of infants, particularly the capacity for memory. Prior to Freud, our culture's denigration of childhood was evidenced in the ways parents were allowed, if not encouraged, to treat their children as property with the full support of society. Culturally, it was beneath the upper-class citizens of the Western world to care for their own children; strangers of lesser means were hired to raise the children of the elite—a practice still in place.

In his book *Echoes from the Womb*, Dr. Ludwig Janus poignantly makes this connection:

> We still remain estranged from the very small baby within us and unquestionably rely on external norms and authorities to determine what happens to our newborn and unborn children. As long as we deny any personal awareness of our life before birth, of our birth and earliest baby years and repress the significance of early experience for a fuller understanding of human life, then we are also condemned to distancing ourselves emotionally from our unborn and newborn offspring. The next generation then remains unprotected from blind repetition of the same mishandling and trauma which lie buried but quite alive and active within our unconscious minds. . . . Earliest experiences remain within each of us. Our whole existence is based upon the vitality and the dynamic experiences of

our very beginning. This period is physically and psychologically the foundation of our life and our experience and of our relationship to the world.[21]

For centuries primitive cultures have believed that what mothers see and experience, babies reflect. Now modern science is corroborating this ancient wisdom. When we are not protective of mothers' experiences during pregnancy, our communities may give birth to the reflection of those experiences.

5

Jack Be Nimble, Jack Be Quick:

THE DISRUPTIVE BEHAVIOR DISORDERS

"So they went. At first Pooh and Rabbit and Piglet walked together, and Tigger ran around them in circles, and then, when the path got narrower, Rabbit, Piglet, and Pooh walked one after another, and Tigger ran around them in oblongs, and by-and-by, when the gorse got very prickly on each side of the path, Tigger ran up and down in front of them, and sometimes he bounced into Rabbit and sometimes he didn't. And, as they got higher, the mist got thicker, so that Tigger kept disappearing, and when you thought he wasn't there, there he was again, saying "I say, come on," and before you could say anything, there he wasn't."

—A. A. MILNE

The House at Pooh Corner

I was born colic. As a baby they said I was cranky all the time. All the time. I was constantly fussy. Mom said I was the worst of the three of us. I was just always moving, always in trouble. . . . I was in second grade . . . no, it might have been first. I was in school, and they sent me to the school nurse. The school nurse contacted my grandma and said I needed to go to a doctor and be checked out, so I went to Dr. Roberts, and he diagnosed me with attention deficit disorder. The doctor told my grandma Ritalin would make me relax and calm me down. So I took the drug, but I didn't like it from the first time. It made me feel like I was just like bugging out—real hyper, not really showing it, but inside me I felt hyper. But yet I was kinda tired, too tired to move. And I felt like I was ready to snap or something, like I was ready to jump up and bounce off the walls and yell and scream. And I didn't like it. . . .

My grandma would give me a cup of coffee, black coffee, with no sugar. And she found that in the morning my teachers said I was very calm in the morning. At first I was sneaking coffee behind her back, and when she caught me, she asked the doctor. And the doctor said, "Well, it might just have a reverse effect on Jeffrey." So she decided to experiment . . . she would give me my Ritalin pill with coffee . . . and she would call my teachers. She found out I was behaving just fine in the morning before lunch. But at lunch time I was supposed to go to the nurse's office to take my medication again. And they found out that anywhere between 1:00 and 3:00, when school let out, I was just bouncing off the walls, that I'd get real smart-alecky with the teachers, have a real smart mouth and I'd turn into class clown. My teachers would comment that it was like Dr. Jekyll and Mr. Hyde. So my grandma asked the school to give me coffee at lunch time. . . . Half the time I only took the coffee. . . . They thought the Ritalin was working. I hated taking them, they made me feel funny because I was so antsy in class. And I was the class clown, and teachers was always having talks with me in the classroom—not with other students but just with me. You know, getting me to focus and to stay quiet long enough to learn something. So when we'd come in from the playground, if the teacher would see me and another kid rolling around on the ground, it would automatically—it may just seem paranoid, like the world was out to get me or something—but it always seemed to me that the blame would just automatically fall on me. . . . In junior high, I got into the wrong crowd, the little rebels . . . the little kids who flunked all their classes and the little kids who smoked cigarettes out behind the gym. And the school started having disciplinary problems with me. I was definitely a discipline problem. I was always being sent to the office. I was always being suspended from school since I can remember. . . . From the first grade on up to the ninth grade, I was always acting out and in trouble.

JEFFREY, AUGUST 1996

Jeffrey almost always got the worst beatings as a kid. And I have no idea why. I mean maybe because he was always a towhead. He knew how to piss people off real quick, and he did it on purpose. He knew how to get to their, you know, their little spot. And he did it on purpose. I just don't think he really cared. . . . He wanted attention, any kind. . . . I guess I just wasn't as rambunctious as Jeffrey. Jeffrey was always moving around, always had to be doing something, and it just bothered them that he was moving around so much and always annoying someone. And I mostly just kind of kicked back. I just watched things. I guess you'd have to say I was always the observant one. I always just kind of stood back and saw what was going to happen, so if I saw a bad outcome, I knew not to do it that way. And Jeffrey, he just always jumped right into it.

You know, Jeffrey saved me from a lot of trouble because I would have probably done some of the stuff the same way he did it. But the only thing was, I learned from his mistakes. So a lot of times, he was

102

the one who kept me out of trouble. But it was always me yelling at him when he'd done stuff wrong. I'd be like, "You can't be doing this stuff, Jeffrey." A lot of times he wouldn't listen to me, and so I'd have to beat on him for a while—like sometimes—the only way I could get Jeffrey to listen to me was to make him hurt. We'd wrestle around, and I'd sometimes have to twist his arm behind his back and make him cry. And then I'd have to apologize . . . "Jeffrey, God, I'm sorry. You know I don't like doing this. But why won't you listen to what I'm trying to tell you? You're going to get hurt if you do this." A lot of times he'd be like he'd want to jump out of this tree that's so far up where it would hurt him or something—just stupid things like that. And I'd have to beat his butt to get him to listen.

JOHN, AUGUST 1996

Jeffrey was evaluated for Special Education in 4/85 while he was in the 3rd grade. He has been on Ritalin as a result of a plan to intervene for his high activity levels. He was identified as S.E.D. [severely emotionally disabled] in 9/85 based on depression, nonacceptance by peers, a rigid use of denial and fantasy as defense mechanisms, and conflict with authority figures. . . . Jeffrey still demonstrates some social-emotional and behavioral problems indicative of S.E.D. . . . The educational effect is apparent based on poor report card grades and regular education classroom observations. . . . He continues with a medication program for his activity level.

SCHOOL ASSESSMENT TEAM REPORT, JANUARY 6, 1989
FROM JEFFREY'S CHILD WELFARE CASE FILE

He isn't paying attention. He can't sit still at school. He doesn't stay at his desk or table or in his circle. He talks out of turn and wanders the classroom. He may be very anxious to please—or seem to be in a fog. He has difficulty taking turns. He often interrupts or talks when he shouldn't and gets into trouble, because he doesn't seem to think things through. He is impulsive. He lacks good judgment and is attracted to goofy or high-risk behaviors. He may be the class clown or the butt of other students' humor. He doesn't learn from his mistakes and overreacts to frustration. He may be bright, but his schoolwork goes uncompleted. By second grade, he may be on Ritalin or another stimulant medication.

Every classroom has one or several of these children. Many are very bright, and their intelligence helps compensate for the early delays in focus and perseverance. Even so, behavior at home is most likely difficult. When a child is ceaselessly on the go, fearless, seemingly unaware of her impact on others, and shows no sign of common sense, she requires constant supervision. Parents often feel exhausted and angry, their feelings of affection stretched thin or greatly compromised.

Such a child is the Richmond, California, six year old who is the youngest child in the nation ever charged with attempted murder. The charges were filed after he savagely beat a neighbor's month-old baby with a stick as the infant lay sleeping in his bassinet, leaving the baby with permanent severe brain damage. This little boy is barely old enough to read. But he is old enough to kill—or to try. His behavior did not emerge from a void. Newspaper reports, which generally do not cover psychiatric issues in depth, nonetheless contained important clues to this child's aggression: he couldn't sit still in school, was repeating kindergarten, had a history of learning disabilities, was a special education student, and was known as aggressive—already a bully. His attempt to kill did not come without warning. Even without reading the newspapers, professionals who see these children daily know that such children typically have a history of exceptional behavioral difficulties manifesting from around the age of two years.

We still live in a time when such children may be viewed within a community as simply "difficult"—disciplinary failures. Some of them may, in fact, be children with difficult temperaments since the first weeks of their lives. But most likely the children described above will have attention-deficit/hyperactive disorder, cognitive deficits, and learning disabilities. Some who match the description may also be fetal alcohol syndrome or fetal alcohol effect (FAE) children. Some may be oppositional-defiant (ODD) or conduct-disordered (CD) children showing strong resistance to discipline, troubled relationships, and already working their way up the ladder to more serious aggression. Some may be experiencing abuse at home, or come to school out of chaotic and neglectful circumstances that leave them physically and emotionally malnourished. All are at risk of academic and social failure. Because of the way our society functions, the primary grade school teacher is typically the first person to officially notice. By that time, behavior patterns are well established. Self-image is already crystallizing, and resources to turn these factors around are scarce.

In growing numbers, these children are overwhelming preschools and grade schools across the nation. Thirty years ago, when such children began to be seen as more than just failures of parental control, they were called hyperactive. Then, as now, the diagnosis covered a multitude of behaviors. Refined sugar or food allergies were seen as the likely explanation. According to the prevailing theory then, they were most likely to be blond, blue-eyed boys. "Hyperactive" soon gave way to "hyperkinetic" or "minimal brain dysfunction," an older term coined in 1902. Now we use "attention deficit disorder" or "attention-deficit/hyperactivity disorder," a diagnosis that includes three types: predominantly inattentive, predominantly hyperactive and impulsive, or a combination of inattention and hyperactivity. While ADHD predominantly affects attention, it may compromise learning and typically has some negative impact on a child's judgment. It is the element of hyperactivity, however, that is more commonly the root factor in aggressive or violent behavior, due to the added behavioral elements of impulsivity and restlessness.

If we fine tune what is really meant by ADHD, we find that the label actually covers disabilities in several discrete brain functions that most of us take for granted in both learning and social situations. There are five basic capacities involved in the attention disorders. The first is the capacity for planning, which includes the ability to be reflective, to think before acting. Children with ADHD are likely to proceed without thinking. Problem solving suffers as a result. These children seem compelled to rush through tasks and to make careless mistakes. Parents comment that they always seem to "do it the hard way."

A second ability ADHD affects is selectivity. In normal school and social learning, tasks often call for the ability to determine saliency or the relative importance of certain information over other details. ADHD children excel at picking up the wrong information at the wrong time. They may focus on irrelevant information, often becoming masters of trivia. They cannot pick out what is important from a sea of detail.

A third capacity affected by ADHD is the ability to resist distraction from competing stimulation. Distraction comes in many forms: sound, sight, and touch. Filtering out extraneous distractions is difficult if not impossible for these children. They have trouble controlling their own fidgety movements and what they say, constantly talking out of turn. This inability to inhibit verbalizations and movement poses problems in the classroom and on the playground.

The fourth capacity affected is continuity of attention, which is essential to learning and completing work and to sustaining friendships. ADHD children are unpredictable. Sleep and arousal patterns may be affected, so that they are wakeful at night and not alert during the day. Yawning and stretching and other signs of fatigue are common in the classroom. There are fluctuations in the attention behaviors of these children ranging from over-concentration to flightiness. Parents frequently comment that concentration is no problem if the subject is one the child really likes.

A final area impaired by attention deficits is the ability of these children to self-monitor how they are doing on a task. Self-awareness and self-regulation pose huge obstacles. Teachers and parents become frustrated by the fact that ADHD children don't seem to be as responsive to positive or negative reinforcement as other children. A parent's sense of efficacy and competence is diminished by a constant struggle with discipline. When attention problems are compounded by hyperactivity or impulsivity, the child is also excessively physically active and impulsive. This is the child who is not only constantly on the move, but who lacks social radar: the ability to read and appropriately respond to other people in his environment.

The neurological and behavioral characteristics that combine in ADHD clearly render a child vulnerable to early learning and social problems. When this disorder affects children born into constructive and supportive home environments, it provides a serious challenge to parents. However, when ADHD-affected children are submerged in familial environments that are chaotic, neglectful, or abusive, there is a greatly increased likelihood that they will also develop oppositional defiant disorder or conduct disorder.

More than 65 percent of children with ADHD also develop oppositional-defiant disorder.[1] Further complicating the lives of these children are conduct disorders which appear in 20 percent to 30 percent of ADHD children, primarily children with co-occurring environmental risk factors. By adolescence, 40 percent to 60 percent of ADHD children will be so diagnosed.[2] ODD adds a pattern of hostile, defiant behaviors to the attentional problems. John's description of his brother Jeffrey's behavior as a kid who deliberately annoyed people, who knew their "little spots" and deliberately pressed them, is typical of the ODD child. These children have a low tolerance for frustration, are easily annoyed, and lose their tempers easily. They are argumentative with adults and blame others for their mistakes. They are stubborn and have trouble compromising, especially at home. To warrant an ODD diagnosis, a child must be displaying this behavior so that people around him are consciously and chronically affected; the child's home, peer, and school performances clearly suffer. Children with ADHD and aggression (ODD or CD) display significantly greater levels of physical aggression, lying, stealing, and peer aggression than children with just ADHD or purely aggressive children.[3]

Conduct disorder is an intensification of ODD behaviors. CD children may be physically cruel to people or animals. They show a lack of empathy and have little regard for the feelings or needs of others. They often perceive people as more hostile or threatening than is realistic. They may lack guilt or remorse. The CD child is generally a chronic bully and a fighter. He may use weapons. His self-esteem is low, but he acts tough. He may steal and may deliberately destroy property including fire setting. As these children get a little older, they may break into houses, force sex, be truant or runaway and ignore or override societal rules. As adolescents, these are the kids who drop out of school, get arrested, and have high rates of unplanned pregnancies and sexually transmitted diseases. One study showed that children with ADHD are on the average five times more likely to develop CD before age twelve than children not affected by ADHD.[4]

Children having both ADHD and aggressive behaviors typically have greater levels of parental and family psychopathology than children with only one or the other.[5] This is not to imply that ADHD is a condition produced by the social environment. It is, in fact, a brain-based condition attributed to heritable genetics about 50 percent of the time and to insults to the neurological system occurring primarily prenatally and at birth 50 percent of the time. But when aggression is added to ADHD, other environmental factors, including lack of parenting skills and abusive or neglectful parenting are attributed at estimates ranging as high as 30 percent.[6] Those ADHD children who are also maltreated are the children who are especially set up for impulsively violent behavior.

By adolescence the pattern typically includes substance abuse, ongoing psychological problems, and violent behavior. The combination of biology and early aggressive behavior together with a nonsupportive environment appears to be the seedbed of serious child and adult violence. Research from varying scientific orientations, employing various terminologies and explanations, all converges on these children. Beginning with ADHD, developing an aggressive profile in preschool, moving into oppositional-defiant and conduct disorders at an early age, and breaking the law early—typically before the age of twelve—is a common description in the histories of violent offenders.[7] A 1995 study of homicidal youths found that 84 percent of the young murderers studied met the diagnostic criteria for conduct disorder. Over half had also been diagnosed with ADHD.[8]

When strongly antisocial behaviors, especially physical fighting, are chronically present before the ages of seven to nine, the child is much more likely to be violent as an adolescent and as an adult. These are the children—impulsive, hyperactive, failing in school, and already showing aggressive behavior—who most warrant intervention to prevent adult crimes.[9] When these kids come to our attention as adolescents, we fail to connect the fact that by ages five or six the aggressive behaviors that signal the syndrome were fully discernible. Parents, foster parents, and behavioral specialists familiar with such children say they can see differences in such children by age two or two and a half. "He never walked, he just started running," is a typical comment from parents. These children often achieve physical milestones early. While being physically active and even aggressive may characterize normal two-year-old behavior, there is a different quality to the interactions of ADHD children. Parents feel anxious, often fearful and angry, because they sense that the child is not "hooked in" and responsive to their communication. When a parent describes his or her relationship with this child, they report that there is little sustained reciprocal eye contact or communication of any kind from the child. The parents appear to have a damaged or nonexistent sense of connection to the child. There is a sense of desperation, of feeling that the door to understanding and influencing the child is closed. They express extreme frustration and often feel angry and powerless.

Regardless of the reason for such developments, these parents need sensitive and specialized support to achieve emotional, disciplinary, and social changes in their child's behaviors. Parents of children so affected have much more difficulty than parents of normal children in meeting their children's needs for limit setting, structure, organization, and rational discipline. Practitioners who want to assist children must assist parents simultaneously. The tendency is often to blame the parents, especially if they have additional problems that confound the diagnosis, such as drug or alcohol abuse. For many reasons, including lack of training and lack of program resources, such children may go undiagnosed until preadolescence, when their juvenile offenses bring them to the attention of judges rather than therapists.

Together these three diagnoses—ADHD, ODD, and CD—make up the three "disruptive behavior disorders" that first appear in childhood and adolescence. They are all primarily diagnosed from a series of behavior checklists completed by parents, teachers, and a professional diagnostician. The diagnosis is subjective. There are no objective brain-based tests that are routinely used to detect the presence or absence of these behavioral disorders. It is the underlying element of impulsivity that provides the common link between the three disorders and later violent behavior. Impulsivity places children at relatively greater risk of physical aggression.

LARRY, LARRY, QUITE CONTRARY

Ten years ago there was likely a single diagnosable behavior-problem child in a given classroom. Now there are typically several. Current estimates are that 5 percent to 6 percent of the childhood population age four to sixteen are likely to be ADHD. Some estimates run as high as 20 percent. A survey of the entire province of Ontario, Canada, found the prevalence to be 9 percent in boys and 3.3 percent in girls.[10] Between 19 percent and 26 percent of ADHD children have at least one type of learning disability in math, reading, or spelling.[11] In addition, as many as 52 percent of ADHD children, compared to up to 35 percent of normal children, have poor motor coordination, especially fine motor coordination, as measured by such activities as peg-board tasks and maze drawings.[12] Teachers are frustrated. Parents are worried. So, too, are the experts. In the 1970s, Dr. Jim Satterfield undertook a longitudinal study of 110 ADHD and 88 normal control children in Los Angeles. Satterfield distinguished two groups of ADHD children in his study, which was controlled for social class, intelligence, academic achievement, and other demographic variables.[13] One group had high levels of aggressive and defiant behavior,

110

while a second group was simply inattentive and overactive. The boys with high levels of aggression and defiance had high rates of felony arrests in adolescence. But even the ADHD boys who showed low rates of aggression but were inattentive and overactive had a 26 percent arrest rate in adolescence—a rate more than three times that of non-ADHD boys, for whom the arrest rate was 8 percent. Satterfield found that 43 percent of the ADHD children who were treated only with stimulant medications were arrested for two or more felony crimes before their eighteenth birthdays. By the time they were adults, 20 percent of this group were arrested for felony crimes. Dr. Satterfield believes that the children most at risk of later criminal behavior are those ADHD children who also develop conduct disorders.

In a subsequent study, Dr. Satterfield, in partnership with his wife and colleague, Breena Satterfield, followed one hundred ADHD boys ages six to twelve through a three-year multimodality treatment regimen that included stimulant medication coupled with parent training, family therapy, and individual social skill training for the children. The multimodality treatment with this group cut the juvenile felony rate in half. Breena Satterfield, an outspoken advocate for intervention and prevention with these children, says sorrowfully, "In this country, we give them midnight basketball, but by that time it's too late!"[14]

Still, the treatment afforded these children in most communities is simply a course of stimulant medication, typically methylphenidate, or Ritalin. It was only twelve years before his death sentence—at age six—that Jeffrey was diagnosed with ADHD. And, like thousands of others, his treatment consisted solely of a Ritalin pill twice a day. For a child like Jeffrey, this prescription was equivalent to administering an aspirin for a heart attack. In considering the impact of ADHD on the lives of affected children, Breena Satterfield says:

> There are two curriculums in life. One is the academic one, the one you learn in school. The other one is the informal social curriculum, the one where you learn to say hello and goodbye and to pay

111

attention to other people and their needs and how to get along in society. Both can be compromised by attention deficits. But it is this second one that these kids have particular trouble with. Social judgment is a continuing struggle.[15]

Numerous studies done in the last two decades confirm that children who are both hyperactive and impulsive, physically aggressive at an early age (preschool or early grade school), and engage in a persistent pattern of physical fighting that continues to middle childhood are at the greatest risk of later violent crime.[16] There is strong evidence that conduct disorders at preschool age predict similar disorders in middle childhood. One longitudinal study showed that when problems began by age three with hyperactivity, attention difficulties, impulsivity, and aggression in combination with familial stress, the aggressive behaviors were most likely to persist through middle childhood.[17] Additional studies have confirmed that where such behaviors are strongly in place in primary grade school, particularly when aggression involves hyperactivity, inattention, and impulsivity, approximately 80 percent of children go on to delinquency, adult crime, and alcohol abuse.[18] The variety of acting-out behaviors, their frequency and intensity, are predictors of later violence.[19]

The vicious beating of five-week-old Ignacio Bermudez, Jr., by eight-year-old twins and a six-year-old boy made headlines across the nation in April 1996. The three boys broke into the Bermudez home to steal a three-wheel tricycle. The six year old had previously told others that the Bermudez family had been hassling him and had looked at him the wrong way and that he had to kill their baby. The three boys broke in to the house while the family was away shopping for groceries, leaving Ignacio in the care of his twenty-one-year-old stepsister, who was in the bathroom and did not hear them enter the house. In an attack that police estimate lasted only a couple of minutes, the six year old tossed the baby from his bassinet to the floor, kicked him, pummeled him with his fists, and beat him with a stick, while the twins stood by. The little boys left with the trike. Ignacio was hospitalized with internal injuries and his skull cracked in two places.

The *Los Angeles Times* characterized the crime as "an event that may never make sense." But given the facts gleaned from a flurry of newspaper accounts and what we now know about biological vulnerability in combination with an early abusive or neglectful environment, this appalling event tells a familiar story. According to news accounts, the child had learning problems, was repeating kindergarten, and was "not functioning at a 6 year old level." He was diagnosed with learning disabilities and a hearing impairment and was a special education student at the grade school he attended. He was hyperactive. He couldn't keep still in school, often tripping other children in the aisle. Families ordered their children not to play with him, and those who did often regretted it. His grandmother told reporters that he was "often hyper," and his grandfather said, "He was an energetic kid. . . . But he's not an evil kid. . . . Kids run, they play. He didn't sit in the house, and he ain't no choir boy." He had a history of behavioral problems, was always getting into trouble, and was known as a bully, a kid who "liked to hit other kids with sticks." One neighbor told reporters, "He was always sneaking out of the house on his mother. He would travel the streets with stick in hand, threatening other children, trying to knock them off bicycles, pointing it at them like a gun." In school he was the class clown, was disruptive, was always getting into trouble for acting up, and was sometimes sent home for his misbehavior. He was also reported to be cruel to animals. When questioned by the police after the beating of Ignacio, this child lied about his role in the crime, while the other two boys readily confessed in tears.

The newspaper descriptions of this six year old's family point to multiple risk factors that were present from the beginning of his life. At the time that he was born into a neighborhood struggling against problems of crime, drugs, and violence, his mother was relying on relatives for financial support and child care. His grandmother, a convicted drug dealer, was thirty-four at the time he was born. While there was no direct evidence of abuse in the newspaper accounts, the family has a history of explosive violence. His mother has a history of alcohol and drug abuse. In the year preceding her son's arrest, she was in a drunken brawl over "family matters." The police were called to the scene and had to use pepper spray to subdue her. His father was eighteen at his son's birth. When the child was four, his father was killed as he stood on a corner in the neighborhood. Unidentified assailants fired five bullets through the father's head as he reached for his weapon. At age seventeen his uncle was accused and later acquitted of killing a taxi driver. The little boy was often alone. He wandered the streets in the evening and was unsupervised. Neighbors reported that once during the prior year, when he was five, his mother appeared two hours after dark, wanting to know if they had seen him. His mother worked long hours in a day care center, often leaving him in the care of his grandmother. "That child is a victim of his home, not of his neighborhood," one neighbor told reporters.

The stories of Jeffrey and the six year old, though different from each other, have several dynamics in common. They both began with a biological vulnerability to impulsivity and to attention and learning problems. Then negative environmental factors in the lives of both boys exerted their influence from their earliest hours and days. Jeffrey experienced abuse, and both boys experienced chronic neglect and had mothers who were depressed or otherwise unavailable, to name but a few factors. The patterns of caretaking and modeling both boys experienced from birth and throughout earliest childhood placed them on a behavioral path that soon broadened—into a conduct disorder in the six year old's case and into oppositional-defiant disorder in Jeffrey's. Both were clearly identifiable as troubled little boys before age five. More important, the nurturing and teaching that could have ameliorated their biological vulnerabilities were unavailable to them in their first two years.

114

THE SHEEP'S IN THE MEADOW, THE COW'S IN THE CORN

We know that ADHD tends to run in families. Less clear, however, is whether this familial link is created by inherited genes or by genes that have been environmentally altered through circumstances such as prenatal exposure to drugs or alcohol. Studies of heritable genetics have found that there are four times as many hyperactive children with hyperactive parents as there are hyperactive children with non-hyperactive parents, and that ADHD children have more uncles and fathers with ADHD than do children not affected.[20]

A second line of research, which is exploring the potential impact of environmental toxins on genetic development, offers another explanation for the cause of ADHD. Several studies point to correlations with parental abuse of tobacco, cocaine, crack, heroin, and alcohol either before or during pregnancy. Alcohol and nicotine, in particular, have been implicated.[21] Some researchers hypothesize that these substances may harm the sperm, or egg prior to conception as well as the fetus.[22] Epidemiological studies indicate that the presence of ADHD is particularly high in states where alcohol and drug use is widespread.

Another explanation for ADHD is minimal brain injury or damage related to difficult pregnancies or deliveries. Unusually long or short labors, very young mothers, fetal distress before or during delivery, toxemia, and eclampsia have all been examined as possible causes or contributors to these symptoms.[23] The correlations clearly exist. How toxins or experiences may cause minor brain changes is the subject of several ongoing studies. Children born prematurely are, as a group, showing higher rates of ADHD, especially when they are very tiny at delivery (less than 1,500 grams) and have spent months relying on technology to get started. The exact biological processes behind this correlation are still being researched. What we know is that, while it may be exacerbated by them, ADHD is not caused by social factors such as family chaos, poverty, or poor parenting. Although ADHD may be diagnosed improperly by virtue of the similarities between the behaviors of children neurologically impaired and those reacting to serious environmental problems, true ADHD has a neurological basis. And it appears to be on the increase.[24]

There is a line of research, however, that shows us how the earliest environment can exacerbate or ameliorate predisposing factors, primarily through its impact on the developing frontal lobes of the baby's brain. Changes in the frontal lobes, as measured by PET scans, occur primarily in the second half of the first year. Following this period of exceptional potential for adaptation or "plasticity," there is a period of stabilization. The establishment of synaptic connections occurs more slowly after this period. This is followed by a third period of brain development in which modifications of brain connections allow for ongoing changes in the "neural maps" throughout life. The human brain remains adaptive to specific environmental stimulation and continues to change even though the number and plasticity of connections are now reduced by selective elimination in the sixth through the twelfth month.

As brain physiology changes, so does the baby's behavior. Through the first six months after birth the infant's emotional regulation gradually moves from a primarily reflexive response to physical stimulation such as cold, hunger, or pain, to an awareness of internal feelings and the ability to associate feeling states with specific external stimuli. By six to eight months of age, the baby is gradually able to recognize the connections between external stimuli such as food, feelings such as hunger, and his or her own actions to regulate those feelings, such as crying or fussing directed at a caregiver. By this age, the infant can perceive distress and signal to a parent to respond. These new abilities—to perceive and regulate basic physical and emotional states through planned behavior, which is linked to maturing cognitive abilities—are expanding dramatically in the first year after birth. Through directed, goal-oriented behavior, including eye contact and vocalizations, the baby can communicate feelings intentionally and obtain information about how others are feeling. All of this activity is being mapped in the frontal lobes in relation to the interactions occurring between the child and his or her caregiver.

Developmental scientists researching the suspected environmentally based causes of the three disruptive behavior disorders note that it is the parent or first caregiver who helps an infant establish self-regulation, first by directly maintaining and regulating the baby's states of physical and emotional arousal and later by teaching and directing the child to self-regulate those feelings.[25] Babies quickly develop a repertoire of signals that they use to communicate their needs to caregivers. Competent mothers and fathers become good at reading their child's hunger cues and feeding them, mimicking the sounds their babies make to "talk," comforting when the baby is crying, and lowering stimulation when the baby becomes irritated or drowsy.

But when parents are depressed, mentally ill, retarded, or otherwise unavailable, it can have a profound effect on the parents' responsiveness and subsequently on the infant's ability to learn to regulate physical and emotional feelings. This is particularly true during the first year of life. For example, depressed mothers display frequent negative emotions such as sadness, anger, and irritability. A depressed mother's face may remain stilled or unsmiling regardless of her infant's attempts to engage her. The baby's feelings may go unrecognized and may overwhelm the child. Such a mother may also respond to her infant in an erratic, poorly timed way. In response, babies of depressed mothers show less motor activity, less eye contact, and withdraw more often. They also show less positive behaviors such as smiling during interactions with their mothers.[26] Through tiny subtle exchanges like normal eye contact, and the timing of vocalizations and touch, mothers and caregivers teach their infants a series of coordinated interactive behaviors that shape the babies' efforts to regulate their own feelings. The baby of a depressed mother learns, as all babies learn. In this case, however, the baby learns a series of miscoordinated interactive failures in which the reciprocal and synchronous aspect of normal interactions is missing or greatly reduced. The result is often withdrawal by the baby, as well as diminished expectations of attention and comfort from others. Babies generalize the behavior mirrored from the depressed mother to strangers.[27]

A totally different pattern exists when the parent is abusive. Here the caregiver's behavior may be even more unpredictable. The parent not only fails to respond positively to a baby's signals but also erratically inflicts pain when the baby signals for comfort. In this situation, children learn that they can't make the world work to meet their needs effectively and that they need to be vigilant for signs of coming assaults. Depressive, or otherwise neglectful, or abusive patterns each teach an infant a maladaptive series of behaviors that can exacerbate the neurologically based predispositions toward attentional and impulse-regulation deficits. These pathological interactions form the basis of the child's "cortical map" or basic learned programming in the frontal lobes of the brain during the first year after birth.[28] There is growing evidence that some ADHD children may also be suffering from the impact of early trauma, a post-traumatic stress condition characterized by changes in the chemistry and structure of the brain.[29]

Several common variables stand out in the histories of children who develop conduct disorders. First, the family is rarely "intact." The parents were never married, are fighting, or are separated or divorced. Rarely do these children emerge from a loving pair of parents. Second, there is a high degree of maternal psychopathology, especially depression and including substance abuse. Low intellectual function or education level of the mother is also a frequent factor. She is often young at the birth of her first child. The father, if present, typically has a problem with employability, with health, or with criminality. The income and occupational levels of the family tend to be below the norm for the community. Neighbors and other observers often report child neglect or emotional or physical abuse. Parents of CD children typically practice disciplinary methods that are erratic, authoritarian, and harshly physical. The parents report lack of pleasure in parenting this child since early life.[30] One study of twenty-five homicidal youths found that 88 percent of those who had committed murder had one or more disruptive behavior disorders.

118

Eighty-four percent were conduct disordered. In examining their histories, the researchers found that 96 percent were from chaotic families defined by abandonment, parental incarceration, parental substance abuse, chronic fighting, or promiscuity. Ninety percent were abused emotionally, physically, or sexually. One hundred percent of these homicidal children had serious school problems.[31]

Conduct-disordered children are difficult kids to work with. Dr. Jeffrey Rowe, senior staff psychiatrist with San Diego's Children's Hospital Outpatient Psychiatry, described his CD patients and their thought processes at a recent conference in San Diego.[32] Coming from a small town in the Midwest, Rowe was at first a bit afraid of his CD patients, primarily adolescent boys. "These are kids who hurt other kids and people, break stuff, steal, and lie. If they see a bike and want it, they hop on and pedal away." When asked why or what other options they might have considered, a typical response is, "I never thought about it." These children are short-term thinkers, impulsive, without forethought or self-monitoring. They are not people pleasers and have trouble seeing how anything looks from another person's perspective. In fact, they often don't know that other people have a perspective different from their own; egocentrism and lack of empathy are typical. For conduct-disordered children, emotional responses are always big—and are generally out of proportion to reality; one young man who was one of Dr. Rowe's clients shot his friend for letting his dog defecate on his bed. Cause-and-effect thinking is limited; when CD children lie, they don't understand why you won't trust them the next time. Everything that happens is experienced as outside of their control. If they get bad grades, it's the teacher's fault. If they don't have a job, it's the president's fault. Instead of the truth, they say what they think a person wants to hear or whatever is necessary to keep them out of trouble. "Don't listen to their words," Rowe cautioned the audience of professionals. "You have to look at their feet. It's where their feet go that makes the difference."

A large longitudinal study done in Montreal, Canada, of boys five to thirteen years of age showed that the "behavioral style" or person-

119

ality that correlates with highly delinquent behavior is clearly in place by the time a child is old enough to begin kindergarten, leading researchers to conclude that prevention efforts should target preschool children with "at-risk behavior profiles."[33] The authors of this study confirm what several researchers have maintained for over a decade—that deviant behavior in early childhood is stable over time. In another large study, the Dunedin Multidisciplinary Health and Developmental Study, parent assessments of their three year old's behavior was found to be predictive of delinquency in preadolescence.[34] Very early disruptive behavior is relatively stable and often translates into delinquent behavior in preadolescence and adolescence.[35] Looking forward from childhood to adulthood, 40 percent of males and 35 percent of females with a diagnosis of CD in childhood continue to show an antisocial personality disorder in later life. One study concludes that "three quarters of children with a clinically significant conduct disorder will go on to exhibit pervasive and persistent social malfunction."[36] In this study only 13 percent of males and 9 percent of females went on to show satisfactory functioning in adult life.

Based on these studies, it is clear that we are missing opportunities to intervene early with aggressive and disruptive behavior, primarily with two- to four-year-old boys. An example of the successful application of this knowledge can be seen in the pioneering work of the Oregon Social Learning Center. Dr. Gerry Patterson, the iconoclastic researcher who founded the center, began by working with disruptive and predelinquent preadolescent boys. These were typically children who were having trouble in school, in home, and in foster care. Their backgrounds reflected loss, neglect, physical abuse—and an early start at giving back what they had absorbed. Patterson and his staff identified a series of distinct skills these children lacked. He has developed technologies for teachers, parents, and foster parents, as well as social skills for these children, models that are currently used nationwide to intervene with predelinquent children. While most of his counterparts have retained their focus on this age group, Patterson began to work his way back in his intervention efforts, first to grade school, then to preschool. His current grant proposal is focused on infants.

Although the diagnosis of ADHD, let alone ODD, is generally not given until children reach school age, Dr. Patterson has developed a strong body of research documenting the emergence of ODD during the preschool years, especially in two and a half to three year olds, who are often overlooked because chronic oppositional or openly hostile behavior is somehow viewed as normal at this age. It is still typically the case that these diagnoses are withheld until ages five or six, when the expectation is that excessive oppositional behavior will subside for a majority of children. Some level of defiant behaviors is common between the ages of two to four—this is part of the normal process of establishing autonomy and independence—but for the majority of preschool children showing inattention or defiance, this type of behavior does not intensify and extend over the course of several months. Typical preschool behaviors include resistance to adult commands and a trying on of adultlike autonomous behaviors and phrases like, "I'll do it myself!" These behaviors are signs of growing independence and the child's desire to test or see how far he or she can push. When met with clear limits, behaviors that are aggressive or that threaten the safety of the child or other children or their property should shift within a few weeks or months. When a pattern of hostile, destructive, or chronically defiant behavior in the home persists for twelve months, it warrants an evaluation for ODD.[37]

Patterson feels very strongly that parenting behaviors rather than neurobiology are at the core of antisocial behavior:

> I feel the evidence for parenting-skill–based research as causative factors is much more convincing than the brain-based or biologically based research is. In the last decade, we've mounted six or seven prevention trials using random assignment to demonstrate that changing parenting skills changes antisocial behavior. These effects persist in follow-up. I simply don't see anything in the brain-based

research that suggests that changing the brain chemically, etc., can have long-term persistent effects on antisocial behavior. . . .

Specifically it is child noncompliance that's at the core of his or her antisocial behavior. This is a kind of generalized situation, where such a child doesn't respond well to requests or commands given by any adult or child for that matter. The matrix surrounding this core consists of a high level of skills in the child's use of aversive behaviors to control, manipulate, and shape those around him or her. The child's shaping and manipulation of his or her social environment is a 16–hour-a-day process that makes those around the child absolutely miserable. The other behaviors in this that are tied in with noncompliance become things like temper tantrums, yelling, screaming, crying, and finally hitting. By the age of 3 or 4, these coercive skills are identifiable, and these are the things the child takes into new settings to repeat the whole process. . . .

I don't really believe that most antisocial children have inherent brain vulnerabilities. A few may have, and this may, indeed, amplify the kind of training and coercion they are receiving. It might even set it in motion for some families. But I think investigators would be hard pressed to demonstrate that anything like the majority of extremely antisocial preschoolers have inherent brain vulnerabilities.[38]

This is probably not an either-or argument. Neurobiologists point out that neurobiology conforms to the environment, so that the young brain quickly reflects the cumulative impact of child-parent interactions. When parents expect very different behavior than their child presents, the result is chronic frustration and negative feelings for both parents and the child. Whether this stems from a mismatch of temperament, lack of developmental knowledge, or lack of discipline skills, the result will still be reflected in the child's developing brain. Brain biology and environment appear to be flip sides of the same experience. Relationships change the brain, especially in the first months of life.

A local program has been developed near Patterson's Oregon Social Learning Center in Eugene, Oregon, that builds on his research and teaches the skills he has developed for parents and teachers. The program, called First Steps, serves preschool children showing early signs of bullying or other aggressive behavior. Its purpose is to divert young antisocial children from a path leading to delinquency and violence. Working with both school and home, the program involves thirty program days at school and six weeks of in-home parent training. Here the little preschooler, typically a boy four to six who is known for bullying his classmates, can be taught how to take turns, how to ask before taking what he wants, how to wait in line without pushing or shoving, and how to get attention in constructive ways. This is a very structured, reward-based collaboration between parents and the classroom, which, done at this early age, appears to break aggressive patterns for more than half of the First Step pupils continuing into grade school. Parental commitment and intense consistent routines can make great differences in these early years. The program is too new to have generated longitudinal data on what happens as these children reach later grades, and Patterson is fully aware that the real first steps toward aggression occur at even earlier points in development.

When we trace the problem of violence backwards from adult crime to juvenile crime to aggression in grade school to preschool aggression and impulsivity, we still have not looked back far enough. It is the root cause that escapes our focus. No one has identified a single sweeping cause for ADHD or for ODD or CD. The current thinking is that biological factors combine with social factors such as neurotoxins, child abuse, child neglect, and other larger environmental factors to produce these problems. But when we look at these factors, the seeds of the majority are planted in the first thirty-three months of life. As important, the potential for making real change and protecting innate strengths lies in this period. Even brain vulnerabilities present from birth can be greatly ameliorated, and in some cases functionally eliminated, by environmental protective factors. The real difference in violent outcomes lies not in whether or not there was ever physical damage to the brain, but in the strengths in the environment of the infant and young child, particularly the family. For the most seriously violent children, family has been the source of rather than the refuge from trauma. When children are terrorized by violence within their homes from an early age—a condition on the rise[39] in the United States—the results come back to haunt us.

6

Tea for Two:

THE ROLE OF TEMPERAMENT

"What is REAL?" asked the Velveteen Rabbit. "Does it mean having things that buzz inside you and a stick-out handle?"

"Real isn't just how you are made," said the Skin Horse, "it's a thing that happens to you when a child loves you for a long, long time, not just to play with, but REALLY loves you, then you become real."

"Does it hurt?" asked the Rabbit.

"Sometimes," said the Skin Horse, for he was always truthful. "When you are real, you don't mind being hurt."

"Does it happen all at once, like being wound up," he asked, "or bit by bit?"

"It doesn't happen all at once," said the Skin Horse. "You become. It takes a long time. That's why it doesn't happen to people who break easily, or have sharp edges, or who have to be carefully kept."

—MARGERY WILLIAMS
The Velveteen Rabbit

The main difference that I see between me and John is that John was always one to stand back from a situation. He would detach himself and evaluate whatever circumstances in our environment that life brought our way. Whereas me—I wouldn't take that time, that, you know, maybe split second, you know, to stand back from a distance and look at the situation and assess it and figure out what would be the most effective way of going about things. I would just kind of jump in with both feet, just deal with it at the moment and take whatever consequences came—whatever hit me—instead of stopping like John did and looking.

JEFFREY, AUGUST 1996

We could all go out and do this one thing and we could talk about it later, and Jeffrey and my grandma, well actually my grandma, would say something about how it was, and it didn't actually happen that way . . . I'd see it a different way. And I would ask someone else, like one of my friends or whatever, and they'd say, "Yeah, that's exactly the way I saw it." And I'd say, "Well, did you see it the way my grandma saw it?" And they'd be like, "Well, no, I didn't see it like that." 'Cause you know they [the family] have this funny thing. It's like when we do things or we experience things or when certain things happen, it's like they twist it around to being something either better or sometimes they even make it worse than what it really was, you know. And a lot of times I just try, I've always tried, to keep an open mind and see what I see. It was like most of the time I had to agree with them. I'd just say okay because I didn't want to get in a long argument with them. But I'd be like, "That's wrong. That's not the way it was. But have it your way or whatever."

JOHN, AUGUST 1996

127

A personal opinion on me and my brother. . . . See, the way I look back on things, I look back on it and remember the feelings that I had. I remember it like it's happening again when I remember it. But the way John remembers things is that he detached himself from everything that was going on and he just kind of took it like, "Oh well—that's just some more bull shit." There was just so much chaos. . . . The way that he dealt with it and the way he accepted being bounced around was to distance himself. We're like total opposites. John all his life has known what he wanted in life, and he can tell you. The way he puts it really makes a lot of sense. He thinks it goes back to Walt and Bev [foster parents when John was five]. He's seen a functional family, and they took really good care of us. He's seen a lot of love—we hated being taken from there.

JEFFREY, AUGUST 1996

Any of us who have stood and really looked at a nursery of newborn babies or have parented more than one infant or observed other families with more than one baby knows that babies are not alike. In spite of some basic physical likenesses, newborns are almost as different from each other as are individuals of all ages. One baby will cry ceaselessly at being bathed or dressed. Another sleeps through it all. Researchers studying this reality have confirmed that babies vary markedly in their dispositions from the beginning, and that a number of their characteristics remain stable over time.[1]

Differences in behavioral style or temperament have captured people's attention since ancient times. Dr. Jerome Kagan drew on this history to name and frame his fascinating book on child temperament: *Galen's Prophecy*. In this volume, Kagan explains that the Greeks and Romans framed human behavior as falling into types that stemmed from varying balances among the four humors: blood, phlegm, and yellow and black bile. Observed differences in human rationality, emotionality, and behavior were accounted for in terms of the relative distribution of the humors in interaction with the bodily qualities of temperature and moisture. In the second century, a philosopher named Galen outlined a behavioral typology that remained influential until the end of the nineteenth century, when philosophers reframed Galen's "choleric" as "bilious," "phlegmatic" as "lymphatic," and "melancholic" as "nervous," while "sanguine" held its own. Remarkably, however, throughout the centuries of evolving thought, individual physiology was seen as responsive to environmental forces such as climate and diet. Although the early typologies sound prosaic in light of current thinking, they have a lot in common with current biosocial views of human behavior. The interaction of biology with the environment is at the heart of current explanations of human behavior, and several schools of thought have opened windows of knowledge onto how this process works. Chapter 5 looked at the roots of violent behavior through the window of the disruptive behavioral disorders first appearing in childhood: ADHD, ODD, and CD. Another group of researchers, studying these and the whole range of nondisordered children, are examining temperament. "Though the terminology and orientations are different in these two branches of research, both groups appear to converge with strong interest on children who are aggressive, impulsive, and difficult to discipline from early in life."

Temperament is often confused with personality, but the two are not the same. Personality consists of the combination of temperament and learned experience, especially as it relates to habitual behavior and ways of coping with the world, along with ideas about what the self and others are like. Temperament, a subset of personality, refers to children's basic orientations to emotion and arousal. These orientations are woven into our genetic endowment, underlie personality, and shape how we respond to learning experiences. At the core of temperament is central nervous system circuitry and chemistry that determine our most fundamental emotional and behavioral responses to life situations. Temperament traits include biologically rooted predispositions to respond to situations of danger or challenges, positive opportunities, and impediments with a given emotional style. They also describe our sensitivity to stimulation and our attentional responses. Temperament appears early in life and is greatly influenced by environmental experiences even before birth.

MARCHING TO THE BEAT
OF A DIFFERENT DRUMMER

This concept of the interactive nature of temperament with the environment, especially for infants with their parents, was a difficult concept to sell in the human sciences fifty years ago. Following a long period of belief in genetic determinism, the influence of the nurture side of the nature/nurture argument was in full swing. When it came to babies, it was commonly accepted that environmental factors made all the difference in who they became. Any variation in infant behavior was attributed to the child's treatment at the hands of caregivers. Mothers, who were generally the primary caregivers, were assigned the burden of guilt for a child's behaviors. This was the milieu in which Drs. Stella Chess and Alexander Thomas, married psychiatrists, began their own family. In bringing up their children, they began to question whether the development of a child's behavior was solely a one-way process. The child's experiences in the home did not seem to be inscribing personality on a blank slate. Drs. Chess and Thomas noticed that often parents with good skills had difficult children and that competent children sometimes emerged from families with multiple problems. They began a lifelong search for explanations for these developmental disparities.

Beginning in 1956, Chess and Thomas undertook the New York Longitudinal Study to investigate whether and how a baby's inherent characteristics influence his or her developmental outcome. Starting with babies at the age of three to six months, Chess and Thomas and their associates observed and interviewed 133 parents and their children in standardized contexts and at regular intervals into the children's late teen years. They have continued periodic follow-up interviews with the children, who are now in their late thirties and early forties. The original research findings from this study have influenced hundreds of studies including a current temperament study done by Kaiser Permanente on 8,000 children in northern California.[2]

Dr. Chess and Dr. Thomas identified nine characteristics that appear to underlie the variability in infants' responses. The nine dimensions—still used today—are: activity adaptability, approach/withdrawal, rhythmicity, threshold, intensity, mood, persistence, distractibility, and sensory threshold. Every child has all of the nine specific traits in varying degrees. Temperament characteristics, while influenced by caregiving, are not caused by the quality of caregiving. Based on an assessment of variations in these traits, Drs. Chess and Thomas grouped characteristics into three categories of temperament, which describe most but not all children: easy, difficult, and slow to warm up.

"Easy" children are characterized by regularity, high adaptability, a preponderantly positive mood of mild or moderate intensity, and regularity of sleep and feeding patterns. They are adaptable, pleasant, smile at strangers, and are easy to be around. Forty percent of the children in the study sample fit within this temperament category. On the other end of the spectrum were the "difficult" children, about 10 percent of the children studied. These are the children who are irritable and withdraw at exposure to new people or situations, who are slow to adapt to change, display a frequently negative mood, and have irregular sleeping and eating patterns. They cry more frequently and may throw tantrums with little provocation. In the middle are children who have a mild positive or negative response to new stimuli, but who can be engaged with extra effort. These "slow to warm up" children comprised about 15 percent of the New York Longitudinal sample. The remaining 35 percent fell into none of the three temperament groups designated by the researchers.

Chess and Thomas assert that each child has a characteristic style and relatively predictable orientation in response to new people, situations, and events. The researchers are careful not to assign a positive or negative value to a particular temperament style. No one style is predestined for aggression, violence, or any other particular outcome. The focus of this body of research is the degree to which there is an alignment between the child's temperament and the traits valued or called for in his or her environment, particularly by the parents. Drs. Chess and Thomas call this match between the child's traits and the parenting environment "goodness of fit."[3] How any of us become who we are is not a result of just genetics or just environment. Rather, it is the result of the interaction of both variables—especially temperament with parental responses.

The value of the temperament perspective lies in its capacity to identify children who may be seen as difficult by their caregivers, so that parents can be provided with the emotional support and education necessary to establish goodness of fit. While temperament theory would not identify difficult children as posing increased risk of violent behavior, there is evidence that babies perceived by their caregivers as having difficult temperaments are at higher risk of child abuse and the resulting behavioral problems arising from conflict between parent and child that can precede violent behavior. This is especially true when such difficult children are born into chaotic and unstable environments in which their parents are stressed by multiple problems and are uneducated about how to best work with their children. Temperament can be one ingredient in a compromised beginning that in turn sets the stage for performance and self-image problems. Early assessment and guidance can make major differences.

Consider the story of Anthony, born into a middle-class environment, a first baby for Elizabeth, an outgoing young lawyer, and her boyfriend. Anthony had a difficult time from the beginning. Following a normal and drug-free birth, he was unsuccessful at nursing, even after weeks of effort by both his mother and a lactation specialist. A series of bottle-fed formulas seemed to disagree with him, and he spit up frequently. He was irritable and had an intense, high-pitched, "angry sounding" cry, which seemed to his mother to be his primary effort to communicate. He had difficulty sleeping, and even small noises awakened him. He was interested in watching the family dog and things around him but did not want to "talk" with or look at his mother. He would not cuddle or mold to her body when she held him, and he felt rigid to her—"like a board." His sleep patterns were irregular, and he reversed night and day for his first four months after birth. He responded erratically to Elizabeth's attempts to comfort him. When he cried, he often could not be comforted by holding. When she put him down, he would scream until he was picked up, quiet for a few seconds, and then suddenly arch his back to be put down. Elizabeth said she never knew what to do to please him. New situations like a trip to the grocery store sent him into his angry cry. Elizabeth increasingly felt herself a failure as a mother, a perception validated by her critical and sleep-deprived partner.

Having anticipated a loving baby who would provide the affection she longed for from her boyfriend, Elizabeth was constantly anxious and distraught. Her pediatrician, perceiving nothing unusual in the baby's behavior during office examinations, encouraged her to try antidepressants. Attributing all of the problem to herself, she felt even less self-confident. Her irritability with Anthony began to mirror his. Finally, a long-pursued referral to a pediatric development specialist turned the tide. The doctor found that Anthony had digestive difficulties (reflux) combined with an irritable and reactive temperament. She helped Elizabeth to better understand Anthony, to appreciate his high need for motor activity, and to better interpret his cues. Instead of seeing Anthony as a baby who didn't have much interest in verbal exchanges with her, Elizabeth began to view him as a baby who was extraordinarily curious about the big world and determined to use his limbs to get there. As a result of this new, non-blaming, and value-neutral information, Elizabeth shifted her perception of Anthony and shifted her self-blame to an understanding of her baby's needs and a constructive course of action. Anthony was intensely sensitive to sights and sounds and required a subdued level of stimulation. Elizabeth adapted his environment, lowering the stimulation level by limiting visitors, using a blanket to reduce visual stimulation in new places, and using gentle music to provide "white noise" during naps. She continued to take him to new places in order to stretch his capacity for tolerance but learned to do so at a pace that Anthony could manage without becoming overloaded.

Anthony and Elizabeth began to enjoy each other. At six months, they showed little resemblance to the mutually frustrated dyad they had been just a few weeks before. Anthony was still a challenging baby. He is to this day (18 months) very active and still gets overloaded easily by too much stimulation. But by the time Anthony was seven months old, Elizabeth perceived him and herself as competent and well matched in intensity and intelligence. She takes great pride in his progress and his unique personality. Babies with easy temperaments now appear to Elizabeth to be somewhat "sluggish" when she compares them to her own little boy's "high-spirited" approach to the world.

Because negative patterns of interaction are often difficult to change once they are established, the temperament research presents another powerful example of the opportunities for maximizing positive outcomes present in the first two years of life. It provides a way to help parents understand their child's unique qualities and defuses the tendency for parents either to blame their own failings or to see their child's temperament traits as deliberate misbehavior. The ability to prevent a continuing cycle of parent-child conflict at the outset or to derail it before negative patterns are well established depends on getting to difficult children and their parents as soon as possible after birth.

While education and emotional support for parents do not change a child's temperament, they can help reduce the early rage so likely to occur when a pattern of escalating negative interactions is triggered as a result of a poor match between child temperament and the environment, particularly caregiver expectations, perceptions, and skills. Several clinical sites around the country are finding that such an approach is effective and that the cost of assessing temperament and following up on difficult infants is a fraction of the cost of waiting until entrenched problems result in child abuse or school problems.[4]

Since the early research by Drs. Chess and Thomas, several branches of temperament research have developed, each varying somewhat in the names and numbers of temperament dimensions identified and some preferring to group dimensions into two or more typologies. Dr. Jerome Kagan, who has written extensively on this subject, focuses on two primary dimensions: reactivity and inhibition. Several other researchers, such as Drs. Robert Cloninger and Felton Earls, have outlined slightly more elaborate systems, each with three or four dimensions. While there are some variations between these systems of temperament classification, each includes a basic response style to new situations and a measurement of the degree of emotional reactivity or intensity the child experiences in those situations. In Kagan's typology, children are essentially viewed as responding positively (eagerly, exuberantly) or negatively (fearfully) to new people, events, situations, or things. Fearfully oriented children are viewed as "inhibited" or cautious. Those children comprise about 15 percent of all children. On the other end of the continuum are fearless children, who are viewed as "uninhibited" or bold. Those children, who are mostly boys, comprise about 30 percent of all children. Most children fall somewhere in the middle. Dr. Kagan introduces his newest book on this topic, *Galen's Prophecy,* with the examples of Walter Matthau and Jack Lemmon in *The Odd Couple.*[5] Lemmon's character, Felix, typifies the sensitive, carefully restrained individual, cautious to the point of neurotic, while Matthau, as Oscar, is gregarious and constantly at risk of behaving like the proverbial bull in the china shop. Oscar and Felix clearly represent the extremes in temperament differences—most of us fall somewhere in the middle—but they illustrate the concept of the basic inborn emotional orientations that are with each of us from the beginning.

Dr. Kagan attributes our propensity toward cautiousness or boldness to inherited biology, particularly brain neurochemistry. Researchers suspect that children like Anthony who are easily overwhelmed have an "excitable limbic physiology."[6] This biology is actively influenced by environmental conditions, interacts with experience over time, and can shift. The key in the beginning is our relationship with our primary caregiver.[7] The child's temperamental profile at any given time is the result of the interactive process between innate, physiologically determined tendencies and the responses the child experiences in the environment.

While we know that infants enter the world constitutionally predisposed to certain temperament qualities, the pivotal role of the home in shaping those qualities can hardly be overemphasized. In one study by Doreen Arcus, approximately 60 percent of infants assessed to be highly reactive at four months of age did in fact become very fearful toddlers at fourteen months. The remaining 40 percent of the babies had experiences with their caregivers that the researchers believe balanced or offset fearful temperaments.[8] Arcus observed that maternal holding and limit setting had key roles in sustaining or discouraging fearful behavior. Children who developed relatively less fearfulness were those whose mothers held them less frequently when their babies didn't require it for comfort. These mothers also used firm and direct limit setting, clearly stated commands, and followed through to enforce their baby's compliance by redirecting, distracting, or removing the baby from an undesired situation. The researchers' interpretation of these observations was that parents who created challenges by setting limits and allowing children some opportunity to console themselves actually stretched the children's ability to cope with unfamiliar situations.

Research with rhesus monkeys has shown very similar outcomes. When little monkeys who were bred for fearlessness or less reactive temperaments were placed with mother monkeys who were inhibited by nature, the young monkeys showed little change in behavior or in neurochemistry as measured by norepinephrine levels and electroencephalogram (EEG) tests. The inhibited behavior of the mothers had minimal influence—her fearfulness rolled off the backs of the bold babies. But when little inhibited or fearful monkeys were placed with uninhibited mothers, both their biology and their behavior shifted over time to reflect that of their foster mother's. They became less fearful, and their levels of norepinephrine decreased.[9]

Tracing the developmental path to aggression or violence through the lens afforded by the temperament theorists is a complex process. This branch of psychology is relatively young and there is much disagreement about terms, definitions, and constructs. Some temperament theorists, such as Dr. Kagan, identify typologies (e.g., "inhibited/ uninhibited") that describe behavioral extremes for the purpose of study and providing parental support. Others, finding typologies too limiting, prefer to study dimensions such as "irritability" or "fearfulness."

Regardless of these differences, the temperament literature offers some valuable insights in discerning children at risk of behavioral problems. Children at greatest risk of later aggression may be those who begin life with high degrees of irritability, are persistent, are low in their responsivity to caregiver feedback, and show marked levels of early distress to limitations, such as dressing and diapering.[10] The rating of children on these dimensions has been done primarily through standardized parent ratings. Parent ratings are key in temperament research because it is the parents' perception of the child together with the parents' own temperamental traits, values, and expectations that may, in fact, edge the child's developmental course toward later aggression or other negative behaviors. When such children are perceived by their parents as angry or naughty, the result can be a high degree of conflict or "poorness of fit" between the child and his or her parents. The child's irritability elicits an irritable response from the parents, which in turn increases the child's irritability. This increases the parents' perception of difficulty and their own irritability. In an environment without social or emotional support for parents encumbered by additional stressors, such as poverty or mental illness, this early pattern of negative interactions is the beginning of what can develop into a path to chronic anger, frustration, and later aggression. So while certain inborn characteristics may begin the cycle, specific parental responses that also begin at birth lead the child to emphasize some behaviors more than others.[11] The interpretation of the child's behavior and the contingent responses by the parents to the child's behaviors greatly influence the progression toward expressing prosocial or antisocial behaviors.[12] According to Kagan, aggressive children are bold children who are indulged, abused, or poorly socialized so that they become bullies.[13]

A central lesson being learned during infancy and earliest childhood is how to soothe oneself or to self-regulate strong emotions. This begins with the model provided by the parent. When the baby gets upset and her mother responds by going to the child, picking her up, verbally soothing, holding, and rocking until she calms, the child begins to learn how to do this for herself.[14] During a specific window of time, between ten and eighteen months, the orbitofrontal area of the prefrontal cortex is creating connections with the limbic system that will enable the child to modulate distress. Norepinephrine is a key ingredient in activating the limbic system. In addition, parental behaviors have a direct impact on the maturing vagus nerve, which regulates the heart, sends signals to the amygdala from the adrenal glands, and prompts the fight-or-flight response.[15] When the baby is initially alarmed, her brain is generating stress responses with strong signals from the limbic brain to the cortex. A host of stress-related neurochemicals surges in the child's central nervous system. The child feels upset. When the mother soothes the child quickly and sensitively, the chemistry of alarm in her brain subsides and is brought back into balance. The baby feels better and connects this feeling with the presence of the mother. A repeated course of soothing interactions creates a "map" or model in the child's brain that anticipates similar interactions in the future and will later enable the baby to generate soothing for herself. But for the child who is left to cry, or whose distress is followed by unpredictable or abusive responses—a blow, an angry voice, or rough handling—no such connections are made. Rather than associating the presence of the caregiver with a positive or soothing experience, the child remains fearful or experiences mixed feelings such as anger combined with some relief from physical distress (e.g., hunger). The baby does not experience regular and immediate release from the chemistry of fear and does not learn a smooth and immediate route to modulating these strong feelings of fear or anger. Such a baby may be left flooded with strong emotions she can act out only by screaming or flailing.[16]

Learning changes the brain. The brain directs behavior. When these basic processes—such as the ability to regulate strong emotion—are learned from negative models and are built into an individual's personality, learning, as well as relationships, can be impaired. The child who continues to throw tantrums and is aggressive with other children in response to wanting his way or the child who freezes, withdraws, and becomes mute in the face of perceived conflict are both reflecting learned models of what has worked with their early caregivers. These models build patterns, which, if not interrupted, can jeopardize future relationships and—if strong enough—steal the child's attention from a focus on school. The foundation for our primary patterns of coping with strong emotions is laid early in life. As Daniel Goleman says in his book, *Emotional Intelligence:*

> Each period represents a window for helping that child install beneficial emotional habits or, if missed, to make it that much harder to offer corrective lessons later in life. The massive sculpting and pruning of neural circuits in childhood may be an underlying reason why early emotional hardships and trauma have such enduring and pervasive effects in adulthood. It may explain, too, why psychotherapy can often take so long to affect some of these patterns—and why, as we've seen, even after therapy those patterns tend to remain as underlying propensities, though with an overlay of new insights and relearned responses.[17]

By preschool, all children are experiencing anger, and displays of aggressive behavior are normal. But, depending on the child's temperament and the responses of early caregivers, many children who have not learned to put strong negative feelings into words have developed a characteristic pattern of either "internalizing" or "externalizing" these strong emotions, especially anger. Internalizing children are those who hold or repress the negative feelings. They feel powerless to act, may be quiet or tearful in the face of conflict, and may unknowingly turn their fury toward themselves. Temperamentally cautious, fearful, or highly sensitive children are the most likely to develop this pattern. In an abusive environment in which a caregiver is emotionally unavailable to help such a child with the regulation of strong negative emotions, internalizing children may develop generalized anxiety and later depression or panic disorders. These are often the children who seem the easiest to socialize because they comply to avoid negative consequences, to which they are particularly sensitive. They may more readily internalize self-discipline and show earlier signs of conscience.[18] But, like little pressure cookers, they also may repress negative feelings and then explode in aggressive behavior.[19] In an overly punitive or critical environment, the price to children who internalize is self-directed emotional violence resulting, at a minimum, in the erosion of confidence and competence and, in the worst cases, in suicide.

At the other extreme are the children who externalize their angry feelings, who act out their anger in aggressive ways against other people and things. These are the hitters, yellers, biters, kickers, and destroyers of property. Externalizing preschoolers present a challenge to their classrooms. They may be viewed as leaders or troublemakers or both. What such children usually have in common is a bold temperament, relatively less fearfulness, and less sensitivity to potential negative consequences of their behavior. Neurochemically they may have relatively lower rates of norepinephrine, allowing them to proceed undaunted by a reactive nervous system.[20] They set their own course. Such children, when growing up in homes where parents are skilled at setting limits and use praise rather than punishment, are more likely to develop prosocial behaviors. Bold children allowed to run over others or who meet with harsh punishment may become aggressive bullies. When this pattern of externalizing feelings is accompanied by poor impulse control and an inability to focus attention, it may trigger an assessment of attention-deficit/hyperactivity disorder in the average preschool or grade school.

The information arising from temperament research is particularly useful in infancy and toddlerhood when it enables the early identification of children with challenging characteristics who may be experienced by their parents as seriously difficult. If a child with these temperament qualities can be supported by parents during infancy, especially when parents are experiencing multiple additional stressors (divorce, single parenting, poverty, physical or mental illness), the provision of information, (especially around how to discipline, together with emotional support for both the parent and child's needs), can offset or moderate children's tendencies to externalize or internalize.

When this early opportunity is missed, and when externalizing or aggressive behaviors become chronic, the stage is set for the more serious behavioral disorders of ODD and CD. At ages two and three years, even when early parent-child patterns have been negative, a great deal can still be done to change this path.[21] But if allowed to persist to ages four and five, chronic noncompliance, restlessness, and aggression with peers can become strongly entrenched. These are strong predictors of antisocial behavior problems during adolescence and adulthood.[22]

Researchers are exploring several theories that may explain the biological basis of temperamental differences. Biosocial researchers hypothesize that, since norepinephrine is involved in the loop between the limbic system and the cortex, which is the seat of control, children who have very high norepinephrine levels are more reactive to extremely low doses of stimulation. These are the children who, like little Anthony, are reactive to small changes and subtle levels of stimulation and respond irritably by fussing or crying. These babies are likely to be more cautious, though not necessarily shy.[23] Conversely, children with low norepinephrine levels experience very low levels of arousal, so that they require higher levels of stimulation to achieve responsiveness to external cues such as parental warnings.[24]

Another theory about the biological basis of temperament points to structural differences in the brain. Asymmetries between the right and left hemispheres of the brain account for predominant moods that affect all of us. Emotional development appears to be inextricably linked with brain development—both inherited and environmentally shaped. Temperamental tendencies to be outgoing or shy, joyful or melancholy appear to be associated with differing degrees of activity in the right and left frontal lobes. Work by Dr. Richard Davidson at the University of Wisconsin and Dr. Nathan Fox at the University of Maryland has confirmed that the left frontal region is activated during experiences of emotions such as joy, interest, and anger, while the right frontal region is activated during the experience of sadness, distress, or disgust. Drs. Davidson and Fox hypothesize that these differences in frontal lobe activation, as measured primarily by EEG testing, are due to innate biological differences that reflect a predisposition to experience certain emotions in certain situations.[25]

Dr. Davidson found that the activity of the frontal lobes predicted whether or not ten-month-old infants would cry when their mothers left the room. The correlation was 100 percent. Every baby who responded by crying had more brain activity on the right side, while those who didn't cry had more on the left.[26] Davidson has also found that adults who have a history of depression have lower levels of brain activity in the left frontal lobe. He believes that people who have overcome depression have learned to increase their levels of activity in the left frontal lobe, a hypothesis as yet untested.[27] Where the researchers seem to have little disagreement is on the fact that basic temperamental orientations are clearly affected by experience over time, as was the case with Anthony and Elizabeth.

Dr. Mary Rothbart, a developmental psychologist working with Dr. Michael Posner at the University of Oregon, looks at constructs within temperament research to examine factors, or what she calls "systems," that are protective against or negatively correlated with aggressive behavior. It is here that the temperament research seems to have the greatest value of all—in discerning temperament traits early and in supporting and educating parents with such information and skills as to enhance each child's temperamental strengths and to counterbalance liabilities. Dr. Rothbart and her colleagues delineate three systems discernible in very young children that she believes are key to the development—or not—of later aggressive behaviors. The first of these she calls the "fear system," a child's tendency toward caution or timidity versus impulsive behavior. Children who are naturally constrained upon exposure to new people or experiences seem to be less likely to engage in aggressive behavior than a child whose reactions to a novel person, toy, or situation are unrestrained. This is a temperament quality that can be measured as early as ten months of age.

Confirming Rothbart's observations, a recent study reports that even children diagnosed with ADHD, who also have anxiety disorders or high fearfulness, do not perform poorly on measures of impulsivity or response inhibition. This group of children, by contrast to those with aggressive behavior disorders (ODD and CD), do not go on to develop criminality in adolescence and adulthood.[28] Fearfulness appears to serve as a protective factor against impulsivity and mitigates against later aggressive behavior.[29] In a study by Dr. David Farrington of Cambridge University, seven year olds with shy or inhibited temperaments living in neighborhoods with high crime rates were less likely to become delinquents in adolescence than bold, uninhibited boys.[30] According to Rothbart, fearfulness helps regulate impulsivity due to a higher sensitivity to negative consequences. Children who respond intensely negatively to new people, places, things, and situations often begin to demonstrate fearful behavior between the age of ten and thirty-six months. This same sensitivity to unfamiliar conditions later acts to inhibit negative or aggressive behavior when there is a perceived possibility of punishment in connection with an action. Dr. Grazyna Kochanska at the

University of Iowa has found that fearfulness in young children is associated with early development of conscience, especially when their mothers use gentle rather than forceful strategies for their socialization. While it is neither constructive nor realistic to attempt to teach bold children to be fearful, parents can work with these children to teach clear limits, provide firm and consistent guidance, and emphasize praise for honoring limits. The development of conscience in more fearless children is also associated with their early attachment to their mothers. And for children generally, positive experiences with their mothers are related to later cooperation and development of conscience. Fearful children also can be encouraged to stretch a bit beyond their self-imposed limitations. Both groups can work to learn to put negative feelings into words, to empathize with other children, and to solve problems.

A second system discernible at a very early age that appears to be involved in later aggressive behavior is what Dr. Rothbart calls the executive attentional system or the child's ability to choose one behavior while inhibiting another. Rothbart calls this system "effortful control." In measuring this capacity, Dr. Rothbart's research staff uses an adapted version of a traditional cognitive learning exercise called the Stroop task. For adults, the Stroop task amounts to answering questions about the color of ink used to spell a word. The word might be "blue" and the color of ink on the computer screen red. In order to answer the question accurately, the subject must inhibit the strong tendency to read the word and instead respond with the color of the ink. For little children ages two to three, this task is adapted by showing them a picture of an animal or other object on the screen and asking them to match it with a picture on one of two keys, one to the right and one to the left. If the animal appears on the right side of the screen and the key with the animal's picture is on the left, the tendency to respond incorrectly on the same side must be inhibited. This ability to inhibit one response while choosing another seems to be involved in the ability to inhibit impulsive aggression.[31] Dr. Kochanska has found that children with higher inhibitory control show greater evidence of conscience development.[32] Here is a skill that parents can teach and reward with simple focusing games that can be played at home.

A third system that may be protective against aggressive behavior is the capacity for what Rothbart calls "affiliativeness." Affiliativeness encompasses the concept of sociability and the ability to get along well with other people. Closely related to the concept of agreeableness, this system typically describes the child whom people enjoy. Here there is convergence between temperament theorists and attachment theorists who assert that the primary bond between the infant and the caregiver, if established in a normal and healthy manner, lays the foundation for empathy, or the sense of connection with other people as a part of one's self. Some researchers believe that affiliativeness is better framed as warmth, or an openness to the experience of love. There is some speculation about whether this is an inborn or an environmentally created trait. Regardless of its source, the capacity to connect with other people is clearly a factor that protects against aggression and can be taught in the earliest months and years and, as found by Kochanska, may be especially important for relatively fearless children. All of these systems—fearfulness versus impulsivity; effortful control, or the ability to choose one behavior while inhibiting another more obvious one; and the capacity for affiliativeness or connecting with others—are capacities that appear to be protective against the development of aggression. These qualities may also be assessed and enhanced by parents prior to age three.

ONE FLEW OVER

Even in the most difficult families, where child abuse or alcohol or poverty and neglect have taken their toll, it is not unusual to observe that one child will somehow emerge relatively more competent or successful than the rest. The stories of Jeffrey, John, and Julie, though they were siblings, provide a study in contrasts. (Jeffrey and Julie are full siblings; John is a half brother.) At nineteen Jeffrey is on death row; Julie, now seventeen, is embarking on her third pregnancy; John is in college at age twenty-one and is gainfully employed by his "dad" (foster father). Their stories reveal very different temperaments, aptitudes, and coping mechanisms. While all three children were bounced through several foster homes, only John had the capacity to engage emotionally with two different sets of foster parents. He attributes his abilities to hope for more, to visualize a different life, and to actually create that life for himself to his closeness to those foster parents, one family at age five, another during adolescence. There is growing evidence that John's insights may be valid.

The theory of resiliency is based on the observation that certain individuals manage to succeed in spite of the odds. The resilient child is the child who emerges competent and confident from a family when everyone else seems to be a victim of "risk factors" or negative circumstances such as chronic poverty, alcoholism, criminality, community violence, or child abuse. With the exception perhaps of the fear system, Dr. Rothbart's emphasis on the systems of effortful control and affiliativeness as protective factors against development of aggression or violence, coincides with concepts emerging from the resiliency studies that are asking why some children do not succumb to negative environments. It is notable that the systems viewed by the temperament researchers as those most protective against later violence are "higher" cortical functions attributed to the frontal lobes, the adequate development of which is seen by neurobiologists as key to protection against later violent behavior. In effortful control, the ability to focus on relevant information in school (similar to the ability to focus attention and to delay action) is a key resiliency factor.[33] The ability to perform successfully in school allows a child otherwise at high risk to succeed in this arena, gain prosocial employment, and avoid a criminal lifestyle.[34]

An agreeable and affiliative or social personality is a second factor cited in the studies of resiliency.[35] Such children are optimistic, positive in their responses to others, get along well with their peers, and engage adults outside their families, such as teachers and neighbors who provide alternate role models and opportunities in addition to affection and validation. Resilient children are somehow capable of generating relationships and collecting glimpses of a different sort of world, which they integrate into a very different life for themselves than that from which they are emerging. They are empathetic and their connections with people enable them to internalize socially constructive behavior. For example, Jeffrey's brother John still consciously treasures the kindness of the foster parents he and Jeffrey lived with for seven months when John was five and Jeffrey four. In talking about Bev and Walt, John says:

> It made a difference. It made all the difference. I don't know how to explain. It was like that seven months of time is when I got all of my morals. It's when I learned every single thing as far as basics. And it's so strange, I mean, because I've thought of this a lot. . . . It's been a long time and I think about them almost every day of my life. I think about what they did for me. I wish I could talk to them right now.

John, similar to many resilient children, internalized a social compass early that proceeded to guide him beyond his original risk-laden environment. Like Dr. Rothbart's three protective systems, resilience can be made as well as born. Resilience is a concept best viewed as more environmentally than biologically generated. Like risk, it seems to occur as a consequence of the interplay between the child's basic traits and the environment. Risk for behavioral problems is created by the combination of a child's innate vulnerability (e.g., Jeffrey's ADHD) with negative environmental factors (e.g., his mother's depression and consequent abuse and neglect). John is an example of this process in reverse. His strengths were key to reducing the negative effects of difficult circumstances such as his placement in foster care. When a child is exposed to risk factors that challenge but don't overwhelm his strengths, when his experience results in feelings of competence and confidence, he can actually become stronger. When the risks overwhelm the child's strengths, the outcome is most often destructive.

Taken together, temperament research and resiliency research corroborate what we know through common sense observations—that the capacity for connecting and getting along with other people, the capacity for focused thinking and problem solving mitigate against impulsive violence in human society. These capacities are fundamentally sown and nurtured in the earliest months of life.

7

Baby, Get Your Gun:

THE IMPACT OF TRAUMA

AND HEAD INJURY

There was an old woman
Who lived in a shoe.
She had so many children
She didn't know what to do.
She gave them some broth
Without any bread.
She whipped them all soundly
And put them to bed.

—MOTHER GOOSE

Citizen reported that on the evening of 10–22–84 loud scream-ing was coming from within (S) [Jeffrey's mother's] apartment and sounded like a child was being hit. Citizen also stated that this type of action took place more than once. . . . Writer and Officer Johnson left (S) residence and went to [V's] school to interview him and examine for abuse. . . . When [V's] pants were pulled down, writer found that both buttocks had been bruised. The right side was very red and blue in color and it was quite obvious that (V) had been struck numerous times. . . . Writer left school and contacted CPS and said they should interview (V) and consider placement. Writer to issue CTA (citation) to (S) for Assault IV into District Court.

POLICE INCIDENT REPORT

Mostly we were always really afraid. Sometimes if somebody was just coming up to give us a hug and they'd say our names loudly—and they were coming up to give us a hug—we would cower. We would actually throw our hands up and cower. And I did that all the time until I moved in with Richard, my [foster father]. And when he saw that, he just broke down and started bawling, and I didn't understand why. I figured he was mad at me, and I thought he was gonna come hit me. So I just threw up my hands like, "You're not gonna hit me so just get away!" And he just started crying. . . . And I didn't under-stand why he was crying, why that was going on. . . . 'Cause after a while you don't realize that it's not wrong anymore. You see all this stuff and you don't realize that it's not wrong anymore to hit some-body. . . .

My mom beat my brother up. That one time she beat him with a braided belt, and she put bruises like from his knees all the way up to his neck. I mean, like, I don't know. She had hit him a lot, I mean, and it was like colors you never thought that human people could ac-

151

tually make in their body. You know what I'm saying? I mean it was like all the colors on his back and on his backside and different places. I was totally amazed. I mean, I'd never seen anything ever quite like that. . . .

You could go home and watch Cops on TV and see every single thing on that has happened to us at one time or another. Every single thing! I mean, you name it. There's been guns pulled. There's been knives pulled. There's been people cut open. You name it, it's happened. To me, it's not really—this is sad to say—but it's not really anything new, and after a while you just kind of become callous to it. After a while you're just sitting there looking at it, and it's like, well, nothing new, I guess. And you hear your family, "Well, such and such deserved it."

JOHN, AUGUST 1996

Sometimes it's more difficult than others. I think everybody has to deal with it, you know. Everybody has to deal with anger. It's how we deal with it that's important and how we learn to deal with it. What makes us decide to deal with it or what makes us not decide to deal with it—to just let it flow . . . and run into uncontrolled rage. There are different levels of anger from upset, to mad, to pissed off. Then there's raw fear, you know, and uncontrolled rage. And I borderline up there. When I get mad, I borderline up there, then I follow my impulses. If I can't control it up there, then I follow my impulses. If I can't control my impulses, then I do things that I regret later. . . . I do follow my impulses . . . because that was the way I learned to survive when I was little. . . . Like, if I knew I wasn't supposed to be running from an asswhupping, but I'd be running anyway. What I was doing was wrong, but I would follow the impulse rather than stop and think about the consequences of 'He's got to catch up to me sooner or later'. I didn't care about that. I just wanted to get away.

JEFFREY, AUGUST 1996

152

On a stifling hot and humid day on July 15, 1976 a school bus was highjacked as it rolled along a back country road near Chowchilla, California, a small, middle-class town in the San Joaquin Valley. The children, ranging in age from five to fourteen, were returning from a day of outdoor recreation and activities, including a performance by the sixth-grade class of *Born to Be Free*. The bus driver slowed on his route to pass a white van that was blocking the road. As the bus passed the van, suddenly two men, one with a stocking over his face and the other wearing a mask and carrying a gun, leaped from the van and forced their way on to the bus. They ordered the driver and the older children to the back of the bus.[1]

The kidnappers then drove the bus for some distance into a steep gully and at gunpoint ordered the children to get out. The older children went first. One by one they filed off the bus and disappeared from the view of the younger children into the white van, which had followed the bus. When the van was full, one of the men slammed the butt of his gun into the stomach of ten-year-old Terrie and ordered her to stop just before getting in. The white van pulled off, and a fourth man in a green van drove out of the slough and pulled alongside the bus. Terrie, the youngest children, and the bus driver filed into the second vehicle.

The children sat crammed in the vans on hard, wooden seats. The windows were boarded, and any communication with the kidnappers was blocked by a solid barrier erected behind the front seats. They were driven aimlessly in the heat on bumpy roads for eleven hours in total darkness without food, water, or an opportunity to go to the bathroom. At one point the vans stopped and then backed up. Some of the children thought they would be driven off a cliff; others smelled gas and thought they were going to be burned alive. None of them knew what had happened to the other half of the group.

Finally, about three in the morning, the vans stopped and the children were ordered outside at gunpoint. One by one they were interrogated beneath a tentlike canopy placed near a ladder that led down into a hole. Their inquisitor wore a mask and was eerily illuminated by a flashlight placed under his chin. He demanded that each child tell his or her full name, and he confiscated some personal possession—a toy, a bathing suit top, or the contents of a pocket—and then he ordered the child to get down into the hole. The rectangular space under ground, which later turned out to be a large truck trailer buried several months before, was lit by flashlight and prepared in advance for the children's arrival. There were stale cheerios, soggy potato chips, a jar of peanut butter, musty water stored in cans, and a pile of old mattresses.

The children timidly explored their environment and settled in. A few kids held up towels to shield other children as they went to the bathroom in two wheel wells with signs over them marked "boys" and "girls." Suddenly, they heard the sounds of shovels above and rocks and dirt began hitting the top of the hole. Some of the children begged and shouted, while others whimpered as they were buried alive. The bus driver implored the kidnappers to have mercy and then fell to his knees praying as the shoveling continued. As the dirt and rocks continued to clunk relentlessly on top of the hole, he lay down and cried. They were all "goners," he told the children.

As the hours dragged by, the children remained quiet and listless. Some of them slept. The rest sat doing nothing. This torpor continued until some time during the day of July 16, when one of the younger children leaned too hard against a makeshift pole and the roof began to collapse. This new crisis galvanized the older children, who with great effort and ingenuity finally dug their way out and led the others to freedom. Jack Wynne, the bus driver, having lifted the littlest children out, took off on foot to find a telephone. As they emerged from their crypt, the children found themselves in a strange valley nearly one hundred miles from home with no idea of what had happened or why. (To this day, no one knows why. The four kidnappers were caught and convicted, but they have never revealed their motives or why they chose this particular group of children.)

The sheriff and his deputies took the children—by bus—to the Alameda County Prison for questioning. They received a fifteen-minute physical examination by a prison doctor and a pediatrician, who found them, much to the relief of the waiting world, to be in "good shape." The medical team did not call any psychiatrists, psychologists, or social workers because the children seemed calm and normal. None of them was hysterical or crying, and none of them seemed to be acting strange, except for the smallest kids, who had repeatedly slipped off the bus and tried to hide when the sheriff and deputies came to rescue them.

After eating hamburgers and apple pie, the children spent the night in the prison and were then taken home in the morning—on a bus—with no warning of or protection from what they were to encounter: a town gone insane with FBI agents, news personalities and reporters from around the world, television cameras, microphones, sightseers, and frantic parents, siblings, and relatives, all waiting for the bus as it pulled into the parking lot next to the Chowchilla fire station.

No psychiatrist or psychologist even spoke with the children until five months after the incident, when Dr. Lenore Terr, a clinical professor of psychiatry at the University of California at San Francisco, approached one of the families. She had read a newspaper article published in the *Fresno Bee* reporting that the children were still suffering from terrible fears and nightmares. Terr undertook one of the first major studies of the long-term effects of trauma on children and found that at one-year, four-year, and five-year evaluations every single child of Chowchilla was still seriously affected.

As incredible as the blindness to the psychic injuries of the Chowchilla children may seem to us now, at the time of the incident—just twenty years ago—we believed that children were resilient and would weather most trauma given time. The two doctors who initially examined the children had no idea that anything serious was wrong. They didn't even know what symptoms to look for, since the possibility of serious psychic injury, let alone any specific symptoms of trauma in children, was totally absent from medical literature.

As the story of the Chowchilla schoolchildren illustrates, we have come only recently to begin to understand that, for children of any age, long-term damage can occur from a single searing trauma or prolonged exposure to chronic stress or fear. But we have yet to understand that when serious trauma occurs to babies and toddlers during their most explosive phase of brain development, the injury reverberates beyond anything we have ever imagined possible. Fear and anger produce changes in the levels of hormones that are associated with aggression and violence, including noradrenaline, which puts the brain on red alert and serotonin, which has a calming effect when the perceived danger subsides. When stress is especially severe or prolonged, permanent changes may occur in hormone levels that alter the brain's chemical profile and affect patterns of information processing. The result may be maladaptive behavior patterns, including both aggression and depression. Children so traumatized come to perceive the world as a dangerous place.

Jeffrey's older brother, John, describes how he and Jeffrey cowered from the hugs proffered by foster parents who held out their arms spontaneously to receive the boys. For children who have associated adults' sudden arm movements with being hit, this fear is a normal response. Children who are seriously traumatized stay watchful to anticipate and be prepared for the worst. They are apt to misread gestures and respond accordingly.

When the environment continues to teach a child to expect danger rather than comfort, the results can be disastrous. Such was the case of Robert "Yummy" Sandifer, who was shot through the back of his head at age eleven by two members of his gang.[2] In commenting on Yummy after his death, Cook County public guardian Patrick Murphy said, "He was in trouble the moment he was conceived."

Yummy was born to an eighteen-year-old mother on welfare. He was her third child. By the time she was twenty, she had five children. At the time of Yummy's death, she had seven children by four different fathers. The court records show that she had a serious drug problem and had been arrested forty-one times. Yummy's father, also

156

a teenager, went to prison for theft three months after Yummy's birth. At the time of Yummy's death, his father was in prison again, for dealing drugs. The court records show that Yummy had a history of serious physical abuse and neglect. At twenty-two months, he was treated at a Chicago hospital for scratches and bruises on his arms and torso. His mother said he had been beaten by his father. When Yummy was three, the police found him at home alone with two other brothers under the age of five, apparently a routine occurrence. He was removed from his mother's custody and placed with his grandmother when investigators found cigarette burns on his neck, back, and buttocks, scratches on his face and abdomen, and marks on his legs from beatings with an electrical cord.

Yummy's criminal record began at age nine. Police believe that he committed more than two dozen felonies before his death two years later. He was prosecuted eight times for various felonies and convicted twice. The charges included attempted armed robbery, auto theft, arson, and burglary. He was kicked out of a group home for fighting and stealing. He was turned loose by a frustrated judge who could no longer detain him under state law after a dozen homes refused to take him.

In a story published in the *Toronto Star* on September 3, 1994, George Pappajohn reported on a psychological examination of Yummy conducted at a state-run shelter for children ten months prior to his death. During the testing he had to be reassured constantly that it wasn't a police interrogation and that he wasn't in trouble. At one point when he heard a walkie-talkie outside the door, he jumped to his feet to look for police. In writing of the incident, Pappajohn said:

> He seemed to see the worse—even in himself—and to expect it from others. . . . Even though the troubled child in the lime-green jeans and food-stained sweatshirt was in the care of the Illinois Department of Children and Family Services, not in court or jail, he thought of himself as "servin' time." . . . Robert's past was marked by abuse and chaos, but he made the transition from victim to victimizer by

157

the age of 9. In language both clinical and heartbreaking, the psychological report fills in that picture. . . . "Robert is a child growing up without any encouragement and support," the examiner wrote. . . . "Since he is so bound up in trying to manage negative feelings of inadequacy on the inside, and the pressure his environment is exerting from the outside, Robert is emotionally flooded. . . . His response to this flooding is to back away from demanding situations and act out impulsively and unpredictably. . . . He is caught up in a never-ending cycle of emotional overload and acting out. His anger is so great that his perception of the world is grossly distorted and inaccurate."

What happens to children to turn them into vicious killers? How does a baby turn into a child who wants to hurt or even kill another baby? How can a child grow into an adult who enjoys torture and killing? The answers, which are just beginning to surface, are not simple. But neither are they impossible to understand once we reflect on how the brain works. It is the brain that mediates this metamorphosis from baby to killer. And it is the environment that shapes the entire process.

THE HOUSE THAT JACK BUILT

We humans have evolved and maintained our primacy on the planet because of our amazing ability to successfully adapt to the varying environments in which we find ourselves. The brain presents us with a microcosm in which we are able to see how biology shapes itself in response to individual experiences. Like the capacity of photographic paper to respond to varying patterns of light, our brain is constructed to respond to specific environmental needs and will adjust its chemistry to reflect environmental demands. In early childhood, or even in later life, responses such as extreme vigilance, chronic anxiety, and depression are adjustments that protect people in difficult settings when their survival is threatened. But when such responses are generated in the first years of life, they may be developed at the cost of other more constructive potentials such as trust, confidence, and curiosity, which atrophy when not reinforced by the environment.

Neurons, the basic cells of the brain, connect with each other to form networks; networks connect with each other to form systems; systems work together to facilitate specific functions such as vision. Every neuron in the human brain is geared and waiting for stimulation to call it into action. Experiences in the environment determine which of these cells will be called into use and for what purposes so that an internalized reflection of specific responses needed for survival in a particular environment is created in the brain of the developing child. The more a certain type of stimulation is experienced, the more the corresponding cells in the brain will be called upon or sensitized. Once sensitized, the same neural activation can be called forth by less and less intense stimulation.[3]

When the brain is first forming, both the quantity and quality of tissue and chemistry can be changed by sensitization to trauma. The same experiences can change the brain of an older child, also, but in the beginning, in infancy and toddlerhood, while it is at its most malleable, the brain actually organizes itself around these conditions. Hypersensitivity can become wired in to basic brain chemistry and bodily functions. And attention and capacities in the brain originally available for learning other skills may be deflected to help defend against future trauma.

FROM STEM TO STERN

As discussed in chapter two, the brain grows from the simpler or more basic functions to the more complex. So the brainstem, which regulates basic functions like heart rate, body temperature, and blood pressure, grows before the mid-brain, which controls sleep, appetite, and arousal. This is followed by the limbic area, the center of emotional activity. And finally, the cortex, the seat of rational and analytical process.[4] In the normal brain, there is a balancing system in which the "lower" or more primitive areas of the brain—the parts responsible for excitatory processes—are modulated or held in check by the "higher" or executive functions in the cortex.

Early developmental experiences that build cortical functions, such as exposure to language or music or a loving relationship with a parent, are investments that protect against the expression of violent or impulsive behavior. Conversely, experiences that increase reactivity of the lower areas of the brain, such as physical or sexual abuse by a parent, will increase the capacity for impulsive emotional responses and the likelihood of later violence.[5] Dr. Bruce Perry, executive director of the Civitas Child Trauma Program and chief of psychiatry at the Baylor College of Medicine, has specialized in treating traumatized children and teaching how trauma in the environment alters the developing brain. Dr. Perry's research is at the forefront of our evolving understanding of the impact of early trauma and its relationship to the early precursors of impulsive violence.[6]

Because development occurs in stages that build upon each other, that which occurs first tends to echo through subsequent development. For example, negative experiences such as chronic maternal stress or drug consumption that occur prenatally and affect the development of the brainstem or mid-brain will subsequently affect the development of the limbic and cortical areas of the brain as they mature.[7] This is not to say that all children, or even most, who are young victims of abuse or neglect will become victimizers. In fact, most will not. And all neglect, abuse, or trauma does not have an equal impact. Children are not affected equally; ameliorating factors vary greatly in the lives of individuals. Most of us have had some degree of negative childhood experience. But growing numbers of children across the world are victims of severe trauma ranging from sexual mutilation, to incest, to war and natural disasters. In this country alone, conservative estimates of the number of children exposed to trauma exceed five million each year.[8] These are the children who are victims of or witness to physical, emotional, or sexual abuse, or to domestic or community violence such as gang murders. For American children, the gestation of violence takes root primarily in the home. When trauma or neglect happens early in life and is left untreated, the injuries sustained reverberate to all ensuing developmental stages. Adult and adolescent community violence begin with violence inflicted on the babies these individuals once were.[9]

ROUND AND ROUND IT GOES

In the late 1980s Cathy Spatz Widom of Indiana University conducted an extensive review of the literature to answer the question "Does violence beget violence?" Her conclusion was that, although it is not invariably the case, there is strong evidence that a history of maltreatment is associated with aggression and violence. Her review documented what those of us who are parents have often experienced in spite of our best efforts: that we tend to parent as we were parented.[10] Widom reviewed several studies of intergenerational transmission of abuse and concluded that, over all, abuse tends to breed abuse. Dorothy Lewis, who also looked retrospectively at histories of violent criminals, reported that the more offenders were victimized by chronic violence in the home, the more violent crimes they committed.[11]

The cycle Widom documents is obviously generated by nurture, by the experiences the child has in the environment. But in addition to understanding the social and psychological imprinting of abuse, several researchers, including Perry, now paint a brain-based picture of how being victimized in childhood can lead to becoming an adult victimizer. Again, this is not an either-or argument. While we tend to think of mind and body as separate domains with separate lines of influence, they are not separate at all. The mind is constructed in the brain, which is a physical entity with physical connections—in fact, controlling connections—to the entire body.[12] Nature and nurture are united in the brain. All that we experience changes the brain, and the brain in turn changes physiological responses in the body. Heart rate, blood pressure, and muscle tension are all examples of changes that occur in response to experiences. Each relationship, each person, each situation we experience is reflected by responses in the brain, which is constantly adapting itself and the rest of the body in response to environmental input. So when we look at the transition of the baby from victim to victimizer, the first step is understanding the neurological as well as the psychological impact of chronic fear, pain, or terror in earliest life.

TOO LITTLE TO FIGHT OR FLEE

The phrase "fight or flight" was coined by W. B. Cannon in 1929 to describe the classical adult response to threat.[13] But for the infant, neither of those options is available. Faced with overwhelming fear—such as parents yelling or hitting each other—or having cries signaling hunger or discomfort met by pain, the infant brain presents a different menu: becoming very alert or becoming numb—hyperarousal or dissociation.

According to Perry, in the initial stages of fear, an alarm reaction is triggered in young children, just as it is in adults. The sympathetic nervous system goes into full swing, increasing heart rate, blood pressure, respiration, and muscle tone and creating a release of stored sugar. The child becomes hyperalert so that all information irrelevant to the perceived danger is tuned out. Next, if the threat materializes, the autonomic nervous system, the immune system, the hypothalamic pituitary axis (HPA), and other stress systems in the brain come into play. Norepinephrine is released, and all the regions in the brain that regulate arousal within the brainstem and mid-brain are turned on. If the threat is perceived frequently or is very intense, the systems contributing to hyperarousal will become sensitized, ready to flip on at the least provocation.

Following even one intense exposure, the systems involved in stress modulation will be reactivated by reminders or thoughts of the event, including dreams. If it occurs often, the response may generalize to more reminders of the event so that a loud noise will be enough to terrify a child traumatized by gunshots, or any man may

162

terrify a child traumatized by rape. When chronic hyperarousal is elicited in the earliest weeks and months of life—for example, by physical or verbal abuse experienced directly, or by witnessing episodes of terrifying domestic violence—sensitization will cause the dysregulation of the stress response systems. Traumatized children will show sleep problems, anxiety, or impulsive responses. In extreme situations, the fear responses go into overdrive, resulting in overreactivity, oversensitization, and difficulty concentrating. Hyperaroused children may suffer from high blood pressure, rapid heart rate, a rapid and irregular heartbeat, slightly elevated temperature, and constant anxiety. The neural thermostat becomes stuck on high. The child becomes hypervigilant for signs predictive of the feared event, constantly on the watch for nonverbal cues that may signal threat in the environment and in a physiological state of preparedness to face the danger. According to Dr. Perry, when this process occurs in very young children while the brain is still at its most malleable and is just organizing, trauma that is originally experienced as a brief "state" of arousal can, after chronic intense experiences, become a "trait" in the child. The brain organizes around the overactivated systems to ensure the child's survival.

Religious cults that deliberately employ physical, emotional, and social violence to condition their young to mindlessly follow directives have provided unfortunate natural experiments revealing how children respond to chronic trauma. Dr. Perry examined eleven of the children involved in the Waco, Texas, Branch Davidian crisis. He compared their noradrenaline levels after they were released from David Koresh's compound with those of a group of inner-city Chicago children he had examined earlier. Perry characterized the abnormally high noradrenaline levels in both groups of children as the "chemical signature of post-traumatic stress disorder." These children, while seated, had heart rates of 100–170 beats per minute; the average for their age is 84. Their brains were pumping noradrenaline and other stress hormones—their chemistry reset for survival in a dangerous setting.

Originally an adaptation to a threatening environment, these responses become maladaptive in a nonthreatening environment such as school. With noradrenaline keeping the body in a constant state of readiness, these children are quick to erupt. With this neurophysiological state hardwired into brain function and chemistry, IQ, school performance, and social relationships generally suffer. This is commonly the scenario when children have been physically or sexually abused.

By kindergarten, the world of nonabused children is expanding to include their focused learning of numbers, letters, and a kaleidoscope of interests. But children who have been unable to develop trust and security with a primary caregiver in the first two years, show a depressed interest in the world—and in themselves. The playfulness we anticipate in very young children is often absent or dulled. Dr. Dante Cicchetti, of the University of Rochester and Mt. Hope Family Center, has studied the self-image of abused children extensively. In one study, children at nineteen months of age were placed in front of a mirror after a spot of rouge was painted on their nose. The nonabused control children reacted with delight upon seeing their decorated face, while the children who had been maltreated viewed their faces without expression or made negative faces at themselves.[14] Cicchetti's studies also show that abused children are more dependent and have less knowledge and ability to think effectively. Lacking security in the present, they are also less likely to seek to explore or to engage in new situations.[15]

Each of these factors creates additional barriers to success in school. By age thirty months, maltreated children use proportionately less descriptive language and are less likely to verbalize or describe their feelings than children who have not been maltreated. They also talk less about themselves, their activities, and other people.[16] Numerous studies show that in early grade school abused children perform less well than nonabused children on various developmental measures, have attentional problems, lack impulse control, and perform less well on measures of verbal IQ.[17] Instead of providing the foundation for self-control, for empathy, and for focused cognitive learning, abuse in earliest life undermines all three.

Because we each view the world through our own filter, based on our individual experiences, it is not surprising that abused children tend to suspect others of hostile intent. Even neutral behaviors may be viewed as arising from cruel motives. This negative expectation is associated with greater aggression in elementary school, which is in turn associated with peer rejection.[18] The combination of aggression and peer rejection predict academic, social, and behavioral problems in middle school.[19]

When a traumatized child sits in a classroom next to a nontraumatized child, even if they are of equal intelligence, the traumatized child will not be available to focus on the cognitive information being presented by the teacher in the same way that the nontraumatized child will. The traumatized child will be hypervigilant, still on red alert for signs of impending threat. A margin of his or her focus will be on reading subtle cues in the nonverbal behaviors of those in the vicinity—constantly prepared to take quick protective action for survival. Cortical functions that would otherwise be available for the lesson presented by the teacher are deployed for self-protection. There is a jumpiness—a quickness to act—in response to often misperceived intentions of others. In grade school, such children may be diagnosed as ADHD or even ODD. Learning and relating are often drastically affected, resulting in learning disabilities and impaired self-image and confidence.

Dr. Perry explains that as they grow older, hyperaroused children become ostracized. Standing outside of the mainstream of nontraumatized children, they inevitably find each other. The violent cycle begins to intensify as disenfranchised preadolescent and adolescent children hang together with others like themselves. Lacking the healing effect of a nurturing home or normal environment, gangs or groups of children with in common trauma and deprivation look to each other for social acceptance and appreciation of the very traits that first segregated them from their peers. Hypervigilance, impulsivity, pervasive expectations of threat, and quickness to be the first to act are the exact skills called for in gangs and illegal activities. That which has been a liability in school is an asset on the streets, where the environment is similar to the traumatic environment that first shaped the child's adjustment. Like all children, these children migrate to a familiar setting where they feel acceptance and valuing of their abilities. In a chapter of his book *Violence and Childhood Trauma* entitled "The Vortex of Violence," Dr. Perry describes the too commonly heard retorts from young offenders that reflect this now deeply ingrained mindset: "Listen, man, I just did him before he did me." "I could tell he was going to jump me—he looked me in the eyes." "If I didn't shoot him, he would have shot me."[20] Alcohol further lowers the adolescent's capacity to control fear-based thoughts and impulsive behavior. Such a child may permanently see the world as a hostile place where one has to be ready to defend oneself. Cradled in trauma, the adolescent is positioned to begin the cycle again.

Jeffrey, who sits on death row, fits this profile. Based on the testimony of family members, he was a baby terrified by chronic traumas ranging from multiple, often abusive caregivers, to violence between his parents, to drug-induced stabbings, to regular beatings, which he ultimately volunteered to take for both himself and his brother. After he was diagnosed with ADHD, stimulant medications had little effect on his hypervigilance, impulsivity, and inability to focus in school. Obviously a bright, verbal, and insightful young man at nineteen, when he was interviewed for this book, Jeffrey reflected that he learned in grade school that his only possible friends were "the little toughs." Drugs and alcohol played a role in Jeffrey's life from his earliest memories, compounded his school problems, and appear to have been a major contributor to his first and only serious crime. Although Jeffrey was only sixteen when he was imprisoned, he was clearly identified as one of the troubled kids on the fringes of his community, and he had already fathered one child.

Any child, regardless of gender, intelligence, or temperament, when exposed to repetitive terror, will develop a chronic fear response. The form the response takes will vary—commonly by gender. Boys, as they grow older, tend to develop an "externalized" or aggressive,

166

impulsive set of symptoms: the "fight" response. Males are more likely to be violent. Girls will typically "internalize," responding to such trauma by dissociation, or "freezing." We can see how this works by observing traumatized babies.

The baby or young child will typically cry in response to threat, hoping to elicit the help of a caregiver. When the caregiver is neglectful or is the source of the trauma, and crying does not result in help or results in further pain, the child either moves further into arousal with more vocal and motoric efforts to engage help or will stop crying altogether, or freeze. Lack of movement and sound in the face of increasing threat allows for the opportunity to camouflage, to scan for additional information, and to think how best to respond. In children who have been sensitized by previous trauma, freezing may be the first response to anxiety. Because sensitization means that events or people or fragments of memory that bear any resemblance to the original threat may elicit the same anxious response, such children may freeze or act defensively in situations that observers find puzzling. Thus, a child like Jeffrey's brother John, who has been hit by his parents, may throw up his hands to protect himself at the approach of a well-meaning foster father intending a hug. Or a child asked by a teacher to do a seemingly simple task may, fearing abuse, appear to be deaf and dumb, refusing to budge—appearing oppositional. If the terror continues, the child may move from freezing to complete dissociation, appearing to "go away" or to disengage mentally and emotionally from the immediate environment.[21] The child is there in body but not in spirit, mind, or heart. Dissociative states vary along a continuum that ranges from short episodes of daydreaming to total loss of consciousness. Individual children (or adults) dissociate at varying points in their response to terror. Some will immediately faint at the first sign of arousal, while others will only dissociate late when reaching a state of complete terror.

Both hyperarousal and dissociation involve brainstem-controlled central nervous system activity that produces an increase in epinephrine and other neurochemicals. But unlike hyperarousal, dissociation results in decreased blood pressure and heart rate. In dissociation, there is an increase in dopamine-secreting systems, which work together with opioid systems in the brain to produce a calming effect, lowering pain perception, and altering one's sense of time and space. The younger the child is at the time of experiencing terror, the more likely she or he is to respond with dissociation rather than hyperarousal. Freezing or dissociation is the most likely response to be employed if one is helpless, feels powerless or is immobilized. When we are terrified and know there is nothing we can do to escape, dissociation is our only choice. This is why women and children, especially young children, are more likely to move to dissociation than arousal to survive violence perpetrated by men. Fight is futile. Numbness and compliance work. For self-protection as they grow older, many children employ a combination of hyperarousal and dissociation.[22]

The chronic overactivation of neurochemical responses to threat in the central nervous system, particularly in the earliest years of life, can result in lifelong states of either dissociation or hyperarousal. In the case of hyperarousal, overdevelopment of the stress response systems in the brainstem and mid-brain alters the development of the higher cortical functions, creating a predisposition to behave in aggressive, impulsive, and reactive ways. The oversecretion of cortisol is believed to actually destroy synapses in some parts of the brain, particularly in the orbitofrontal system, an area involved in reading emotional responses in other people.[23] As mentioned earlier, the overuse of the alarm response in young children can result in posttraumatic stress disorder or ongoing symptoms of fear characterized by intrusive memories or flashbacks, fear of vaguely similar occurrences, invasive dreams, interrupted sleep patterns, hypervigilant or avoidance behavior, numbing, detachment, or a decline in cognitive performance.[24] PTSD, while frequently diagnosed in adult victims, is rarely diagnosed in very young children.

It is ironic that we continue to overlook the reality of the impact of serious trauma on babies. While we know PTSD is a common response to severe trauma in older children and adults, we fail to recognize the much more pervasive damage being done to a baby's developing brain at a time when the impact of trauma can shape the entire organization of key brain functions.

Perhaps the most disturbing implication from the research on the brain's adaptation to chronic fear and anger is the growing evidence that it may be altering the course of human evolution. Not only can the changes in hormone levels be permanent in an individual's lifetime, the altered chemical profile may actually become encoded in the genes and passed on to new generations, which may become successively more aggressive.[25] Increased rates of child abuse and other forms of unpredictable and uncontrollable trauma in our culture mean that more and more children are having this experience. Dr. Perry calls this process, along with its growing social implications, "devolution."[26]

There is now some speculation that an increase in violent crimes committed by females may be an early sign of this accumulation of violence in our nation's social fabric. Dr. Robert Cairns, a psychobiologist from the University of North Carolina at Chapel Hill, undertook a research project to breed increasingly aggressive male rats by successively breeding the most aggressive lines. In the course of the study, he observed that sisters of the aggressive males were also more aggressive. Based on his study results, Cairns believes that in rats, genes for increased aggression can be transmitted to offspring by parents who are exposed to stressful environments. Cairns speculates that this same dynamic also may be occurring in the human population. After looking at the arrest records of two populations of teenage girls from 1900 to 1960, Cairns concluded:

> The pattern is emerging of girls, who are increasingly victims of child abuse, who grow up angry and have children with men who are likely to also be aggressive. As a result, succeeding generations of children are being born to aggressive parents and into aggression-producing environments. It really suggests that if there are red signals that our

society has to be wary of [they] should be those temporal increases in female violence. This has been ignored, but is maybe the most important of all.[27]

WHEN JACK FALLS DOWN AND BREAKS HIS CROWN

It has long been an established fact that injury to the head, even a single blow, can cause subsequent recurring violent behavior. The medical literature is filled with anecdotal accounts of patients who suffered remarkable negative personality changes after a head injury. Raff Brinker, the father in the classic children's story *Hans Brinker or The Silver Skates,* written in 1924 by Mary Mapes Dodge, is a fictional account of this phenomenon. At the time the story is told, Raff Brinker has changed literally overnight from a loving, cheerful father and husband to a silent and strange man who is subject to periodic episodes of murderous violence directed at his wife. This metamorphosis occurred in the story when he fell and hit his head and was taken home unconscious after trying to repair a dike in the middle of a storm.

While accidental injuries that lead to violent behavior are rare, they are clear evidence that the brain can be profoundly altered by a physical blow, which can cause small lesions at specific sites.[28] A number of studies on adolescents and adults show a correlation between head injuries and aggression and violence. Several retrospective studies on juvenile and older death row inmates show that a high percentage have a history of serious head injury. A 1986 study on a group of violent adult offenders who had been sentenced to death found that all of them had a history of head injury.[29] A second study by the same group of researchers two years later on a group of fourteen violent juveniles on death row corroborated this earlier finding; all of the juvenile offenders had a reported history of serious head injury.[30] Males with problems of aggression in marital and dating relationships also often reflect this history, with correlations between head injury and wife battering ranging from 52 percent to 92 percent.[31]

While there is debate among some researchers as to whether the head injury causes violence or those who are prone to violence suffer an abnormally high degree of head injuries as a result of their lifestyle, a growing body of information demonstrates that head injury may play a much greater role than is currently understood in predisposing an individual to delinquency and crime. Head injury from either blows or the early shaking of an infant may diminish coping skills, judgment, and control.[32] To date, the studies on the links between head injury and violent behavior have been done on older children and adults. The role of early head injuries resulting from child abuse has been virtually overlooked. To an angry or frustrated parent whose patience has snapped, the head of the infant or toddler is the part that cries or is rebellious and talks back. As such, it is a primary target for hitting. Rough shaking or blows can cause shearing and multiple microscopic lesions throughout the brain. These early injuries are often cumulative from multiple incidents of abuse and, except in the most extreme cases, are hard to detect because they leave no external marks. The damage from such injuries often does not appear until later as the affected neurological system matures.

The extent of this problem is both insidious and serious—the majority of all infant head injuries and 95 percent of serious head injuries to children are due to child abuse.[33] Even violent offenders who do not report a history of head injury may have suffered early neurological damage if they come from abusive homes. Many of the studies that report a high incidence of head injury in violent offenders from other accidental causes also report high rates of serious child abuse. Such individuals have had a double dose of damage to the brain and are more likely to become violent. Ultimately, it is likely that we will come to discover that the link between child abuse and violent behavior may be both biologically based through early damage to the brain and psychologically and socially based through the modeling of violent behavior.[34]

The majority of studies on the link between injury to the head and aggressive behavior focus on damage to either the frontal lobes or the temporal lobes. The frontal lobes are the seat of the capacities for planning, self-regulation, and sustained effort as well as of higher abstract thinking and judgment. The temporal lobes, by contrast, contain the limbic system structures important for regulating emotion and behavior. Individuals who have sustained injuries to their frontal lobes show impairment in their control of emotional expression and an absence of empathy or awareness of the impact of their behavior on other people. They are often highly egocentric and unable to appreciate pain to anyone but themselves.[35] While impairment of the frontal lobes does not always lead to aggression or violence, it is particularly serious when the injury occurs early in life, before internal controls have developed.[36] There is strong speculation by researchers, such as Dr. Charles Golden of Nova-Southeastern University in Florida, that frontal lobe injury is a primary cause of sociopathy or cold-blooded criminal behavior. Dr. Golden believes that the apparent increase in violent behavior is linked to several aspects of modern living, including car accidents, child abuse, especially of youngest children, and the increased capacity of medical science to save the lives of premature and birth-injured infants.

Temporal lobe injuries, by contrast to frontal lobe injuries, are associated with "episodic dyscontrol," in which violent behavior erupts seemingly out of nowhere, is unpatterned, and occurs without provocation or premeditation.[37] As many as 30 percent to 50 percent of individuals with a criminal history may have sustained injuries to their frontal or temporal lobes.[38] Although head injury is one way in which the human brain may be altered toward aggressive behavior, it cannot be assumed that all brain-injured individuals become aggressive, let alone violent. In most cases, brain damage creates only a greater likelihood of impulsive behavior. The larger environment plays a key role; with rare exceptions familial and social factors exacerbate or greatly lessen the likelihood of violence. Conversely, even in cases in which no acute brain injury has occurred, negative environmental factors, such as trauma, may produce neurological changes of such magnitude that violent behavior may be the result.

In grappling with the issue of violence, it is crucial to understand that both the physical structure and the chemical profile of the human brain may be adversely and permanently altered from prolonged stress or injury during the most rapid period of brain growth, which occurs during the first thirty-three months of life. When children have been traumatized or head-injured, the key to preventing such early experience from setting a course toward impulsive, aggressive, and violent behavior is the presence of a nurturing and responsive caregiver.[39] One healthy individual willing to protect, teach, discipline, love, and play constructively with a child can greatly offset the adverse effects of trauma in a very young child. But when the child's caregiver is equally affected by the threat or is the source of trauma, the risks to the child's development are greatly magnified. When the caregiver is physically present but is emotionally unavailable or distant, the convergence of early chronic trauma or head injury with impaired attachment becomes the seedbed for impulsive violence. One person can make the difference.

8

The Hand That Rocks:

THE IMPACT OF EARLY

EMOTIONAL DEPRIVATION

Piglet sidled up to Pooh from behind.
"Pooh," he whispered.
"Yes, Piglet?"
"Nothing," said Piglet, taking Pooh's paw.
"I just wanted to be sure of you."

—A. A. MILNE
Winnie-The-Pooh

[Jeffrey's mother] was walking down the center of the highway toward on-coming cars causing traffic problems, as the cars were having to swerve around her. She said she wanted to die . . . and she was attempting to throw herself in front of cars. She had no smell of alcohol and was very depressed and despondent.

EYE WITNESS ACCOUNT IN JEFFREY'S CHILD WELFARE CASE FILE

After I came home from the hospital, I couldn't hold nothing down. I had a problem with retaining any kind of food . . . and [Mother] said she would feed me and I would just vomit it right back up. And she said that she was real scared. She took me to my grandma and grandpa's house. And she was crying. She didn't know what to do. She was scared that I was going to die. . . . I don't think she had the money to take me to the hospital . . . so she went to her dad for advice. And her stepmom told her she should leave the baby with her and get out of here and don't come back for two weeks. So that's what happened. . . .

When my brother was only two and three years old himself, he says he got up and used the cooking stove to heat water and did things like changing my diapers. My mom would go into bouts of depression and sleep forever. The house would be like just sick, and John fixed bottles by himself. . . . My earliest recollection was the ambulance coming to take her away. . . . I remember my brother and me sitting on the porch. I was still wearing a diaper, that's how young I was. . . . I remember my brother wrapping his arms around me and holding me tight. And a police woman told us our mom had to go to the hospital. We didn't know what for. We thought she was dead.

JEFFREY, AUGUST 1996

When we arrived at the home, John and Jeffrey were observed outside with nothing on but their underpants. The temperature was 53

degrees. It had been raining earlier, and the ground was still wet. . . .
The condition of the family's trailer was deplorable. Clothing was scat-
tered throughout the floor. Dog feces was observed on the floor and cloth-
ing. Moldy dishes and baby bottles were on the kitchen counters. Dirty
diapers, tin cans and a collection of garbage was on the kitchen
floor. . . . The only food in the house was milk and cereal.

CHILD PROTECTIVE SERVICES

CASE WORKER REPORT, OCTOBER 23, 1979

They were so much alike—my grandma and my mom—in so many
ways. When my grandma was younger, she had her kids taken away
from her. And then there's my mom not doing the things she should be
doing, so my grandma figures she should take us away from her. Well,
my mom was of course no angel. She was doing a lot of drugs. My
grandma decided we shouldn't be living with her. . . . So we went from
bad to worse—back and forth until at least the third grade, plus at
least six foster homes by the time I was six years old. Yeah, we went back
and forth between my grandma and my grandpa 'cause my mom was
young and she wanted to party and stuff like that. She left us at times.
Official foster care began later. I must have been two or three years
old when I went to my first foster home, and I don't even remember
why. . . .

Walt and Bev are the reason I turned out the way I am. . . . We
had a lot of structure. I remember every night we went to bed at the
same time. Every night, no if, ands, or buts about it. There was an
older boy—he was in high school, every night he stayed up and watched
the 10:00 news, and we always wanted to stay up and watch the 10:00
news, too. . . . One night we got to stay up and watch the news with
them. . . . And like, I remember going to preschool or kindergarten.
I'd never gone to school before. . . . And every day Bev would wash my
pants. I had to wear corduroys, and I loved those corduroys 'cause they
made the neatest sound. I just loved them. I thought they were the coolest
things in the world. . . . They always told us that they loved us. They
always told us, every time we went anywhere. From the very beginning,

they expected a kiss and a hug. And it was always funny to me. I was like, "I don't want to kiss you! I mean, I hardly ever kissed my mom, why would I want to kiss you?" And it was hard for me to get over for a little bit, but after a couple of weeks it was like, "Yeah, I'm going to kiss them." So, you know, I'd give them a hug and a kiss and we'd get out of the car and go do our thing. I remember every time, I mean, this is how much love they had in this house. . . .

I know half the time [going to foster homes] was because we were getting beat up by either my mom or one of her boyfriends or actually sometimes even her friends, her lady friends that would be living with us. . . . I don't know if they found drugs . . . or just plain neglect, like not having food in the house or, you know, having clean clothes. I mean, we lived in this one house this one time, and when you'd walk into our room, you'd literally walk through a pile of clothes. . . . We had a bunk bed and it would actually go from the door—you couldn't open the door because the clothes were all the way up to the top of the thing, and Mom never washed them. . . . She was too busy. She was out doing her drugs. . . . Sometimes she'd be with her friends. You know, this one lady, Bobbie, I remember when she lived with us. She and Bobbie were always going out, and this is a biker lady. I mean, she had four kids of her own. So you can imagine us three kids plus her four all in this one room. . . . And their little baby always screaming, and some of the little girls and boys wetting their beds and never getting it cleaned up. You know, sleeping in wet sheets and different things like that. It was just gross. It was disgusting. I remember times, you know, there was garbage all over the floor in the kitchen. You would try to walk through the kitchen, and you could not, no matter how hard you tried. It was literally piled on the floor with garbage and stuff. I mean, you couldn't hit the linoleum. . . .

I had a friend when I was in the fourth grade, and his family was perfect. I always wanted to go over to his house. Always. Every weekend I would actually ask him if I could stay the night. . . . He had his own room, and his parents were super nice. They always made sure he had breakfast. They always made sure he had his lunch and dinner, you know, three meals. They always told him that they loved him and all this stuff. They all could talk. They could all sit down and actually have a conversation together without having an argument. You know, just talk about fun things.

JOHN, AUGUST 1996

Eleven-year-old Ray DeFord lived in a dingy apartment house in Aloha, Oregon, with his six pet rats, a python called Satan, and a knife he called "protection." Neighbors described him as a strange and disruptive child, referring to him as a "junior Charles Manson," and ordered their kids not to play with him. "He would throw rocks at my children," one neighbor said. "One time he punched my son badly, and I complained to his mother. She wouldn't say anything. She laughed."[1]

Based on neighbors complaints, the deputy sheriff went several times to the DeFord's home prior to July 2, 1996, to talk to Ray and his parents. Ray beat up two neighbor children ages five and nine, packed rocks in socks to sling at children, and kicked kids in their backs as they got off the school bus. He was never referred for services or taken into custody, however, until July 3, 1996, when he became the youngest child in Oregon history to be charged with murder the day after he set fire to the apartment complex where he had lived for five years. The fire killed eight neighbors—five children and three adults—all from the same small village in Mexico. Fourteen more people were taken to the hospital with injuries, and dozens of people were displaced by the fire.

Ray is an only child, born three years after the marriage of his parents sixteen years ago. His mother is mentally retarded and is unable to read or write. His father, while more mentally capable, had been a fugitive from a New Mexico prison for fifteen years at the time of the fire. He is partially paralyzed from a stroke that occurred two years before Ray was born. The neighbors describe Ray as both abused and neglected with parents who alternated between letting him do anything he wanted and sudden brutal punishment. "He was born, fed and unloved," a neighbor told reporters. He wore tattered and ripped

180

bell-bottoms and T-shirts. He was dirty and unkempt and had frequently been shunned in school by children who refused to sit near him for fear of catching "Ray germs." The neighbor children often ridiculed him when his parents, both without jobs, searched through the apartment garbage-collection site for redeemable bottles and cans to supplement their disability checks.

Ray is not at his age level in reading. He failed the first grade and was in special classes for slow learners, where he reportedly fidgeted at his desk and stared into the distance. Ray has been diagnosed as slightly mentally retarded with ADHD. He reads at a first grade level, is unable to do any math except for counting his fingers, and doesn't know how to respond socially. According to expert testimony given in court, Ray was injured on the head at eighteen months of age "before the soft spot had hardened" when his father beat him with a clipboard for crying. He also weaned his son by placing Ray's baby bottle in a pan of rubbing alcohol and setting it on fire.

Those who know Ray say that he learned not to cry and that his father continued to abuse him. Ray's thirteen-year-old friend Jed told reporters from the *Oregonian* that once Ray's father, Tom, invited Jed and a few other boys to Ray's home when Ray was eight. While the boys were there, Tom smoked marijuana and then began shooting Ray in the legs with a BB gun for laughs. "Look at his parents and you'll get the whole story," Jed told reporters. Tom encouraged Ray to drink beer and whiskey and to smoke marijuana. He often allowed Ray to play with flammable liquids and fire in his presence and taught his son how to make cyanide out of bleach, detergent and Coca-Cola. By the time he was five, Ray was threatening children who teased him about his clothes and hair with sharpened popsicle sticks and with knives he took from his kitchen. Detective Michael O'Connor, who interviewed Ray after his arrest and who arrested Tom eight months later, said that Ray talked about the people who had died but showed no remorse during the several hours he was questioned.[2]

Even the casual reader of Ray's story in the newspaper can see the painful reality of abuse and neglect that constituted Ray's daily life. We have grown accustomed to such children acting out the fury they have absorbed. But questions remain: Why did this particular boy and not another who experienced equal pain wreak such havoc on innocent people? What keeps other children in similar circumstances from committing such crimes? The answers lie in understanding not only the separate factors involved in creating or preventing the creation of a Ray, but also in understanding the ways in which biological and social factors work together from infancy to set a course that may be lethal.

A review of the research on violent and homicidal children reveals that the majority of children like Ray have neurological impairments or diagnosable psychological illnesses. The majority of violent adolescents also have substance abuse disorders. Few have received treatment for these problems.[3] In one study, 96 percent of homicidal children had come from chaotic family backgrounds, usually including family violence (81 percent). Ninety percent had been abused by a family member as a child. One hundred percent had a history of serious school problems, including 86 percent who had failed at least one grade and 76 percent with documented learning disabilities.[4]

As reviewed in earlier chapters, many children who become impulsively violent had, as babies, subtle neurological abnormalities. They began life with "difficult" or extremely sensitive temperaments or showed early signs of attention-deficit/hyperactivity disorder, which progressed to more serious behavioral disorders. They may have been exposed to extreme trauma. But these beginnings are not in themselves causal. Neurological differences only render a child more vulnerable to negative environmental circumstances. Whether children become poets or ax murderers depends on the interaction of biological and social factors—the complex interweaving of risks and protective qualities in a child's life.

One way to picture the interaction between the biological (particularly neurological) traits of the child and familial or social factors creating violence is to imagine each individual as a small lake. Each lake is different; the size and depth and breadth of our lakes vary. Each is unique in its dimensions since birth. The parameters of our lakes are determined by biological and genetic factors. The water in each lake is the fluid force of potential, the basic competence and confidence we each bring to life. Positive experiences in our environments serve as the wind and rain that enlarge the size of our lakes—we may grow deeper or broader and develop our potential capacities. The water in our lakes increases from these experiences. But negative familial or social factors are like rocks in our lakes. Some rocks, such as multiple family moves, are small; most of us have several of these. Others, such as early physical or sexual abuse, are huge rocks that may rise above the surface of the water. Numerous large boulders in a very small or shallow lake have a far greater impact in reducing the total volume of water than the same number of large rocks in a large and deep lake. A child who begins life with an expansive lake will be less likely to experience immediate overflow from a huge rock outcropping (e.g., loss of a parent) than a child who starts with a lake rendered small and shallow by negative biological factors such as neurological impairment. All lakes will be affected by boulders, and if there are several, the water can become dammed or overflow, leaving the lake nearly empty. Those children with small and shallow lakes from the beginning are most at risk.

Biological and social factors are highly interactive in human development, particularly in earliest development. Biology is one strand of influence on human behavior, affected both by heritable genetics and by environmentally imposed factors such as the prenatal impact of alcohol or drugs, birth trauma, or later head injury. Social factors, particularly the sensitive nurturing of a committed caregiver interact with and actually alter biological elements such as brain chemistry and brain tissue. Reducing the relationship between biology, experience, and behavior to its most basic form: Children reflect what they have absorbed biologically and socially. Though the processes are complex and often the injuries are unintended, when it comes to our babies, we reap what we sow. Never is the opportunity so great to make so much difference for our children. And never is it so potentially damaging to our communities and to our nation to be unaware of this reality.[5]

FIRST LOVE

The interactive process most protective against later violent behavior begins in the first year after birth: the formation of a secure attachment relationship with a primary caregiver. Here in one relationship lies the foundation of three key protective factors that mitigate against later aggression:[6] the learning of empathy or emotional attachment to others;[7] the opportunity to learn to control and balance feelings, especially those that can be destructive;[8] and the opportunity to develop capacities for higher levels of cognitive processing.[9]

In the 1960s, John Bowlby theorized that children form models or templates of themselves and relationships with others based on their experiences with first caregivers, most often mothers.[10] These templates form the organizational core of children's beliefs, expectations, and motivations, which continue to guide and shape the child's sense of himself and of his role in subsequent relationships. Bowlby recognized that the emotional dance we go about creating in intimate relationships as adults has a strange way of echoing our first relationship. Americans spend untold fortunes and countless hours in therapy trying to figure out why they have continued to seek and then how to avoid marrying the ghost of their mother or father. As the result of early emotional learning, we tend to replicate familiar relationship patterns and confirm the view we formed early of how relationships work. In the same way, generally without awareness, we bring our own histories as infants to our roles as parents.

Bowlby's theories were a blending of views adapted from psychoanalysis and ethology, or the study of animal behavior. Bowlby had been particularly impressed with the work of Konrad Lorenz, who noted that ducklings and goslings "imprint" or attach to the first moving object they see after hatching (human, goose, or whatever). Early interpretations of Bowlby's work were applied very simplistically to human children, resulting in the still popular but poorly validated concept of "bonding." This is the notion that, immediately after birth, babies, like goslings, imprint or bond in gluelike fashion to their caregiver, presumably the mother, and that birth bonding is critical. In fact, we now know that for human babies attachment does not occur all at once and does not happen just at birth. It is a cumulative process of minute interchanges between a child and a caregiver over a period of many months, perhaps even years. Even the traditional emphasis on mothers is misleading. Key to attachment is the child's ability to secure a close and trusting, reciprocal relationship with one caretaker, male or female. The failure to achieve this at all is even more devastating than suffering a disruption in an existing relationship. The first months of life are especially important to this process.

At the explosive event of birth, the normal newborn is wired to signal her mother with behaviors designed to draw her mother close. Expelled from an existence that maintained her comfort automatically, the baby cries and extends her arms in a primitive message designed to trigger her mother's protective embrace. When the mother responds by reaching for her baby, bringing her infant to her breast, making comforting sounds, and patting or rocking, the baby's temporarily alarmed nervous system is calmed. Inside the baby's brain, the neurochemical responses to the mother's soothing reestablishes the physiological equilibrium, and this new little person experiences a physical state similar to the one preceding birth. The baby quiets and relaxes. The mother in turn relaxes.

From this beginning, these exchanges, initially triggered by the baby's biological needs, will be repeated in millions of tiny gestures and will evolve over time to complex readings of the respective emotions of both mother and baby. The differences between one mother-and-baby pair and another will occur at this moment-to-moment level. Behaviors of the baby trigger behaviors by the parent; crying, for example, can trigger the letting-down of milk for nursing. Optimally, the behavior of the parent, such as holding and feeding, elicits predictable behaviors from the baby, such as nursing and calming, which in turn relieves the parent's tension and results in a balanced, goal-directed partnership. These gestures passed back and forth—cries and agitated movements followed by smiles, caresses, pats, gentle words, warm nipples, dry clothes—or frowns, slaps, yells, cold food propped and left—all occur hundreds of times in the course of a week. Together they leave a cumulative imprint on the developing brain, which, over time, forms a template or pattern for anticipated behavior.[11] Bowlby calls this the child's "internal working model." Bowlby observed the ways in which one generation transfers patterns of caretaking to the next through the working model. He also noted that these are "working" not static models. They can and do shift with education, therapy, and important life events such as marriage and close relationships. This is how child-rearing patterns, including child abuse, are transferred from one generation to the next.

Dr. T. Berry Brazelton has documented this process of intergenerational transfer of basic caretaking behaviors on videotape. He first shows a mother feeding, burping, and holding or playing with her baby. Brazelton points out the feeding posture, the positioning of the baby by the mother to receive the bottle or breast, her timing, and the way she does or does not wait for the baby to show satiation before interrupting for a burp. Her positioning of her child over her shoulder, the way she pats or rubs the child's back or holds her on her lap to burp, are all observed. Then the scene shifts to a different mother and baby. The second mother also feeds and burps her baby, using the same gestures, positioning, rhythms, and even facial expressions. After watching for a while, the audience learns from Dr. Brazelton that the second mother is the now grown-up baby seen in the first sequence. Though this woman has never seen the film of herself as an infant with her mother, her behaviors with her own infant are a shadow image of her mother's behaviors with her. The somatically stored memories of her own experience as a baby were activated with the advent of her own child. To document the variations of parenting behaviors being transferred, Dr. Brazelton shows several two-generation sequences, each different from the other and each graphically illustrating the transference of patterns stored and remembered from babyhood. It is through this subtle process of working models internalized quietly in the nursery that the hands that rock the cradles do in fact influence world outcomes.

MIRROR, MIRROR: THE ORIGIN OF EMPATHY

Twenty-three-month-old Jason was strapped into his car seat looking out the window as his mother slowed to a stop at a traffic signal. As the light turned from yellow to red, an old woman waiting at the corner stepped painfully from the curb and walked across the street directly in front of the car where Jason and his mother waited for the light to change. As the old woman hobbled across the street, bent over with the weight of two bulging shopping bags, Jason began to cry softly. His mother turned to ask him what was wrong. Tears flowing down his cheeks, he pointed at the old woman as she continued slowly toward the opposite curb, "Dat poor old lady," he said.

Two-and-a-half-year-old Tray, short for Thomas, received national media attention and praise last year for his part in a serious domestic drama in February 1996. His mother wouldn't wake up, apparently having succumbed to an undetected heart problem in her home in Vancouver, Washington. She had died in her bed with a book across her face, leaving Tray and his 18-month-old sister, Kiana, who was upstairs in her crib, alone in the apartment. Tray's mother appeared to him to be sleeping. When he couldn't rouse her, he knew what to do. He opened the kitchen cupboard and found dry cereal. For two days he fed himself and carried juice and handfuls of cereal and crackers to Kiana. He used wads of toilet paper to mop up his sister's wet crib and to pad her diaper. When a scheduled but new babysitter came to the door two days after his mother's death, he wouldn't open the locked door. His mother had taught him not to open the door for people he didn't know. When he grew sleepy, he lay down on the toddler bed near Kiana's crib. Concerned at her inability to contact Tray's mother by telephone, though she heard the children inside, the sitter returned the following day and persuaded Tray to let her inside the apartment.[12]

These stories of preschoolers, though unusual, are not rare. By the age of fourteen months, toddlers often show clear signs of empathy.[13] Like violent behavior, empathic behavior does not emerge from a void. Unlike violence, it is built from the loving experience between a baby and a caring adult. Many believe that some form of empathy is inborn: the frequently cited example is of the newborn who begins to cry upon hearing another baby cry in the hospital nursery. But developmental research distinguishes this response from empathy, viewing it as a form of emotional contagion experienced prior to the baby's capacity for empathy. The more sophisticated cognitive processes involved in empathy include the ability to discriminate oneself from another person, the ability to take the perspective of another person into account, and finally to respond to alleviate another person's distress. The first of these functions—recognizing one's physical separateness from others—is generally developed near a child's first birthday. But at that young age, it is difficult for toddlers to discern that other people's feelings are not the same as their own. A one year old will often cry at seeing a cut on Daddy's knee or will examine his own fingers when he sees another child hurt his fingers. But as young as fourteen months, some children will move from showing signs of awareness of another's pain to trying to do something about it, like summoning an adult to help. Between twenty and twenty-nine months, children begin to take steps to comfort others directly—patting, embracing, and taking things to the victim.[14]

Here lies the root of altruism—the core of moral behavior. Without this quality, human societies would fall apart. When the early sensitive exchange of emotional and physical caretaking between a child and a parent is continued and followed by the parents teaching the child about the impact of their behaviors on others, altruistic behavior like Tray's is not uncommon by thirty months. Although individual differences in children's temperaments, personalities, and other potentials certainly influence the ease with which these lessons are absorbed, given parental modeling and direct teaching, young children will reflect empathic and altruistic values.[15]

The foundation for empathy is laid from the beginning. When the early months of an infant's experience include consistent, sensitive interactions in which the caregiver accurately assesses the child's needs and responds quickly in a soothing manner, and when a child's sadness or joy is mirrored in the face of the parent, the child experiences comfort and trust with the caregiver. But when the baby instead experiences unpredictable or dissonant emotions from a key adult, or no response, or a harsh or overwhelming response to efforts to engage the adult, the attachment to the caregiver may be characterized by distrust, fear, or a disorganized combination of conflicting feelings.

Observing the securely attached baby at four to six months of age, we can see and feel his sense of confidence at gaining and maintaining his closeness to his mother, his freedom to express a range of emotions and the expectation that he will be soothed and comforted. The relationship looks fluid and flexible like a waltz between mother and baby. This is the kind of relationship we all love to watch. The pair, like lovers, are enthralled with each other. They seem not to tire of mutual gaze, and even the subtlest gestures are appreciated. The baby's delight at a toy or a funny sound is reflected in the mother's smile. Conversely, her baby's fear or pain evokes the mother's immediate tension and triggers gestures to comfort her child. It is only a very few months before the infant becomes a toddler like Jason, Tray, or Rachel (introduced below), who reflect to the world the quality of the positive connections they have experienced. This emotional attunement is the cradle of human connection. Tiny interactions between each infant and his mother create threads of empathy that together form the warp and woof of the tapestry we call community, a tapestry that is weakened by each thread that is frayed or broken.

Not all mother-child relationships look like a waltz. Research on interrelationships, particularly parent-child relationships, was given strong impetus by Dr. Mary Ainsworth in the 1960s. Prior to Ainsworth, individual behaviors had been the primary focus of psychology's lens. It has only been since her work that transactional, or interactive, dynamics have taken their place alongside individual measures in assessing young children. A student of Bowlby, Ainsworth created a now famous laboratory exercise involving mothers with babies who ranged in age from twelve to eighteen months.[16] In brief sequences, researchers watched babies as they played with their mothers, as the baby was separated from the mother when she left the room, and as the mother returned. During two intervals a stranger was in the room. In one, the baby was alone. Ainsworth called this assessment the "strange situation." It was used to determine the type of attachment relationship infants experienced with their mothers. Ainsworth classified the infants' reactions into three distinct profiles. One group of babies cried when their mother left the room but when she returned, reached up and greeted her with smiles and obvious signs of pleasure. They molded easily to their mothers' bodies when their mothers picked them up and were easy to console. These infants, which Ainsworth called the "securely attached," accounted for 70 percent of the total.

A second group of babies were clingy with their mothers and seemed afraid to explore the room independently. When their mothers left, these babies became agitated and anxious and cried frequently. When the mothers returned to the babies in this group, which Ainsworth called the "ambivalent" babies, they also reached to their mothers for contact, but then they arched away and resisted their mothers' efforts to comfort them. This pattern is associated with erratic, inconsistent, and sometimes intrusive caregiving during the first year.

The third group, which Ainsworth called the "avoidant" babies, looked very independent while their mothers were with them. They explored the new environment and seemed not to look much to their mothers for reassurance. Having shown no preference for their mothers over the stranger, when left alone, these babies showed little response. And when mothers returned, the avoidant babies went their own way or avoided contact. This pattern is associated with parental insensitivity or emotional unavailability. The child's avoidance is believed to be a defense against the parent's lack of responsiveness.

Succeeding studies have added a fourth category, the "type D," or disorganized type. These are children who have typically been abused. They seek closeness to their mothers but in disorganized or distorted ways. These babies may approach their mothers backwards or suddenly freeze or sit and stare off into space. Upon reunion, they show conflicted, sad, or fearful behavior. Unlike the children in Ainsworth's first three categories, who all have the ability to get their needs met in some organized if not ideal manner, type D children are at risk of serious relational conflicts. Type D relationships are characterized by parents who are both the primary source of protection and simultaneously the source of harm or failed protection. Researchers studying maltreated children estimate that 90 percent of abused and neglected children exhibit disorganized attachment.[17] When seeking to prevent violence at its root, it is this group of babies and their caregivers that warrants intense intervention.[18] As we look more deeply at what is going on for "disorganized" babies both behaviorally and biologically, this understanding becomes especially relevant to understanding the antecedents of violence. Over time we realize that far more is being exchanged between parents and babies than meets the eye. This is particularly true when neglect or abuse characterizes this relationship, as the following story of Rachel illustrates.

At age eleven, Rachel is a beautiful and intelligent child. But Rachel steals money from her adoptive mother's purse, her brother's wallet, her teacher's pockets. She destroys her brother's favorite things—most recently his prized autographed baseball card and his new mitt. Recently, her mother found a darning needle pointed upright in her bed carefully lodged in the middle of the mattress pad and bottom sheet. At school Rachel fights physically with other kids. She's bright but won't accept the teachers' authority. Even when she has completed her homework, Rachel won't turn it in. Little things upset her, and when they do, she yells obscenities and pushes, shoves, or hits whoever happens to be there.

When Rachel was barely a year old and still living with her biological mother, a neighbor who was babysitting one afternoon found cigarette burns on Rachel's bottom and reported it to authorities. Although she was not removed from her mother then, her case was monitored by the child welfare system. Almost a year after the first incident, Rachel was again reported with serious injuries when hospital staff at the emergency room discovered multiple bruises and more serious burns on her buttocks. Just before her second birthday, Rachel was removed from her home and placed in protective custody when her case worker discovered that her mother's boyfriend had set fire to Rachel's diaper. Initially, Rachel's mother was angry and demanded that she get her baby back. For the first few months after Rachel's removal, her mother faithfully attended parenting sessions and came for weekly supervised visits in an effort to regain custody of her daughter. But after her mother met a new man, Rachel was left crying and disappointed as her mother failed to appear for several scheduled visits.

Rachel's mother, herself a baby adopted and then relinquished to foster care, was unable to put Rachel's needs ahead of her own. She said that Rachel had always been hard for her, a difficult baby with a bad temper. Rachel's father had relinquished paternity shortly after she was born. After nearly a year of mostly missed visits by her biological mother, Rachel—then in a foster home—was placed in "permanent planning," a child welfare term for the final phase of evaluation of biological parents prior to the state's termination of parental rights. Rachel's mother decided to relinquish her rights to Rachel. After two years of foster care, at age four, Rachel was adopted.

Rachel's adoptive parents met a little girl whom the agency told them had "lacked loving parenting." The reality of Rachel's multiple losses, moves, and disappointments—to say nothing of the physical traumas—was missing from the account. Rachel's honeymoon with her new family was short-lived. Her temper was irrepressible. When she didn't get what she wanted, she would scream and then hold her breath until she turned blue and passed out. She was irritable and loud in most situations, rarely allowing affection from her foster parents, let alone giving it. She was constantly aggressive with other children. After seven years of failed efforts, Rachel's adoptive parents are now near the end of their rope. The school wants her in a more structured fifth-grade setting because she frequently becomes physically violent with other students with little provocation. Her parents intuitively feel that her behaviors are a misguided and now habituated response that Rachel exhibits in an effort to receive attention and to make an emotional connection with adults. But they have no idea of how to cope with her behaviors and fear that they may be forced by her escalating aggression into confirming what Rachel already believes and screams at them: that they will "dump her."

From all we know about Rachel's mother and the agency records of observations that began before her first birthday, the interactions between the infant Rachel and her mother were, from Rachel's view, unpredictable and erratic. Her mother was only able to respond to Rachel when her own feelings were controlled and when her own needs were met. Her ability to comprehend or respond to Rachel's signals was very limited. Rachel's mother was physically available to Rachel sometimes, but her emotional availability and responses had little to do with Rachel's cues. Her efforts to engage her mother as often as not likely resulted in frustration. Rachel was picked up, fed, and talked to sometimes—but often she was also handled with anger, or burned, or left to cry. Having tried and failed to engage her mother, Rachel, learning only that she couldn't predict what would happen, felt angry, fearful, and ineffective. By age one, she would hold her breath and then erupt into explosive tantrums. Her mother was surprised by her baby's fury, which she experienced, just as Rachel had experienced her mother's anger, as "coming out of the blue." Rachel's rages, however, at least succeeded in attracting her mother's attention. There were several visits to the emergency room before she was two with Rachel holding her breath and turning blue, sometimes fainting.

Rachel's behavior at age eleven may be viewed by some therapists as an attempt to engage or connect with her adoptive parents and to release her anger at what she experiences as anticipated betrayal. Rachel—as all children do—developed a working model of what to expect in intimate relationships based on her first relationship with her mother in early infancy. Even in the best of circumstances, creating constructive patterns of relating will clearly be difficult for Rachel. She will require unusual structure, patience, and energy and remains at risk of losing her second primary caregiver. Her behavior, once adaptive to a negative pattern with her biological mother, is now recreating her early formed belief about what happens when she is vulnerable to a caregiver: they hurt her and they leave her. Without intensive and expensive therapy, Rachel is well on her way to school failure, negative peer affiliations, and violent behavior.

While psychologists have long been aware of the concept of attachment in behavioral terms, it is only in the last few years that neurobiology is providing the understanding that actual biological change accompanies the behaviors we see. The biology of attachment again points to the crucial period of the first two years when negative patterns are rooted in structural and neurochemical changes.

Dr. Allan Schore, at the UCLA School of Medicine, believes that there are neurochemical and structural processes in a specific area of the baby's brain—the orbitofrontal cortex—that are designed to be receptive to and programmed by the interactive emotional relationship between the baby and the mother or primary caregiver. This area of the brain appears to link sensual input from the cortex (sight, smell, sound, etc.) with the child's emotionally reactive limbic system and with his internal physical processes (the autonomic nervous system). When the caregiver is able to read the baby's physical states and cues accurately and respond in a timely and sensitive way, this system of the baby's brain associates the caregiver with positive and balanced internal physical feelings. By experiencing the joyful and soothing responses of the caregiver to basic needs, the baby experiences connection and pleasure and confidence in the presence of the caregiver. Over time, these feelings become associated with her presence and antici-pated in future interactions with this person. In addition, the infant learns that strong emotional states can be entrusted to another and ultimately balanced or resolved, in the context of relationship. This reciprocal process of positive emotional exchanges is the foundation not only for attachment, but also for the development of empathy and the constructive ability for emotional sensitivity in intimate rela-tionships. Dr. Schore explains:

> The self is not present at birth. The self emerges over the course of infancy. And it emerges over the course of infancy only if it is part of a relationship with the caregiver. That is, the emergence of self requires more than just a genetically programmed or inborn ten-dency to organize experiences. It requires certain types of experi-ences that are presented and performed by an emotionally attuned caregiver. What this means is that the relationship is the crucible, the nurturing matrix out of which the child's self is cultivated. . . . The mother is providing certain modulated emotional experiences that allow for the attachment bond between the two of them to form, this channel of emotional communication to be created. As a result of this, the child begins to master the central task of the first year of life—learning about his own or others' internal states and how she or he can regulate these states with other human beings.
>
> In an optimal scenario, the infant is an active participant in a relationship with an emotionally attuned primary caregiver who expands opportunities for positive emotion and minimizes states of negative emotion. . . . Experiencing the joy of being the gleam in the parents' eye, and of having the secure feeling that one is under the watchful eye of the mother, directly support and nurture the infant's burgeoning positive self-esteem.
>
> At the end of the first year, these same attachment experiences directly influence the growth of the infant's brain, especially the or-bital prefrontal areas of the right brain that are involved in affect regu-lation and in coping with internal and external stress. Over time, the

cumulative effects of these early interactions set up an internal sense of security and resilience that comes from the intuitive knowledge that one can regulate the flows and shifts of one's emotional states either by one's own coping capacities or within a relationship with caring others. The development of this prefrontal area is responsible for empathy, and therefore for that which makes up "human."

So, a securely attached infant learns in the first two years of life that certain internal subjective states are shareable with others, that one is a human among other humans. This capacity for empathy gives him or her a sense of connectedness with others and therefore a human identity. To be a biological human and to be a psychological human are very different things. To have a human body is one thing, but to be able to feel that one's needs are of value to self and others only emerges as a result of, at the beginning of life, experiencing an ongoing relationship with an emotionally attuned adult human. . . .[19]

In Rachel's case, and in the case of children with type D attachment patterns, instead of a sensitive, "attuned" emotional exchange between the baby and parent, there is "misattunement." Signals intended by the infant to elicit comfort have been met with pain or unpredictable responses that did not lead to pleasure and soothing for the child. Structural and biochemical processes that could have once supported feelings of relief and connection instead were set to handle erratic and stressful responses. By ten to twelve months of age, these patterns are internalized by the child, even in the absence of the caregiver. At the end of the first year, brain maturation allows for the baby to move from solely existential responses requiring the physical presence of the caregiver to the ability to store the memory of the caregiver's face and to recall her emotional responses even when she is not present. At this point, Bowlby's template is internalized, and expectations of future emotional encounters will be based on past interactions with the caregiver.

When all has gone well, the mother's role in the baby's first year has been one of primarily nurturing and approval, coaching and cheering. This is what the baby thrives on, expecting it to last. But sometime early in the child's second year, generally around fourteen months, the necessary role for the mother shifts to that of a socializing agent for the child. Where the circuitry being built in the first year in the orbitofrontal area has been predominantly what Schore calls the "excitatory" circuit, now it becomes essential to build certain "inhibitory" mechanisms. In this new stage it is essential for the mother to provide guidance and discipline; her child's safety becomes dependent on restriction. The caregiver's verbalizations change from the gentle encouragement and coaching of infancy ("There you are. You can do it. Look at you! Good job—what a big boy!") to include moments of disapproval ("Stop! No, No."). When this shift occurs, the baby, expecting his mother's consistent approval, is faced with a misattunement between the pleasure experienced from his own explorations and the disapproval that the mother now delivers.

Resolving this misattunement and achieving a balance between excitatory and inhibitory processes is a major task for the parent and child, which is only beginning during the second year. It is an essential and normal process for a mother to give inhibitory commands. But when the parent of the toddler is excessively disapproving ("Bad boy! You are so stupid! You can't do anything right!") and allows the child to experience shame for long periods of time, then the child's ability to connect intimately with others can be damaged. This is especially true when the first year's task of achieving attunement has not occurred. Schore believes that these effects often continue throughout life:

> I suggest that the orbitofrontal system is an essential component of the affective core. This prefrontal-limbic region comes to act in the capacity of an executive control function for the entire right cortex, the hemisphere that modulates affect, nonverbal communication, and unconscious processes for the rest of life.[20]

Excessive shame results in the child experiencing "hypo-arousal" (underarousal)—the opposite of excitement and playfulness—a dampening of pleasure. This is conveyed to the rest of the child's physical system through the inhibitory circuitry to the autonomic nervous system, affecting all the nonvoluntary functions, such as heart rate. Schore believes that when prolonged cold and shameful experiences with the primary caregiver are experienced too early during the child's first year of life, particularly when playful and warm interactions have been infrequent, these events foster low self-esteem. Not only does the child experience a lack of excitement, closeness, and warmth in this early relationship, but the child's basic brain biology shifts for self-preservation to a dampened level. Now little comfort or sensitivity is expected from other people. Over time, these children become individuals who may show little concern for relationships. Schore asserts that early unregulated humiliation may be a common source of transmission of severe emotional disorders associated with the underregulation of aggression and an impaired ability to empathetically experience the emotional states of others. Schore sees strong clinical evidence that shame-humiliation dynamics always accompany child abuse, and that the loss of the ability to regulate the intensity of feelings is the most far-reaching effect of early trauma and neglect.

In extreme instances of misattunement, scientists like Antonio Damasio, author of *Descartes Error,* believe that the result is developmental sociopathy.[21] If the synapses in this area of the brain are never built due to neglect or are destroyed by neurochemicals resulting from chronic stress, the individual may be left without the ability to connect, to trust, and ultimately to experience empathy. Developmental sociopathy renders the individual unresponsive to the pain or endangerment of others. In laboratory settings, when scenes of horrific violence are shown to such individuals, their autonomic nervous systems do not register the normal physiological responses such as increased heart rates or increased skin moisture. In describing a child who cold-bloodedly murders, Bruce Perry says:

> The part of his brain which would have allowed him to feel connected to other human beings—empathy—simply does not develop. He has

affective blindness. Just as the retarded child lacks the capacity to understand abstract cognitive concepts, the young murderer lacks the capacity to be connected to other human beings in a healthy way. Experience or rather lack of critical experiences resulted in his affective blindness—this emotional retardation. . . . If a child feels no emotional attachment to any human being, then we cannot expect any more remorse from him after killing a human than one would expect from someone who ran over a squirrel.[22]

While the prognosis for Rachel is still unknown, her story is, unfortunately, no longer an unusual one, especially not for teachers or foster parents. Nor is this an unfamiliar story for therapists who specialize in working with adopted and foster children or children who have had multiple "breaks" or separations from their biological parents, who themselves have serious problems such as mental illness or drug addiction. There is something very fundamental in our first relationship with our parents, which reverberates throughout our ensuing relationships—often for a lifetime. When we are at our most vulnerable, when care is a matter of physical and emotional survival, parenting behaviors have a more pervasive impact on both our behavior and on our biology than we might want to consider.

THAT OLD FAMILIAR FEELING:
LEARNING TO REGULATE EMOTIONS

Besides meeting the baby's basic physical needs for food, shelter, and warmth, early caregiving behavior sends subtle messages of emotional comfort—or not—to the infant's brain. Not only are physical systems such as digestion being regulated by the mother's proximity and her provision of food, touch, etc., but the child's neurologically based emotional systems are also setting their balance points. A mother's ability to accurately interpret her baby's cues and her response to those cues have immediate repercussions on the modulation of the stress-related neurotransmitters (e.g., norepinephrine) and on key centers of emotion such as the limbic system in the baby's brain. The baby left to cry for long intervals or the baby whose cry is greeted with a slap is undergoing a very different experience emotionally and neurologically than the child whose cries result in immediate soothing. A caregiver's predictable responses to the baby's distress signals and her sensitive pacing of activities to engage her infant when the baby is alert are not only patterning the emotional behavior we can observe, but also are actually building connections and modulating neurochemicals in the baby's brain. This becomes the biological foundation for the child's later efforts to maintain emotional balance.

Schore's research on the neurobiology of emotional regulation focuses not only on the orbitofrontal system in the brain, which links the neocortex to the limbic system and modulates emotions, but also on the right hemisphere of the brain, where emotions of distress, sadness, and disgust originate. Dependent on the caregiver's ability to accurately and sensitively respond, the baby communicates her internal state through a repertoire of emotional signals. Over time, the actual physical structure and neurochemical profile of the baby's brain comes to reflect the caregiver's responses. According to Schore, the sensitivity and responsiveness of the mother "is literally shaping and fine tuning the circuits in the infant's limbic system, which will ultimately be responsible for the regulation of affect."[23] Through mutual interaction, the mother actually recreates in the baby a psychological and physiological state similar to her own.

The baby left alone to cry or whose cries result in unpredictable or abusive responses may never learn what it feels like to maintain or regain balance through thoughtfully timed external soothing. This is our first model for a constructive, self-consoling pattern when faced with strong negative emotions. Fear or rage may frequently overwhelm a child who has not learned emotional regulation skills. Explosive aggression, freezing, or self-destructive behavior may result from a child's disorganized efforts to handle strong feelings without a constructive experiential "map."

As they mature, all children—like all adults—will be exposed to situations that will generate strong negative emotions of fear, anger, jealousy, or frustration. But here, in our first relationship, is the seat of our physiological and emotional patterning in regulating those emotions. A 1995 study by Dr. Angela Scarpa Scerbo, psychologist at Eastern Washington University, and David Kolko, of the University of Pittsburgh, suggests that the ability to regulate emotion in childhood serves as a protective factor against one's own aggressive behavior.[24] While this ability can be taught in later childhood, the fundamental patterns for handling negative emotionality are formed in the first two years of life. By late preschool, failure to learn to modulate strong negative emotions may have taken its toll on the child's social relationships and on self-image.

Emotional regulation begins with parental responses to a child's behavior. There are four aspects to parental emotional regulation that are particularly important for young children: joyfulness, anger, fear, and empathic sensitivity. Joyfulness is crucial to self-esteem, relationships with others, and trust in a caregiver. Children of depressed mothers who receive relatively little stimulation of this emotion are at increased risk of depression and anxiety; later social and academic problems are also correlated with this experience.

Anger or rage, while experienced by all children, may be inherited behavioral tendencies. There is increasing evidence that irritability tends to run in families.[25] If these emotions are not modulated in infancy or toddlerhood by caregiving adults, children may continue to act out high levels of aggression and overt conflict. The ability to control impulses may also be linked to this patterning and is definitely affected in a positive manner by constructive and consistent adult involvement.[26] By school age, children who lack this skill are often already labeled bullies or troublemakers, and the pattern can be hard to reverse.[27] If allowed to continue, the inability to regulate emotion may undermine the child's ability to focus on learning tasks in school, as was the case with Jeffrey.

Chronic fearfulness may also be genetically based, but like rage it can be modulated by caregiving behavior.[28] Easily frightened children, particularly little boys, may cause great concern for parents in our culture, which typically values outgoingness and boldness. The role for parents here is sensitive support and encouragement to expand the child's experience, confidence, and competence.

Finally, empathy is a strong protective factor against antisocial behavior. By modeling sensitivity to the child's needs and by encouraging the child to be aware of the impact of his behavior on others, parents help children build a foundation for altruistic behavior.[29] Dr. Patricia Brennan and her colleagues, who have looked extensively at protective factors against the development of criminal behavior, identify "orienting reactivity" (measured by skin conductance and heart rate) as a factor that distinguishes nonviolent from violent sons of criminal fathers. Orienting reactivity is a physiological measure of emotional sensitivity, the lack of which distinguishes many violent criminals. This quality may be heritable through an "inhibited," shy, or fear-sensitive temperament. But researchers speculate that it is also shaped by early sensitive responses to the subtle emotional cues of the baby and young child.[30]

BEFORE DICK AND JANE: NURTURING THE FOUNDATION FOR COGNITIVE LEARNING

The ability to learn broadly about the world "out there," to focus on learning in school, and to master a range of interests in the world outside of self all hinge on a child's freedom to direct attention away from internal needs—away from basic survival. When children have not been able to achieve some level of trust in at least one other person, when they are coming to school or to play groups with strong feelings of fear, rage, or grief, when babyhood experiences push them into a state of constant vigilance or escape into a fantasy world, learning is compromised.[31] The ability to focus on abstract concepts requires some degree of emotional security, which may not be available to children who have not found protection and trust in a caregiver during earliest childhood. Internal "noise" from unresolved emotional dramas can undermine learning, even for children of high intelligence.[32] These are the children who, anticipating fearful experiences and with no secure base, will hang back. They will show little interest in exploration and will be reticent or frightened in new situations.[33]

A related ability children learn early from their caregivers is that of constructing an internal dialogue, to put feelings into words. The abilities to regulate strong negative emotions and to express feelings are essential to later problem solving, particularly in situations involving conflict or anger between peers. These skills are optimally taught in the first three years and are modulated in our first intimate relationship, generally long before we have expressive language.[34]

There is a strong correlation between school failure and aggressive or violent behavior.[35] The single best investment parents can make in school success is a warm, attentive, and sensitive relationship with their baby. Here, in emotional nurturing and early stimulation, is the nucleus of "school readiness": the building of self-esteem, and a sense of effectiveness, self-control, relatedness, and ability to communicate and cooperate with others.[36] The child's abilities to relate to other people and to know how to behave in social situations are key to successful transition to school. Restlessness, timidity, and proneness to fighting can undermine achievement.[37] Self-expectations—formulated by children's experiences with parental or caregiver expectations—play a crucial role in school adjustment. At least one study has shown that high gains in first grade were predicted by neither family social status nor children's test scores at the beginning of the year; children's high academic self-image and their social maturity were the key factors determining academic success.[38]

The devastating results to both emotional and cognitive development when a baby is deprived of early sensitive nurturing are clearly evident in the children arriving from the orphanages in Romania. In a January 1997 episode of *Turning Point*, a weekly television news magazine, Tom Jarriel and Diane Sawyer focused on a group of Romanian children who have been adopted by Americans.[39] While some children appear to have done well since their adoption, many continue to show serious cognitive, social, and emotional problems. Due to the lack of adequate records documenting the children's histories prior to their arrival at the orphanages, there are many questions left unanswered about these developmental disparities. All of the children who spent early months in the orphanages in Romania suffered severe emotional, cognitive, and social neglect. But there are wide differences in the ages at which the children came to their new families, the quality of care among the orphanages, and the length of time children languished without stimulation prior to adoption.

Left for months in rows of cribs in the orphanages, without a person to engage them in speech, holding, or play, the children featured on the program were all adopted at what we have traditionally believed to be highly malleable ages, before they were thirty-six months old. Often underweight and lagging in development, they came to loving homes in America that lavished on them the best nurturing, educational, and therapeutic interventions available. Several pairs of adoptive parents were interviewed on camera. Their stories, while different, were linked by a common heartbreak at their inability to restore to their children what they had lost in their first months—not just psychologically, but in terms of actual brain tissue.

Using the newest research by Dr. Harry Chugani of Wayne University in Michigan, the documentary offered graphic testimony of the children's losses. PET scans showed the areas of activity within the brain of a normal child in blues and reds. By contrast, the scans of the little Romanian girl whose story was used to illustrate the differences showed that the area of her brain that controls language was barely active. The area that interprets sound and emotion showed even less activity. "It's a black hole," said the voice-over on the film. Areas that should have been pulsating with color were black and still. Adopted at twenty-four months, this little girl could speak, but she couldn't remember simple messages like the fact that her mother loves her. At age seven, she could not remember a simple three-number sequence.

Another child, a little boy, had no ability to create or maintain attachment to his adoptive parents of four years. He was equally happy to go home with total strangers. Born prematurely, this boy was thought to have been the product of a botched abortion. He had been kept in a cardboard box with a forty-watt bulb, which served as an incubator. At three, when adopted, he was covered with scars and could barely walk. As he matured, he improved physically, but his emotional damage is lasting. He is self-abusing, throwing himself against walls and making himself go into seizures by banging his head on the floor. A French woman, on assignment in Romania with Doctors Without Borders, was interviewed for the program. She explained that the orphanage staff was instructed to provide only basic physical care, especially focusing on sanitation. "No one is responsible for taking the baby in their arms . . . for feeding the baby . . . for playing with the baby . . . for speaking with the baby."[40]

Beginning shortly after birth, interactive "games" between baby and caregiver and the caregiver's responses to the infant's sounds have a direct impact on the development of speech and cognitive thought. The baby begins to learn very early that there is meaning and communicative intent in such exchanges. Early language disorders are highly predictive of later school problems. Studies show that greater than 40 percent of the children who have early language difficulties will have learning problems in school.[41] One study found that maternal attentiveness and mood during feeding when infants were four months and twelve months of age significantly predicted children's three-year-old language performance and four-year-old IQ.[42] The research indicates that this interactive teaching is particularly effective when begun during early infancy. Babies whose mothers engaged them in a teaching process at four months, providing them with opportunities to observe, imitate, and learn, performed higher on IQ tests at age four than children who were exposed to the same teaching beginning at age one.[43] In writing on the importance of early experience on cognitive development, Dr. Marc Bornstein says:

> Infants are thought to be particularly plastic to such external experiences because of the still fluid state of the nervous system, because of

primacy effects in learning, and because of the lack of established competing responses. This perspective helps to explain why many life-long characteristics might assume their basic form in infancy and why infants' caretaking experiences might be so influential in later life.[44]

Not surprisingly, children's attachment classifications as measured at twelve to eighteen months tend to be predictive of school success. Children who are identified as anxiously or ambivalently attached are less likely than securely attached infants to make an easy transition into school.[45] Teachers are more likely to view avoidant children as hostile, impulsive, withdrawn, and quick to give up. They are dis-obedient, overly dependent on their teachers, and poor at getting along with other children.[46] Anxiously attached children, though less troubled by school than the avoidant group, also have limited social skills and lowered confidence levels.[47] In preschool, 75 percent of the children in one study who were identified as having significant be-havioral problems had been identified at twelve to eighteen months as anxiously attached.[48] This relationship between attachment and social behavior continues into grade school.

By preschool, we can already see the child's internal working model in action, replicating with teachers the interactions that the child learned at home. Preschool teachers respond differently to children in ways that reflect the children's attachment histories.[49] Anxious or avoidant chil-dren tend to provoke teachers' anger, whereas teachers are generally tolerant of immature or dependent behavior in the ambivalent group. Anxiously attached children seem to receive messages of low expecta-tion from teachers, while the attitude of teachers toward securely at-tached children remains warm, confident, and matter of fact and assumes compliance with their expectations. Research has shown that teachers' expectations are associated with children's IQ scores.[50] It appears that the child's internal working model continues to play out in grade school where teachers' responses influence their self-perception and subse-quently their IQ scores as measured in first through sixth grade.[51]

WHEN THE BOUGH BREAKS:
THE IMPACT OF MATERNAL DEPRIVATION

The first clue is something that happened when Kaczynski was only six months old. According to federal investigators, little "Teddy John," as his parents called him, was hospitalized for a severe allergic reaction to a medicine he was taking. He had to be isolated—his parents were unable to see him or hold him for several weeks. After this separation, family members have told the feds, the baby's personality, once bubbly and vivacious, seemed to go "flat."

EVAN THOMAS REPORTING ON THE UNABOMBER,

TIME, APRIL 11, 1996

While attachment research has long focused on the baby's behavioral attunement with the parent or caregiver, what we have not known until recently is that another, even more fundamental biological drama is simultaneously taking place within the infant's brain. Based on recent discoveries by researchers such as Dr. Myron Hofer, a psychiatrist at the New York Psychiatric Institute who initially studied the impact of separation on animals, we now know that long before working models are internalized by human infants, attachment behaviors serve the purpose of maintaining homeostatic balance in the baby's physical and emotional systems.[52]

Nurturing behaviors like holding, touching, making eye contact, speaking, and rocking—even before they provide the baby with a template of learned expectations about relating to another—provide for the regulation of basic biological functions in the infant. These functions include the immune system, blood pressure, body temperature, appetite, sleep, and cardiovascular regulation. The infant is so fundamentally dependent for these functions on the mother's continuous proximity that many researchers refer to the mother and baby as one biological system.[53] The baby comes to associate physiological security or homeostasis, which he or she experiences as contentment, with proximity to the mother. The baby's natural opiate network in the brain is stimulated by the normal nurturing and attending behaviors of the mother.[54] This process links attachment to the central reward system—the same system that is stimulated by addictive drugs. These early physiological regulatory experiences, resulting in frequent states of contentment or of frustration or rage or confusion—are the building blocks of later mental representations of the parent and of the feelings associated by the child with similar experiences later in life.[55]

When the baby is screaming, the nurturing mother provides soothing to lower the baby's state of alarm. When the baby appears droopy or depressed, an attuned mother will attempt to raise her baby's state to a more elevated mood. These maternal behaviors, besides providing a moderation of the baby's mood, are also maintaining an even balance of neurochemicals in the baby's brain, resulting in the contentment we observe and the baby's experience of emotional modulation, which over time becomes the child's internalized model for self-regulation of strong emotions, as discussed previously.

If a baby is separated from the mother, he or she experiences the loss not only of the emotional but also of the physiological balance of basic systems that are maintained by the mother's proximity. This is similar if not identical to the kind of loss adults experience at the death of a life companion or a great love. One's entire physiological system may go into shock. We find ourselves unable to eat or eating too much, unable to sleep or sleeping too much, lacking energy or highly agitated, and experiencing heart palpitations, high blood pressure, and memory lapses. As Dr. Hofer says:

> Insofar as mutual homeostatic regulation characterizes our first relationship and insofar as mental representations are built on this experience, some of the characteristics or later mental derivatives from this preverbal stage may be more readily understood. For example, affect states associated with the experience of separation later in life involve sensations of fragmentation and loss of control that

may derive from the early experience of regulation of so many infant systems by the first relationship. The biological, symbiotic aspects of the early mother-infant interaction may also help us understand the power of some of the many bodily sensations—the sensations in heart and stomach so familiar in everyday speech—that are experienced in connection with memories associated with important people in our lives.[56]

The implications of this information for the expression of violence are attracting growing concern. Dr. Gary Kraemer, of the Harlow Primate Laboratory at the University of Wisconsin at Madison, defines violence as "unregulated aggression,"[57] pointing out that society accepts and even encourages some forms of regulated aggression, such as in sports, movies, and video games. But when violence occurs outside socially approved channels, it is culturally categorized as antisocial behavior.

Attachment behavior is the developmental process whereby social regulation of emotion and behavior is first embedded in the human species. Early caregivers are the linchpin in this process. Kraemer, like Hofer, focuses on the neurobiology of these processes. His research on rhesus monkeys, described in chapter 4, demonstrates that deprivation of adequate nurturing in early life leads to the dysregulation of neurobiological processes, one result of which can be violence. When little monkeys are separated from their mothers, there is alteration of the neurobiological mechanisms that the baby uses to deal with stress. The result is exaggerated or blunted emotional responses and enduring changes in the infant monkeys' performance of cognitive tasks. Specifically, when baby monkeys were separated from their mothers and raised in cages with other little monkeys but no mother, they showed several social deficits that placed them at risk for aggressive behavior. When exposed to a social group, they were not as playful, and they clumped or clung more to each other than mother-reared monkeys. They showed less grooming and approaching with other monkeys and were generally less outgoing. When stressed as adults, these monkeys became hypo or hyper responsive—their responses were unpredictable. They were both retiring and antagonistic without provocation. They were often self-injuring. The aggression they showed in reaction to the triggering event was out of proportion in both severity and duration and was directed toward improbable objects. From a temperament perspective, the monkeys were either shy or reckless (extremely "inhibited" or "uninhibited").[58]

Kraemer attributes these extreme behaviors to the dysregulation of the system of neurotransmitters in the brain. The usual biological coping responses were not adequately stimulated by early learning from the caregiver and will remain impaired in future social encounters. In addition, the cognitive performances of mother-deprived monkeys differed substantially from that of the mother-reared monkeys. Mother-deprived monkeys were actually better and quicker than mother-reared monkeys at finding raisins hidden under novel objects. But when the task changed to finding a raisin under a familiar object, mother-deprived monkeys had great difficulty shifting to the new task. They were, in short, able to learn one problem-solving approach "too well." As a result, they appeared to be more rigid and less flexible in learning new tasks.

Dr. Kraemer is concerned that children who are deprived of adequate early caregiving due to abuse or neglect are now flooding school systems across the country.[59] He sees clear parallels between some children requiring special education in public schools and the behavior of mother-deprived monkeys he observes in the laboratory. He believes that many mother-deprived or neglected children are entering classrooms designed for mother-nurtured children, where the coping skills these children have learned are likely to fail. In addition, their neurobiologically based differences are reinforced by peer rejection. Kraemer's research points toward the fact that the traditional approach to educating children who have been deprived of early nurturing by placing them in environments designed for nondeprived youngsters ignores their totally different neurobiological wiring—an oversight that contributes to their growing alienation and aggression.

THE LOOK OF LOVE:
THE EFFECTS OF MATERNAL DEPRESSION

Emotional as well as physical unavailability of caretakers takes a huge toll on babies. Dr. T. Berry Brazelton, demonstrating the impact of even short-term loss by the infant of his mother's accustomed attending behaviors, shows an unforgettable series of videotaped encounters between a handsome four-month-old infant and his mother. The film features a split screen. On the left side we see a beautiful baby boy in an infant seat, propped on a table. On the right side we see his mother's head and shoulders as she faces her baby. For the first minutes, we watch this mother engage her baby in their normal way. The baby widens his eyes, raises his eyebrows, and smiles as she sits down in front of him. His arms and legs move fluidly in a regular rhythm toward her as she talks to him. He coos back at her greeting. He is animated, happy, eager to continue their "conversation." When his mother talks to him, he "talks" back. Her words are timed so that she waits for his response, and then she delightedly continues. The pair take turns with sounds and smiles and touches. The audience is enthralled. Then the scene changes. Dr. Brazelton explains that the mother has been instructed to get up and leave and that when she returns, she is to keep her face stilled, without expression. She is asked not to engage her little boy at all and not to respond to his attempts to engage her. Brazelton explains that she is asked to violate the baby's expectancy, to prove that the expectancy was set.

The baby greets his mother's return with the same smiles and coos and enthusiastic kicks we saw in the first sequence. He clearly expects her involvement. As his mother's face remains unmoved, he stops briefly to look at her and furrows his brow. Then he begins again to engage her as he had before, with even more energy and excitement. When she does nothing, the baby grows louder and kicks harder, causing his little seat to wobble precariously. We see mother's restrained face, still sober and without expression. As the baby heightens his efforts, he cries, looks frightened, and kicks harder, gradually almost throwing himself out of the seat. The mother stays with her task, though her face looks pained. The audience is groaning. Finally, in the last frames, the baby almost falls forward as he tries to sit up, folding his trunk over his legs, as if to throw himself out of the seat to engage his mother's action. He will even risk hurting himself to "get her back." Brazelton notes, "Little girls will withdraw; boys will become violent in their efforts to reengage their mothers." This amazing sequence, lasting only a few minutes, is a condensed version of the progression researchers are now studying in the infants of depressed mothers.

Children like Jeffrey whose mothers are seriously depressed during their first two years of life show dramatic differences in their emotional behavior and in their neural physiology by comparison with children of nondepressed parents. When depression prevails in the first years, by school age the children typically show problems in self-control, peer relationships, attention, and focus.[60] There is also a high correlation between maternal depression and both abuse and neglect.[61] Children of depressed parents are at increased risk of developing depression and anxiety disorders of their own.[62] Preschool-age boys whose mothers are depressed tend to act out, showing more aggression, refusing to mind, and often having problems with toilet training. Girls at the same age tend to internalize their anxiety and often withdraw, though either gender may reverse this pattern.[63]

Dr. Geraldine Dawson, at the University of Washington, is currently examining the links between maternal depression and disruptions in children's early social and emotional development. Depressed mothers find it hard to show immediate positive responses to their babies' efforts, and to engage in interesting and stimulating interactions with them. Because of their depression, they show generally more negative moods. They smile infrequently, their faces are often still, flat, or frowning. These mothers rarely laugh or use animated voices or variety in their vocal tones.[64] Here we see the influence of the hand that rocks reluctantly.

As early as three months of age, when babies are observed in interaction with their depressed mothers, the babies begin to mimic their mothers' depressed mood. They show lower levels of motoric activity, vocalize less, look away from eye contact more frequently, and protest more often.[65] Dr. Ed Tronick, of Children's Hospital in Boston, who has been studying these depressed pairs for more than a decade, says that the mothers' moods appear contagious. The same contagion appears to also influence the interactions between nondepressed mother-child pairs who spend more time in playful states. When normal infants were tested to compare the negative impact of still-face situations (as in Dr. Brazelton's tape) to the effects of brief physical separations from their mothers, they exhibited more protest and despair and were actually more difficult to console following the still-face than the separation situation.[66] The implication is that the impact of emotional unavailability may be even more stressful on the infant than physical separation.[67] When infants of depressed mothers are paired with nondepressed adults, their depressed style of interacting persists, suggesting that they generalize their expectations with even nondepressed adults. Dr. Tiffany Field, of the University of Miami Medical School, has found that babies whose mothers' depression subsides by the baby's sixth month showed normal motoric and mental development by their first birthday. But children of mothers who continue to be depressed for the child's first three years show the strong patterns of emotional dysregulation discussed earlier. Some researchers speculate that these symptoms may be inherited. Others believe that the patterns are learned and can be offset by the early involvement of a nondepressed parent or consistent supplementary caregiver.[68]

With the dawning of the psychobiological research that illuminates the neurological counterparts of observable behavior, researchers like Dr. Dawson are looking increasingly to brain physiology to comprehend the path of depressed moods in infancy. Several studies using EEG measures have now provided evidence that the expression of different emotions is associated with activation of the right or left frontal lobes in the brain. The left frontal region is believed to be relatively more activated during the experience of joy, interest, and anger—emotions associated with "approach" toward the external environment,[69] while the right frontal lobe is activated when experiencing the emotions associated with withdrawal from the environment, including distress, sadness, and disgust. Depression is associated with relatively more EEG measured activity in the right frontal region. In even very young infants, researchers have found right frontal activation during crying and left frontal activation during expressions of happiness.[70]

When infants had much greater right than left frontal activation during normal conditions, they were more likely to cry upon separation from their mothers. These individual differences in frontal EEG activities under normal conditions are predictive of differences in children's tendencies to express primarily positive or depressed feelings.[71] When there is generalized increased frontal lobe activity, researchers believe that it indicates a tendency toward the intense expression of emotions of all kinds.[72] Over time, it may be that the preponderant activation of the right frontal lobe is reinforced by the depressed mother. When the infant's display of positive emotions goes unnoticed or unrewarded, patterns of neuronal activity associated with pleasure may rarely or never be stimulated, while negative, angry, or sad patterns may be built. Some researchers speculate that a critical period may exist for this aspect of cortical mapping and its consequent connections with the limbic system. This process and pattern of right or left brain activation is the biological underpinning of future expectations of reward and punishment within relationships.[73]

An additional underlying concern for children of depressed mothers is that they are generally experiencing greater stress than children of nondepressed mothers—stress that leads to increased cognitive and social problems in school. Rather than being available to their infants for reciprocal eye contact, touch, and verbal exchanges and being attuned to the subtle cues initiated by the baby to maintain emotional and physical modulation, depressed mothers respond to their babies from behind the wall of their own unmet needs. As Geraldine Dawson, reporting on Tiffany Field's work, wrote:

> Depressed mothers and their infants spend more time engaged in
> mutual negative states, such as mother "anger-poke" and infant

"protest," or mother "disengage" and infant "look away." These infants joined their mothers in inattentive or negative states, resonating with their mothers' depressed behavior. With repeated dyadic exchanges of negative mood, inattention, and inadequate responsivity, these infants may develop abnormal, stressful responses to social interactions.[74]

The stressful responses measured by Dawson and Field register as early as three months, when babies of depressed mothers showed elevated heart rates.[75] Interestingly enough, these infants did not visibly behave as though distressed, according to the trained observers. Several subsequent studies found higher salivary cortisol levels in the children of depressed mothers, an indication of the activation of the adrenocortical system, which is activated in emotionally stressful situations.

The psychological unavailability of a depressed mother renders her infant emotionally, socially, and cognitively vulnerable. These babies have a limited range of secure experiences in stressful situations and have little practice in drawing upon others to receive emotional support. With poor models for self-soothing, feeling helpless and emotionally disorganized places these infants at high risk of later aggressive or self-destructive behavior. Without confidence in their ability to elicit soothing from a trusted adult, such children may attempt to soothe temselves by rocking or head banging.[76]

By preschool, unless the child's caretaking is balanced by a competent nondepressed caregiver, children of depressed mothers may develop a tendency to focus on negative emotions and thoughts, show little ability to initiate or even engage in play, and develop rigid or inflexible emotional and cognitive patterns in an effort to maintain control.[77] The present hypothesis being examined by researchers studying children of depressed mothers is that there is a sensitive if not critical period in earliest development, particularly from the child's eighth through eighteenth month, when children are vulnerable to establishing enduring behavioral and neurological patterns from exposure to maternal depression.[78]

As the research has uncovered the implications of maternal depression, new directions in treatment for depressed mothers and their babies are being explored. Particularly effective for both mothers and babies is massage therapy—massage given to mothers and taught to them as a way of positively engaging their babies. Various nurturing efforts to alter the mother's mood to more positive thoughts and emotions are also employed, including music, aerobics, yoga, and visual imagery. In a study by Dr. Field, mothers' anxiety levels and salivary cortisol levels decreased after a thirty-minute massage. After a month of two massages a week, mothers' depression levels were significantly decreased, as were urinary cortisol levels.[79] To increase the mother's sensitivity to her baby's cues and to positively affect the baby's mood, mothers were also trained to massage their infants. Two groups of mothers were compared, one group giving their babies fifteen-minute massages, and a second group rocking their babies for fifteen minutes. Each group performed these tasks twice a week for six weeks. Babies who received massages spent more time than the rocked infants in active, alert states; they cried less and had lower levels of salivary cortisol following massage. The massaged babies also fell asleep more easily after massage than the rocked babies did after rocking. They gained more weight, were more easily soothed, and showed more positive mood in face-to-face interactions with their mothers.[80] Another line of early intervention for depressed mothers is simply the availability of a nondepressed partner: a father, a friend or relative, even a familiar and consistent professional mentor. Field's data suggests that nondepressed fathers and even nursery teachers can compensate for the potential negative impact of maternal depression.[81]

THE HAND THAT GUIDES

We are living in a time when parenting skills and discipline techniques are sold in kits, books, videotapes, and television shows. "Canned" approaches to getting children to mind are proliferating and have been for several decades. The implication of these approaches is that once

216

you learn the system, it's all downhill. Neighbors, friends, and family members may also offer well-meaning advice, generally based on a set of skills that worked with their child or children. When all else fails, most of us resort to what we know best—how it was done when we were little—the ways of our own parents.

For the majority of parents, skills learned from families of origin and from packaged approaches usually work just fine. But for parents who have themselves been abused or neglected, or whose families of origin have been encumbered with emotionally destructive patterns, a deeper level of education together with outside support or therapy may be essential for constructive parenting. In addition, children with unique emotional or physical needs challenge these "one size fits all" systems as well as everything that seemed to work before in the family experience. As we learn more about the individual differences that characterize children at greater risk of impulsive-aggressive behavior, such as ADHD children, and those with bold, uninhibited temperaments who are insensitive to punishment, we are also becoming more knowledgeable about the importance of matching parenting skills—particularly discipline skills—to the individual needs of parents and children. This matching becomes important shortly after birth as the reality of the individual child is recognized by parents. No one set of techniques for motivating and disciplining children works across the board for all toddlers and preschoolers. As temperament research has examined the effectiveness of parenting skills with varying temperaments to assure "goodness of fit," we have learned some surprising things about the importance of knowing and accepting children's different needs prior to learning a system that will enable a child to mind.

ADHD children, for example, inevitably provide even seasoned parents with serious challenges. With these children, parents who attempt to use a communication-based system for discipline will be seriously frustrated as will the child. Such systems as Dr. Thomas Gordon's Parent Effectiveness Training (P.E.T.) work well with many children but rely on focused listening. ADHD children lack the ability to screen multiple sources of stimulation and discern a command, let alone follow through on it. With ADHD children, the need is for clear structure of the child's environment and a regimented, well-explained, and well-rehearsed reward system. Children who are bold or relatively undeterred by parental disapproval also need a clear, reward-based system; punishment-based systems don't work well with children who are unfazed by social disapproval.[82] On the other hand, children who are very sensitive, inhibited, or shy will respond easily to gentle, communication-based discipline systems. Even as babies, such children may immediately be deterred by a loud voice; serious consequences such as a loss of privileges or time out may be overkill, necessary only in rare circumstances.

The basis for any system of discipline begins with first relationships, in which primary caregivers pay attention to and articulate the child's positive behaviors. Conscious awareness by both parents and child of the child's capabilities, strengths, and assets is the first step in a discipline system. For the child's security and self-esteem and for the parents, belief in the core goodness of the child needs to come first. Only when this shared perception is in place is the next step—a disciplinary system—going to be optimally effective. The hand that rocks the cradle first needs to embrace the child.

HOW DOES OUR GARDEN GROW

The interactive "dance"—the timing and degree of reciprocity and sensitivity between an infant and first caregiver—lays the foundation for the exchanges that the baby, then child, then adult will echo throughout life. How we relate to others is birthed in this subtle flow of tiny behaviors exchanged between parents and infants and becoming over time the subterranean sea of learned expectations of self and other. Adult relationships—be they between politicians or business people or a shopper and the grocery clerk in the checkout line—are all influenced by this, our first and most profound relationship. The interchanges between caregivers and infants ripple out to all levels of society, affecting relationships from the playground to the Supreme Court.

On April 22, 1997, an advertisement in *The New York Times* featured a full-page photograph of a baby's face. Scrolling down the left side of the bottom half of the advertisement were the phrases: "Every hug. Every lullaby. Every kiss. Every peek-a-boo. Every word. Every touch. Every warm blanket. Every giggle. Every smile. Everything you do in these first three years becomes a part of them."[83]

Our children are the barometers of our nation's strength, their caregivers charged with a role of fundamental significance. Here in the arms of those first rocking our future lies the potential to protect against the rending of society by unsocialized aggression. In order that our babies grow into voting adults who care about such issues and who have the capacities for complex problem solving, the basic ability to connect with other people, to empathize, to regulate strong emotions, and to perform higher cognitive functions must be the intended lessons of the hands that rock the cradles.

9

Where's Poppa?

The cat's in the cradle,
And the silver spoon,
Little boy blue
And the man in the moon.
"When you coming home, Dad?"
"I don't know when.
But we'll get together then, son.
You know we'll have a good time then."

—HARRY CHAPIN
Cat's in the Cradle

It was Christmas day, and I think my dad was in a really good mood because it was Christmas, and my mom was in a fairly bad mood because she didn't think we were going to be able to buy anything. The night before, there was nothing, and when we woke up the next morning, Mom was kind of surprised because there were three big boxes under the tree. There was two hot wheels and for my little sister, a doll house that she wasn't big enough to play with yet, but we put it together for her, and she played with it for a long time. There was a lot of shock, and my mom made a comment to my dad about not knowing if he was going to be able to afford to get us presents, and she asked where he came up with the money, and he said, "Don't even ask." Nobody's ever told me exactly, and I've never really asked anybody, but I can kind of figure it out. I know my dad. I asked him about it, and he really didn't have that much to comment on it. The only thing he would tell me about it is that he did what he had to do to get by. . . .

My mom was just freaking out all the time, yelling and crying. And my dad said the very first time he hit my mom was four days after I was released from the hospital. He said that he hit her up in the head and across the face because I was crying and screaming so much. I was driving my mom nuts and because she was so frustrated. She started to shake me and my dad just smacked her smooth across the face and jerked me out of her arms and kind of pretty much yelled at her and accused her of trying to kill me and all that. They were yelling and screaming at each other. . . .

My father began drinking and would occasionally spend the better part of his paycheck at the bar and then come home and pick a fight with my mother. . . . They would yell and scream at one another until he'd sober up or until one of them would eventually leave the house. My father began to drink more frequently and became more abusive to my mother, often shoving her up against the wall, pulling her hair,

223

or slapping her. Even when he was sober, they would fight. My father would set me up against the sofa pillows and punch me in the stomach and say, "My boy's tough. He won't cry." Then he'd laugh until I would laugh too. . . .

My mother had a large mayonnaise jar she used to put change into whenever she could, and it was supposed to be our college money. But my dad snuck out in the middle of the night and stole the money. He went to the bar and didn't come home for two days. Then my brother says there was a knock at the door in the middle of the night. When Mom opened the door, my father stood on his knees in the doorway, and all he said was, "I'm dying," and he collapsed forward stone-cold drunk. The next morning he woke up still drunk and told my mom he was sorry for taking "the kids' money." But my mom had not yet discovered the missing money, and John said she finally had enough and totally freaked out on him. He said she was throwing things and screaming louder than her other fights with him. So [John] picked me up and carried me to a closet, and he peeked out the crack of the door while she beat him up. She threw an oscillating fan at him and a television and hit him with both. And then hit and kicked him until he passed out again. Then she fell on top of him and cried herself to sleep.

JEFFREY, AUGUST 1996

Do you know what sticks out in my mind about Walt? It's funny because I never—all my life I've never really been interested in tools. I've never been interested in working on cars or anything. But Walt did something for me that was manly. I mean, it was something that a father should do for every son. He went out for all three of us boys, Jeffrey, me, and his son. He bought us hammer and nails. And we were just stoked. We were so happy. We were putting nails into everything. Everything. All over the backyard. We had nails in the fence that, you know, parts of the fence that shouldn't even come close, you know. We were trying to put them in the house, acting like we were building on

224

the house. And you know what? He never once yelled or screamed at us because we were putting nails into things that shouldn't be. He didn't care. The thing was we thought we were being productive. You know, we thought that we were doing something. He never once said that we weren't being productive. He never once said that we were doing something wrong by hammering nails in anything. And a lot of times I knew that we probably shouldn't be hammering nails in there, but we wanted to feel like we helped build this. You know what I'm saying? Like this is my backyard, too. I helped build that. . . .

My mom told me that my grandpa wasn't really hip on the idea of her having a baby and he'd never accept me—or that's what my mom said—that my grandpa would never accept me because I was a . . . a . . . I don't know if he [my father] was a Mexican. He was of nationality, that's all I know. I don't know exactly what type or whatever, but Mom, she said that [Grandfather] wasn't going to accept me or whatever. Well, when I was born, who was right there holding me first and everything? It was my grandpa. And ever since I can remember, my grandpa—I've always loved his voice. There's something about that man's voice that, I don't know, I can't explain. It's something that I've always . . . I mean . . . I can't get it out of my mind. It's like etched in there. Every time I hear someone talk on the street that sounds even remotely close to him, it's like I immediately pick up on it. And I don't know if it's because it was the first voice I heard or what. But it's the sweetest one that I've heard, that I know in life right now. That is the sweetest voice I've ever heard.

JOHN, AUGUST 1996

Shortly after the last narrative, [Jeffrey's father] was arrested for armed robbery. He is currently out on bail and awaiting trial. He appears to be heading for a prison sentence and he is, therefore, not a resource for the children.

SERVICE PLAN NARRATIVE REPORT,
JANUARY 8, 1991, CHILD WELFARE CASE FILE

Besides being male, few factors distinguish violent criminals more consistently than growing up without their fathers. Sixty percent of rapists, 75 percent of adolescents charged with murder, and 70 percent of juveniles in state reform institutions fit this description.[1] Ironically, however, a review of hundreds of research studies on violent child and adult offenders reveals only a handful that focus on the role of fathers.

Dr. Vicky Phares, a researcher at the University of Connecticut, has written extensively about this disparity. Her review of eight clinical journals focusing on child development from 1984 to 1991 found that 48 percent of the studies of children with parents involved mothers exclusively and only 1 percent looked exclusively at fathers.[2] One review of clinical journals found that seventy-two kinds of child psychopathology were attributed to mothers, while not a single one was attributed to fathers. The same study found mothers mentioned in specific examples of children's problems at a rate of 5:1 compared to fathers.[3] "Where's Poppa?" Phares inquired in the title of an article recently published in *American Psychologist*.

SINS OF THE FATHER

Common sense points toward the understanding that male and female contribute equally to the genetic health or disease of their offspring. But traditionally when something goes wrong, scientists begin from the point of conception to scrutinize the mother—and the egg—to determine causality. Maternal age, nutrition, and personal habits have routinely been the focus for discerning the root of pathology. Fathers and the role of sperm have been absent from the picture. While the mother, through her role in gestation, obviously has more opportunity to provide protection or create risk to the fetus, the role of the sperm is increasingly of interest to scientists, particularly as more attention is placed on the issues of infertility, miscarriage, and birth defects.

During the last decade, geneticists have successfully learned to look inside the sperm and to examine its contents. They have found that 8–10 percent of sperm from healthy men who have no history of heritable genetic disease are abnormal; some carry microscopic alterations in genetic material or the wrong number of chromosomes. There is growing speculation that these differences may be critical factors in miscarriages, still births, low birth weights, some types of cancer, and behavioral and learning difficulties.[4]

The causes of these abnormalities in sperm are not known. But environmental toxins, such as alcohol and lead, have been implicated. As long ago as 1860, a report published in France noted that the wives of men working with lead were less likely to become pregnant and when pregnant were more likely to miscarry than other women.[5] Recent studies point to workplace exposures of fathers subjecting their offspring to an increased risk of cancer or leukemia. Paternal exposure to paint and chemical solvents as well as to low levels of radiation has been similarly linked to cancer in their children.[6] One study indicates a link between fathers who smoke tobacco and an increased risk of malignancies in their children, even when the mothers are not smokers.[7]

The negative impact on the fetus of alcohol intake by the mother has been documented by multiple studies.[8] The genetic effects of paternal alcohol consumption are only just being examined. But the last decade has produced strong data suggesting that genetic factors related to the drinking behavior of biological fathers have a significant effect on the behavioral and intellectual development of their children.[9] Studies of twins and adoptees have demonstrated that sons born of alcoholic fathers are at much greater risk of developing alcoholism than sons of nonalcoholic fathers. The drinking behavior of stepfathers appears to be irrelevant in terms of the development of alcoholism for sons born to either alcoholic or nonalcoholic biological fathers. Sons of nonalcoholic biological fathers showed the same incidence of alcoholism as the general population, while biological sons of alcoholics showed a higher incidence, regardless of how they were raised.

More than seventy years ago, early studies of paternal alcohol consumption in animals reported reduced fertility, infant malformations, and high levels of infant mortality in the offspring.[10] Recent studies show that alcohol influences fertility and male sexual performance and subsequently affects the overall maturation of the fetus and newborn.[11] Several reports suggest that fetal alcohol syndrome may occur in the children of alcoholic fathers with no evidence of heavy alcohol consumption during pregnancy by the mother.[12] Although the small size of these studies and a failure to adequately control for variables such as diet, stress, and the presence of other drugs, renders their results inconclusive, new studies on rodents point in the same direction. These studies found that adolescent male rats that ingested moderate amounts of alcohol and were bred to female rodents that had never ingested alcohol, even when followed by an alcohol-free period long enough to restore hormonal balance, resulted in the abnormal development of both male and female offspring.[13] The offsprings' hormonal systems that influence reproduction and stress were affected, as were their capacities for spatial learning. No gross developmental abnormalities were observed, but these subtle abnormalities may have a negative effect on subsequent learning.[14] It appears that, at least in rodents, alcohol consumption by males during adolescence may have an even more harmful impact on the next generation.

These studies, while done on rats, raise serious questions about the potential long-term and harmful impact of alcohol on sperm. Researchers speculate that toxins such as alcohol may impair sperm directly or may be transported to the ovum in the female via the seminal fluid, where it is carried by binding to the sperm.[15] Another possibility is that alcohol may alter the biochemical and nutritional composition of the seminal fluid, thereby exposing the embryo to toxins at the moment of conception.[16] While the exact effects of alcohol on sperm and the manner in which the damage occurs are not yet clear, the reality of this connection has been established in numerous studies. Perhaps the most alarming research of all concerning the impact of alcohol on fathers was reported by Ron Kotulak in the *Chicago Tribune* in December of 1993.[17] In a series entitled "The

Roots of Violence," Kotulak interviewed researchers who believe that alcohol may so alter a father's genes as to cause the offspring to produce insufficient quantities of the neurochemical serotonin. The lowered levels of serotonin in turn predispose the offspring to violent criminal behavior, especially if they also drink alcohol.

Beyond conception, the fathers' role in shaping their children's development parallels mothers, though it is not the same. When this development goes awry, retrospective studies show that there are often correlations to negative factors that are associated with both mothers and fathers. Researchers have identified four primary pathways whereby parents may be involved in the creation or transmission of specific emotional or behavioral disorders. These paths include genetic transmission, specific interactions between parents and children, parenting practices (including teaching, coaching, managing the child's social environment), and marital behavior, especially conflict between parents.[18]

BYE BYE, BABY BUNTING, DADDY'S GONE A-HUNTING

Where's Poppa? is a question that can reasonably be posed not only to the researchers whose focus on mother ignores changing family roles, but also and more importantly to all of us who are submerged in a culture that takes the trend of predominantly female responsibility for children for granted. Each year a larger percentage of children are growing up in single-parent households headed by women. While all children have fathers, more and more children experience their fathers as men who have moved away and whom they see for "visits," or who have never lived with them at all. Today forty out of one hundred first marriages end in divorce compared to sixteen out of one hundred in 1960. No other country has a higher divorce rate than our own.[19] Current estimates of the chances of a first marriage ending in divorce range from 50 percent to 67 percent. The chance that a second marriage will end in divorce is about 10 percent higher than that for first marriages.[20] A slim majority (67 percent) of American children still live with both of their biological parents.[21] An additional 7 percent live in stepfamilies where two parents are present. Twenty-six percent of American children today are growing up in single-parent families, 23 percent headed by mothers, 3 percent headed by fathers.[22]

But while divorce is one path that has led to reduced father participation in children's daily lives, an even greater number of children never have the experience of living with their fathers. Children born to unmarried women continue to increase in numbers well exceeding the million each year who experience their parents' divorce. In 1960, about 5 percent of all births were out of wedlock. By 1970, the number had doubled to 10.7 percent. In 1980 it was 18.4 percent. By 1990, 28.8 percent of children born in the United States were born to unmarried women—the majority to adolescent mothers. In 1997, while births to teen mothers have declined for four years in a row, births to unmarried mothers in general have not. In 1994, the birth rate among unmarried women increased 4 percent. In the same year, nearly one out of three births were to unmarried women.[23]

So four out of ten children in America do not live with their biological fathers—a number likely to rise to six out of ten for children born in the 1990s.[24] For the first time in history, the majority of children in the 90s can expect to live a significant portion of their lives in homes without their fathers. What this means for children living in single-parent (mother only) households varies greatly. Forty percent of the children in father-absent homes have not seen their fathers at all during the previous year. Forty-two percent have some contact, seeing their father one to three times a month.[25] Only one in six children see their father an average of once or more each week.[26] And more than half of all children who do not live with their fathers have never been in their fathers' homes.[27]

Research on the roles of African-American and Hispanic fathers in their children's development has been sparse. But the data that do exist on African-American men are particularly troubling. One study indicates that one in three African-American men in this country are currently under the supervision of the criminal justice system.[28] At the current rate, this figure is projected to rise to one in two by the end of the millennium. With this alarming percentage of men in prison, growing numbers of African-American children are being raised by women alone. Penelope Leach, a British pediatrician who has written extensively about child development, believes that this pattern of incarcerating parents as a primary response to many less serious kinds of crime may be doing as much harm as good.

> I take it to extremes and say that the fact that a man is a practicing father is one of the things we ought to consider when we're putting him in jail or not. Because those children have a call on his presence just as society has a call on revenge. Given that knowledge, it seems that the needs of children ought to weigh far more heavily than they do in our society's choices about how to best deter and punish crime.[29]

In spite of the data, one study of fathers in an impoverished African-American midwestern community found that 70 percent of the fathers of one thousand children on welfare acknowledged their children and "provided them with kinship affiliation."[30] Another study of African-American teenage fathers who were interviewed eighteen months after the birth of their child showed that 12 percent lived with their child, 25 percent saw their child every day, 28 percent saw their child three to six times per week. Only 2 percent had no contact. Where fathers have never married the mothers, 57 percent consistently visit their children in the first two years. But by the time the children are 7.5 years old, fewer than 25 percent of fathers are consistently visiting their children.[31] While it might seem that father absence translates to a lack of influence by the father on the child, this simply isn't the case. The lack of a father's presence has a direct impact on the child. Correlative data show that children growing up without fathers are five times more likely to live in poverty. They are also more likely to repeat a grade in school, to be suspended or expelled from school, and to drop out.[32] The correlations between absent fathers and poor outcomes for children are numerous. In addition, factors such as maternal depression, child neglect, and other factors associated with either financial difficulties or the impact of multiple stressors on single-parent families are highly related to father absence. As a culture we seem to have convinced ourselves that raising children is the domain of women, but as we look more closely at the dynamics surrounding child abuse, child neglect, disruptive behavior disorders, violence in the home, head injury, and substance abuse—the reality is that fathers, whether present or absent, exert a major influence on their babies.[33]

LIFE WITHOUT FATHER

The killing of five-year old Eric Morse in Chicago in the fall of 1994 captured national attention due to the age of his murderers, who were ten and eleven years old. The boys dangled and then dropped Eric from a fourteen-story apartment window because he wouldn't steal candy for them. The killers, A.J. and P.R., both of whom lived with single mothers, became inseparable friends after their fathers were imprisoned: A.J.'s dad for stalking his mother and P.J.'s dad for drug dealing. For these boys, father guidance and a strong male image, the learning of values and handy skills came in the form of the Gangster Disciples gang, which also provided an opportunity for physical safety and economic survival. In describing the role of the gang in the lives of younger boys, reporter Scott Minnerbrook wrote in an article published in *U.S. News & World Report* several months after Eric's death:

> They are sometimes literally father, brother, uncle or their substitutes and often the only acceptable male role models there are. . . . The G.D.'s take the aggressive young boys under their wings, buy them fancy leather coats, Air Jordan basketball sneakers and gold bracelets and teach them to count money and evade the police. They

treat them to visits to skating rinks in winter and bus tours in summer. They buy presents at Christmas and pass them out to everyone. A favored child, 8 to 10 years old, might be provided with a beeper and given drugs to carry or sell. "The message," police say, is "You belong to us."[34]

When belonging and acceptance—especially by males—are developmentally and culturally programmed needs in young boys, we can predict that an affiliative opportunity will have a great magnetism for male children without other options. While being a good student and having a strong, warm mother may be mitigating factors, the absence of a father or equivalent adult role model places growing numbers of boys at increased risk of criminal involvement. Single parenthood and "broken" families are recurrent themes in the research on criminal behavior. While correlative data indicate that the majority of criminals come from broken homes, it is less clear whether divorce and separation or factors associated with single parenthood and poverty are the cause.

In a review of the hundreds of studies on this topic, Dr. Adrian Raine concludes that there is no causal link between divorce and crime:

> Rather than divorce causing delinquency and crime, it is feasible that delinquency causes divorce. Having conduct-disordered, unmanageable, and delinquent children could severely damage a marriage which may for other reasons be at risk for break up. At the least, delinquency could make a significant contribution to divorce and separation.[35]

Several studies have shown that the underlying link between delinquency and divorce appears to be the father's criminality. Statistically, when paternal criminality was accounted for as a separate variable, the link between divorce and delinquency disappeared. The delinquency of the child may result either from parental modeling of antisocial behavior or from some combination of genetics and various additional negative social factors in the child's environment.[36] Paternal criminality is one of the strongest single predictors of whether a child will also become a criminal.[37] How parental criminality results in crime in the offspring is still not well understood; however, experts believe that parental criminality translates into parental absence, poor discipline, child abuse, and neglect, each of which, beginning in the first months of life, is actually communicated to children as are various parental characteristics through the minute behaviors exchanged between parents and children.

Other studies indicate that divorce does not appear to lead to later criminal behavior by children when it is followed by emotional and economic stability. It is when divorce is followed by additional changes in the family constellation that the children are placed at significantly increased risks for crime.[38] In fact, it appears that when divorce results in an end to marital discord, it may lead to better family relationships and reductions in conduct disorders in children.[39] The marital status of the parents does not appear to be the primary factor affecting children's behavior. Rather, it is the quality of the relationship between the parents and their availability to nurture and stimulate the child that makes all the difference in predisposing a child to or protecting a child against later criminal behavior. An interesting fact surfacing in the current research is that broken homes may actually be less likely to produce criminal children than homes in which the missing parent is replaced by a surrogate. To begin with, preschoolers who live with a natural parent and a stepparent are forty times more likely to be abused than children living with two biological parents.[40] To further undermine the view that "intact" is always better than "broken" when it comes to families and predisposition to crime, recent studies have unveiled the fact that unhappy but intact homes may produce more delinquents than broken homes that are clear of parental conflict. In an ongoing study by the Department of Justice in Rochester, New York, 70 percent of the adolescents who grew up in families where the parents fought with one another reported violent delinquency as compared to 49 percent of those who grew up in families without that type of conflict.[41] Parental discord and conflict appear to be more critical in shaping delinquency than the absence of one biological parent.[42]

As we look even more deeply at the underlying factors shaping children's behavior, it appears that the mothers' degree of warmth and affection are variables that fundamentally mediate the link between broken homes and crime.[43] Where mothers are highly affectionate with their sons, the marital status of the home seems to make little difference in the outcome for adult crime. The highest levels of crime are found among boys who had both a broken home and an unaffectionate mother.[44]

MAKE ROOM FOR DADDY

Dr. T. Berry Brazelton claims that from just a short piece of a videotape of the moving arms and legs of a baby he can tell you whether the baby was with his mother or his father at the time of the taping.[45] Brazelton notes that right from the start, fathers interact differently with their babies than do mothers. While the mother croons to the baby, uses her voice and arms to gentle and envelop the baby in a fluid give-and-take pattern so that the baby's arms and legs move smoothly toward her, dads "poke." Their behaviors with their babies are playful, much more apt to elevate the babies' mood and alertness. Dads use fingers to entertain and rouse the child. A baby's arm and leg movements reflect these more animated gestures in spiky, quick, vigorous movements that are less fluid and less directed toward the adult.

Without a doubt, fathers bring a different set of gifts to a relationship with a child than mothers. They nurture differently, they teach and discipline differently. And children clearly benefit from the combination. Significant differences in parenting style by mothers and fathers continue throughout a child's development. Mothers continue to pick up their babies and toddlers, rolling them in to their bodies, creating an envelope of safety. Fathers will more often put the baby over his shoulder or hold the baby so that it can see the world going on around him or her. Although there are exceptions to every rule, dads tend to be more directive, moms more apt to let the child lead the interaction. Fathers will often take risks with infants that mothers will resist, such as trying to balance a baby in the air in a sitting or standing posture. A father's interactions overall are likely to foster risk taking and independence, while the mother encourages intimacy, protection, and a focus on nuances of emotion shared between them. This early exposure to paternal caretaking appears to result in children who are generally more comfortable with new people and situations as they reach out into the world.[46]

Wade Horn, president of the Fatherhood Initiative based in Gaithersburg, Maryland, talks of fathers' potential contribution to healthy development under two main categories.[47] First, he says, fathers love and support the mothers of their children, contributing stability to a family. He agrees with Raine's conclusion that maternal warmth and freedom from depression are key factors in the prevention of criminality in children. But he sees the father's role as important both in mitigating against maternal depression and in facilitating the mother's ability to be warm and generative with their children.

The second contribution fathers can make in preventing later violence lies in their different style of teaching. Mothers tend to be verbal with their babies; fathers tend to be more physical—wrestling and engaging in rough-and-tumble play, especially with sons. Horn says that fathers have been wrongly discouraged from this form of play by well-meaning but misguided experts who believed it encourages aggression. On the contrary, Horn asserts that new research shows that by rolling around in physical play with their children, fathers are actually teaching their children both emotional self-regulation and the ability to discern essential emotional cues in an interactive relationship. This type of physical play actually provides a mini-practice session in essential skills for handling aggression. When the child gets too rough or excited, fathers will typically tell the child to stop; the child learns that if he doesn't stop, his father will discontinue playing. The child is also physically feeling and looking at the dad up close and reading facial cues, which provides practice in understanding emotional cues. Horn strongly believes that these opportunities between fathers and their young children are built-in ways of teaching important lessons and that fathers should be encouraged rather than discouraged in their intuitive expression of male parenting style. "We should celebrate the differences!" he says.

The Fatherhood Initiative appears to be responding to a widely felt need in our society to reassert the importance of male investment in children. The organization is actively encouraging public education and advertising which emphasizes the message that being strong is being nurturing, that active involvement with their babies is not only crucial to the babies, but is also manly. Horn says:

> Dads do provide something that is unique, and these contributions don't just start when the child is old enough to play soccer but really start at the beginning of life, during pregnancy and the first couple of years of life. . . . We have somehow implied in our society that fatherhood is basically about money. Fathers' contributions to the well-being of their kids is not just as economic providers but as nurturers and disciplinarians and teachers and coaches and role models.[48]

The newspaper comic strip "Adam" and movies such as *Mr. Mom* document the growing trend for fathers to become primary caregivers of young children while their mothers are the primary wage earners. Although roles are changing, primarily in white, middle-class families, so that more fathers are in fact becoming "stay-at-home dads," mothers are still the predominant caregivers of young children. Fathers spend an average of 3.2 hours per day with their infants.[49] A father's time tends to be more typically spent playing with the baby (37.5 percent) compared to mothers (25.8 percent). Fathers tend to involve their infants in more rough-and-tumble play than do mothers, particularly if the baby is a boy, while mothers are primarily responsible for basic care such as feeding and diapering. When mothers play, they are more likely to involve their babies with object play, a toy or book, or a finger.[50] All things being equal, little children seem to prefer to play with their fathers and to seek comfort from their mothers, even as infants.[51]

Though fathers typically asume less routine caregiving, the time they spend with their children appears to pay off. Greater father involvement with five-month-old male infants has been positively correlated with their greater social responsiveness and with higher scores on the Bayley Scales of Infant Development.[52] By the time children are sixteen and twenty months of age, their advanced development appears to be directly linked to the father's positive perception of his child, plus his ability to engage the child in play and to anticipate independence on the part of the child.[53]

From the beginning of life, especially when children are born at high risk (e.g., premature infants) or when they develop physical, emotional, or cognitive problems, fathers can make striking differences in the child's course of development. These differences show up early and are sustained through preschool.[54] One study on the effect of fathers on outcomes for premature infants found that father-involved children are more socially responsive at five, sixteen, and twenty-two months, are more cognitively competent in preschool, and are less prone to conduct disorders or risk of abuse.[55] Involved fathers have more positive perceptions of their children and are better at engaging their children in play and in anticipating their children's characteristic responses. Frequent visits by fathers to their preterm babies in the hospital results in larger weight gains for the babies as well as better motoric and social development. In a study of almost one thousand babies, the mean IQ for African-American preschoolers at age three increased by six points as a result of father involvement.[56] This same study also showed that higher involvement by fathers produced fewer behavioral problems.

Interest in attachment to fathers by babies has typically taken a backseat to that of mother-baby attachment. While it is more typical, especially in two-parent families, for infants to first attach to the mother through basic caregiving, we know that babies attach to their fathers at approximately the same time if fathers are available for regular contact.[57] In families in which the mother is absent, ill, or unavailable, a secure attachment with the father may compensate for an insecure or nonexistent relationship with the mother.[58] When both parents are available, infants tend to reach to their mothers for soothing even in the presence of their fathers,[59] turning to their fathers when vulnerable feelings are pacified. The attachment process between fathers and sons appears to be particularly centered around boisterous physical play, which boys continue to desire and initiate with their fathers as they mature.[60]

Clearly, it is in the best interests of children to have the physical and emotional availability of two people who love them supremely rather than just one. Research has consistently shown that, as a group, children who are securely attached to two parents show better adjustment than those attached to only one or the other.[61] Each parent provides important role models for gender-based issues with children. First loves are typically of one's opposite-sex parent, and these relationships may have lasting repercussions on future loves. When fathers are not in the home, the raising of sons by a mother alone can prove particularly challenging, especially as the child grows to adolescence in a family without alternate positive role models. In a new book, coauthored with John DiIulio, Jr., and John Walters, *Body Count,* William Bennett says, "We have come to the point in America where we are asking prisons to do for many young boys what fathers used to do."[62] In fact, particularly as more mothers enter the labor force, we are asking agencies, bureaucracies, and organizations in growing numbers—schools, day care centers, child welfare, and private treatment agencies—to do for children what parents used to do. And none of these are satisfactory parents.

10

All the King's Horses

Bittersweet memories of time that's slipped away
And new found words for everything I always meant to say,
Concrete walls all about, cold bars made of steel,
Guards with iron shackles, to strap them on my heel.

A scream of pain rings aloud, I hear it from my bed.
I listen closer to the voice and find it mine instead.
The pain is not so physical like the one before you're dead,
This pain comes from deep within the center of my head.

It hurts to think I'm sitting here waiting just to die,
If I could only understand all the reasons why.
I don't know what tomorrow brings, the truth is I don't care,
So I'll sit inside this hell and at these walls I'll stare.

Dying now bit by bit, a little more each day
I write down these last words—the ones you'll ask I say.
So now you've read this poem and today's my execution date.
They'll say it's time to die and I'll tell them it's too late.

—JEFFREY, "LAST WORDS"

NAME	SEX	DATE OF BIRTH
Mother		Jan. 30, 1960
John	M	July 6, 1975
Jeffrey	M	Nov. 21, 1976
Julie	F	Feb. 6, 1979

11–23–78   Request from mother to child welfare agency for housing and for child care while in hospital to have third child. Mother and her boyfriend live with her mother and three boyfriends. No transportation. Referred to child care referral service. Housing grant not available from this agency. Referred to employment division.

1–9–79   Public health nurse requested child welfare contact for [mother] for assistance with parenting, budgeting and supporting services offered; [mother] declined services.

10–22–79   "Accidental" call by mother for ambulance; mother confused; declined ambulance.

10–23–79   Neglect report received and investigated. Mother depressed and unable to care for children though reluctant to have children removed; father contacted but encouraged shelter care. Mother committed self to state mental hospital; children removed to shelter care.

10–25–79   Neglect report was filed; after investigation the report was found to be valid.

11–23–79   Mother returned home. Children returned to home.

Several follow-up contacts made. Family wants no further services. Case closed by child welfare.

11–23–79 Report made for physical abuse—after investigation the report was found to be valid.

11–23–79 Referral made for physical abuse, after investigation, report was found to be valid (the record is unclear on nature of abuse and on agency action taken).

1–10–80 Police department investigating an abuse complaint reported to child welfare that the state of the house was such that the children were susceptible to neglect if left in that environment.

4–2–80 Report similar to January's was repeated from the police department. The home conditions reported and described were much worse, however.

7–7–80 Referral was made for neglect. Mother found walking down the middle of highway, suicidal. Report was found to be valid. Children placed in shelter care.

9–17–80 Case referred to permanent planning due to the "inability of both parents to meet the children's emotional and physical needs." Recommended that "other resources be considered including termination of parental rights and adoption." (Children in foster care.)

A SAMPLING OF THE EARLY RECORDS FROM JEFFREY'S CHILD PROTECTIVE SERVICES FILE DURING HIS FIRST THREE YEARS

I wish [Protective Services] could have been more specialized. They were there when we were in big trouble. But they weren't there any other time. They weren't there when we needed a person to talk to. Somebody to put our arm around and be our friend and somebody that we could trust. If I could have just trusted Mark [caseworker], I would have told him everything. I couldn't. I mean, he can take me out to have an ice cream cone if he wants, that's fine. I'm more than willing to accept that when I'm a little kid. That didn't make him my friend. If he'd been around me more, if he'd made more attempts to show me that he cared about what was going on with me, maybe not even so much asking me a bunch of questions about my grandma and grandpa or whatever. But taking us to the park and a lot of times when I was a little kid, I wouldn't even want to go to the park. Mostly, I'd just want somebody to talk to. . . . If he would have come up with me when we lived at the mountain. If he would've walked out in the woods with me like I did every single day because I wanted to get away from my house. I wanted to get away from the things that were going on there. Those buttes, I have been all over those buttes. There is not one part of those buttes I don't know. Not one part. I mean, I know every single animal that lives out there. Every single type of an animal. Everything. Every single type of bug. Everything. And if he'd have come up and I could've shown him what I knew, and, you know, if he'd shown me a little of what he knew and we could have just been friends, I would've trusted him with anything. . . .

JOHN, AUGUST 1996

If somebody says, "Hey, I see you going somewhere, I see a spark of something in you, I know you're going to do something great when you grow up and, you know, just keep on"—encouraging instead of discouraging. I think that's where it's going to make the difference. . . . My grandma, she was there always from the beginning [for me]. She was steady. But she didn't see it in Jeffrey. She wanted to see it in Jeffrey. She always told him that, but you can tell. You can tell by the way that people talk, you know, it wasn't as firm a belief. I don't know. It's hard to explain. See, kids are sensitive. They can sense every single thing about a person. . . . You can be telling a kid one thing, you could be saying, "You're going to be great. You're going to be the president of the United States. You're going to be doing this and this." But if they don't really, if that adult doesn't really believe it down in their heart that they can really do that, the kid knows. It doesn't matter. Jeffrey didn't get that.

JOHN, AUGUST 1996

I thought it was ordinary for so long, that every kid lived the same kind of life I did. I didn't think it was anything unusual to see a kid get beat up or to see him come to school with black eyes or bruises, maybe a broken arm or something like that. I didn't think that was ever— every kid went through it. I look back on it now, and I realize how sad that is.

JEFFREY, AUGUST 1996

On October 14, 1994, a boy sat next to his lawyer in a Multnomah County courtroom in Portland, Oregon. His shackled feet, clad in Nike hightops, dangled several inches above the floor. As the frustrated judge wrestled with what to do about a ten-year-old child who had "a rap sheet half as long as the boy is tall" and who had been arrested for eleven felonies in the previous five months, his mother made an impassioned plea for a "second chance."[1] Among the felonies James was charged with were car theft, robbery, arson, and assault—nicking a classmate in the neck with a piece of glass, for which he had been expelled from grade school. James was characterized by his juvenile court counselor as "beyond out of control."

The week before the court hearing, the judge had granted a special sanction that allowed James to be placed in a detention home at an age under the legal limit of twelve. The authorities interviewed by *Oregonian* reporters agreed that there were increasing problems with what to do about violent children under twelve. "There's a big hole in the system," said Bill Morris, program supervisor for the County Juvenile Department. "The trouble is, we're seeing more and more kids doing bigger things at younger ages." Karen Lee, a spokesperson for the Oregon Children's Services Division, told the reporters, "This is the quintessential case of where there is nothing in the system for a kid who's got such severe problems at such a young age. There are only a handful of treatment beds and there is a two-year waiting list for every one of them."

At the time of the hearing, the court had amassed a thick file of nearly thirty referrals on a mixture of custody issues and delinquencies during James's young life. They documented a common continuum: born into an impoverished environment, including a period of homelessness; evidence of early physical and sexual abuse; a mother with a history of alcohol and substance abuse; a father who spent his teen years in a detention home and has been in and out of prison since; placement in at least three foster homes; and a fourteen-year-old brother currently in foster care. James has been in Oregon's child welfare system since he was seven months old.

Had James begun life as a puppy entrusted to the local Oregon Humane Society, he might have had a better chance. Thanks to the work of the American Humane Association, puppies in Portland are not placed with families until they have met with a "counselor" who explains puppy needs in depth. If a family plans to take home a very young puppy, they have to testify that someone will be at home to nurture it during the day—at least half time—until the puppy is housebroken. Payment must be made up front for the puppy's shots and worming, and a deposit is required toward the neutering of the animal. This deposit will be refunded when proof is sent to the humane society that the surgery has taken place. Finally, a fenced backyard or a contained area outside must be provided for the puppy. There will be a home visit by humane society staff to check these safeguards.

None of this thinking follows most human babies, with the possible exception of children adopted through licensed agencies. The vast majority of babies in our nation receive no assurances that their basic needs for shelter, safety, and nurturing will be met. And we pay a big price in our society for this disconnection between what we know children need and what we allow to happen to a growing percentage.

The result—especially for children abused or neglected, and then turning violent in our communities—is an amazing web of expensive and often ineffective bureaucracies, which come into play once children who are submerged in predictably destructive circumstances rise to the surface of the child welfare system. Just one confirmed case of child abuse or neglect is likely to trigger the involvement of at least five separate bureaucracies, not including special education or medical services. Police, court, child welfare, and an average of two private treatment agencies are typically involved—and the result, for our most difficult children, is abysmal. For families, the experience usually confirms a sense of failure. And their odyssey has just begun.

GHOSTS AT THE POLICY TABLE

One third of the new homes being built in America are being built behind bars. Yet we continue to produce more criminality than we're reducing, in spite of our desperate efforts to contain the problem.[2] Our nation's approach to the problem of violence mirrors our approach to children generally. We operate within an ambulance mentality. It's as if young battered bodies continue to fall before our eyes from a known precipice. Where once a few fell each year, now they come every hour, faster and faster. Our response to this tragedy is to position ambulances at the bottom of the cliff. As the bodies fall, we hasten to make better ambulances and schedule them to arrive at the bottom of the cliff more frequently. In response to increased gang shootings and delinquency, drug abuse, and child abuse, we hasten to build better headlights, better sirens, better motors, or wider doors on the ambulances. We are so busy responding to the immediate crisis and trying to repair the damage that we never consider how poorly the ambulance system itself is working and what we might do to keep children from the edge of the cliff.

The criminal justice system is another example of this ambulance mentality. We view violence as the problem, rather than seeing it as a late-stage symptom. If we trace the cycle of violence backward, we will see that most of the people now in prison were arrested as adolescents (62 percent). In high school, they were likely to have been involved in alcohol, drugs, and gangs. Typically, these kids weren't doing well in school. They were truant, often delinquent, sometimes runaway or pregnant. People knew they were in trouble.

If we look a little earlier, most of these troubled adolescents were known at grade school as children who had learning, behavioral, or emotional problems; a frightening number were delayed, had physical handicaps or developmental disabilities. If we look back still earlier to the neighborhood, a high percentage of these children were children known to be left alone, inadequately dressed and fed, without adequate supervision—children with parents too absorbed in drugs, mental illness, poverty, or the criminal justice system to parent in an adequate way. Many of these children were neglected or abused. And the neighbors knew; they just didn't know what to do.

Finally, if we look back to the beginning, these are the babies born in hospitals in every community who go home with parents too overwhelmed to show the first signs of cherishing their babies. Some mothers are clearly depressed, or are teenagers without support, or have bruised faces or backs. Many of these mothers had little or no prenatal care, and some brought their babies into the world hooked on or affected by the same drugs they ingested to mask despair.

While none of these factors automatically kicks off the cycle of violence, the correlations are far too great to overlook. But we wait. We wait for the babies of overwhelmed families to be abused or neglected and for these abused and neglected children to fall behind in school and for children failing in school to become delinquent or pregnant. While clearly recognizing the warning signals—parental substance abuse, family violence, teenage pregnancy, to name but a few—we wait. We wait for parents to fail and for children to appear in the system. By that time, for many children, it's too late. And we pay dearly. The educational system, the child protective services system, the juvenile justice system, the prison system, and the welfare system are stretched beyond capacity, and they can't fix the problems. We pay for children growing up damaged and angry. When we talk about crime, bigger jails, expanded police, more drug enforcement, we are talking mostly about the same kids later.

Educational and social supports are rapidly growing industries. Communities across the country struggle with outdated responses and systems that can't begin to deal with the growing numbers of children and families requiring services. From our ambulance perspective, we marshal tremendous resources to deal with the symptoms. But what we are paying for is often ineffective, not enough, or too late to alter the course.

The current service continuum is designed to treat child and family dysfunction once full-blown symptoms are detected. Multiple agencies respond to late-stage symptoms of pathology or dysfunction, assess and label these symptoms, and try to help families and children overcome the problems. But it is not a system designed to identify, let alone support, child or family health. Overwhelmed by the quantity and intensity of need, these systems now can hardly afford to do anything for children who have not already fallen from the cliff or are precariously close to the edge. During infancy and toddlerhood, when we still have the opportunity to preserve full potential and when human learning and relating is at its most vulnerable—and also at its most opportune—our society is not paying attention. Our educational and social service systems ignore the earliest stages of life, an oversight that undermines the effectiveness of the education system and the entire continuum of child welfare, which begins too late.

Dr. Ronald David, of the Wiener Center for Social Policy at Harvard's Kennedy School of Government, when talking about the health care system in our nation, could as well be speaking of the system of services for children when he says:

> What we currently have in place is not a health care system but a disease care system. We have created a medical complex that is pretty darn good at diagnosing disease, managing disease, and sometimes curing disease, but not nearly so good at preventing disease—and sometimes it's only too good at *creating* disease.[3]

AMERICA THE BEAUTIFUL

The number of Americans who have been victimized by violent crime is staggering. Between 1990 and 1994, the number of people murdered in our country (119,732) was more than twice the number killed in the Vietnam War (58,000).[4] In 1994 alone, 10.8 million Americans were the victims of violent crime, more than twice the number injured in motor vehicle accidents.[5] The U.S. Department of Justice reported in 1994 that 23 percent of all households had been victimized by crime.[6] Thirty percent of those crimes were committed by juveniles, a number expected to increase along with the juvenile population in the next decade. Juvenile offenders were responsible for 14 percent of all violent crimes and 25 percent of all property crimes. Two million seven hundred thousand juveniles were arrested, more than a third under the age of fifteen.[7] In 1994 alone, 37,130 children under ten were arrested, some as young as six or seven, and charged with serious crimes.[8] Children are the fastest-growing segment of the criminal population in the United States.

A growing problem in the criminal justice system is what to do with children who commit felonies, including murders, who are under the age of twelve. Most states do not allow children under eleven or twelve to be placed in detention centers or jail. Historically, children under the age of eight or nine are considered incapable of committing a crime because they cannot reason. On March 9, 1995, the *New York Times* carried a story about seven-year-old twin brothers living in a middle-class neighborhood in New Jersey who had stolen milk money from the Sisters of Charity School.[9] The burglary was the latest offense in a series of criminal acts beginning in 1992, when at age four the twins set fire to a neighbor's house. Other offenses committed by the twins during their three-year crime spree were: stealing a bike, items from other students' desks, and construction materials to build a playhouse; tossing a brick through a Kmart window; breaking into a neighbor's toolshed; shattering eight windows to break into Sacred-Heart School; and committing a burglary at the Bethany Lutheran Church. The article told of the legal difficulties and the frustration of neighbors and law enforcement officials in dealing with boys who are "too young to be prosecuted for crimes and yet old enough to diagram maps of burglary targets using the movie *Home Alone* for technical guidance. "The reality is that the kids involved with early minor offenses are most likely to become repeat offenders in the juvenile justice system," the Hudson County prosecutor told the reporter, "and they become repeat offenders when they're adults."

In one study of convicted adult felons in Wisconsin, 62 percent had a juvenile record.[10] While overall crime rates are declining, the number of juvenile murders from 1984–94 tripled.[11] This number is projected to double by the year 2010, when forty million kids now under ten become adolescents.[12] In 1986, a majority of cases in New York City's family court were misdemeanors; today more than 90 percent are felonies.[13] While the majority of offenders are male, there has been a 125 percent increase in arrests of girls for violent crimes during this same decade. Girls now account for one in seven crime arrests.[14] These stories are becoming everyday news—stories like that of a twelve-year-old San Antonio girl with a "fascination for the macabre" who was sentenced to fourteen years in prison for suffocating two-year-old Renney Gutierrez and her five-month-old brother, Timothy; and of the eleven-year-old girl who beat a two year old to death in her grandfather's day care center in Austin, Texas; and of two sisters ages thirteen and twelve in Richmond, Virginia, who killed their mother by stabbing her in the neck because they didn't want to go to military school.

Older teenagers (seventeen to nineteen) are the most violent of all age groups. More murder and robbery are committed by eighteen-year-old males than by any other group. While males fourteen to twenty-four years of age represent only 8 percent of the population, they make up more than one-quarter of all homicide victims and nearly half of all murderers.[15] Guns are playing a larger and larger role in these offenses, particularly in drug-related crimes; 80 percent of juvenile homicides are committed with guns.[16] A quarter of all arrests for weapons offenses in 1993 were juveniles under age 18.[17] Juveniles also account for a majority of all arson arrests in the United States; 7 percent of these are under the age of ten. These figures do not include kids who are simply playing with matches and start fires accidentally. "These are kids who know what they are doing," says John Hall, a researcher with the National Fire Protection Association.[18]

The type of crime juveniles are committing is also changing. A decade ago, juvenile property crimes outnumbered crimes against persons. Now the reverse is true. Most juvenile crime used to be against other juveniles. Now more are committing violent acts against adults. Juveniles currently commit about one-third of all homicides against strangers. Gang activity has spilled out of the inner cities into both suburban and rural settings. "You get more today of what the research calls reactive aggression," says Hill Walker, director of the Institute for Violence and Destructive Behavior at the University of Oregon. "Young people are walking around like powder kegs waiting to explode. Anything—body language or a look—could ignite them."[19]

In Los Angeles alone there are now approximately four hundred different street gangs. Gangs have even infiltrated the armed services at the more than fifty military bases around the nation. An article printed in *Newsweek* in July 1995, entitled "Gangstas' in the Ranks," reported that gang members within the ranks of all four branches of the service are actively trying to recruit military men and women as drug couriers.[20] In addition to learning advanced strategic tactics, gangs are gaining access to grenades, machine guns, rocket launchers, and explosives through military training. Military officials expressed concern to the *Newsweek* reporters that terrorist skills may be greatly honed by military training and said that it has been necessary to issue special manuals to help their criminal investigators track covert gang activity.

Contrary to the prevailing public perception, the largest percentage of increase in gang activity is currently in rural America. The recruitment and training of younger and younger children for running errands and keeping watch for gang activities poses particular concern for children lacking strong attachment to guidance figures or a sense of competence and belonging. For children left unsupervised in any environment, inclusion in a gang may be the only available route to experiencing themselves as needed and valuable, or as members of a peer group, normal needs during adolescent development.

Our nation's response to these problems is to "get tough on crime." As of 1995, five million Americans are living under the control of the criminal justice system. If the current trend continues, as criminologists and law enforcement experts predict it will, the number of Americans behind bars will soon overtake the six million students enrolled in four-year colleges and universities nationwide.[21] During 1994, the number of prisoners in federal, state, and local prisons increased by more than sixteen hundred per week. With new legislation encouraging longer and harsher sentences, especially for younger felons, and lengthening the required percentage of sentences inmates serve, the growth in the prison population is expected to accelerate nationwide in spite of a declining overall rate of adult crime.[22]

African-Americans are disproportionately represented in the crime and prison data. In just five years (1991 to 1996), the number of African-American men in their twenties who are under the supervision of the criminal justice system has moved from one in four to one in three. The "war on drugs" has focused on inner cities, sending young African-American men to prison at vastly higher rates than their percentage of the population or their rate of drug use. According to a report by the National Institute on Drug Abuse, although African-Americans make up just 12 percent of the U.S. population and 13 percent of all monthly drug users, they represent more than 35 percent of those arrested, 55 percent of those convicted, and 74 percent of those sentenced to prison for drug possession.[23]

A 1996 headline in the *Oregonian* informed its readers "Prisons become growth industry in Oregon."[24] Oregon expects to see its prison population more than double in the next seven years. Ten prisons will be built across the state during that period to accommodate this influx, primarily attributable to a new law passed to toughen sentencing, particularly for violent crime. The Department of Corrections is emerging as the fastest-growing arm of state government in Oregon.

254

Arresting, incarcerating, and executing our way out of our epidemic of violent crime obviously can't work in isolation. Since 1985, while the criminal population has tripled, there has been only a 10 percent reduction in the homicide rate of adults over twenty-four. This decade has seen the largest growth in the U.S. prison population since the penitentiary was invented.[25] And there is no sign of a decrease in this trend. A recent analysis done by the Rand Corporation projects that the cost of enforcing California's "three strikes" law, if fully implemented, will more than double the state's criminal justice operating costs.[26]

In addition to the high dollar costs of using increasing levels of incarceration as a primary strategy for cutting crime, there are high social costs, which we are already paying. Families are further undermined when young fathers are put in jail. As we have seen, children growing up without fathers, or worse yet, with criminal fathers, are more likely to feed the same cycle, particularly if they are boys. Prisoners rarely emerge from jail better educated, with prosocial skills or improved job eligibility. The reverse is usually true. This cycle feeds itself in widening circles with each generation, creating a swelling tide of abused, neglected, and antisocial children.

BRIDGE INTO TROUBLED WATER

The juvenile justice system is typically a stopping-off point for offenders between the experiences of childhood and the adult criminal justice system. Besieged by the rising tide of young offenders and contradictory theories and policies on how to respond, the juvenile justice system is in chaos. "The juvenile justice system is not working well for anyone—not for violence-prone juveniles, not for their victims, not for communities," says Andrew Stein, chair of New York State's Commission for the Study of Youth Crime and Violence.[27] On one side of the argument are conservative voters and politicians who push for longer sentences and remanding younger criminals to adult courts. On the other side are liberal voters and politicians who advocate treatment, education, and separate environments for young offenders so that they can be rehabilitated rather than become habitual offenders. Most states have vacillated between countervailing "reforms" passed by politicians anxious to target short-term gains.

Where the opposing forces in this ongoing debate tend to agree is on the notion that juvenile offenders need firmly structured environments. Where they disagree is on the most effective ways to accomplish this. The options range from tougher sentences in detention centers to boot camps to structured one-on-one mentoring by community recreational or religious organizations (e.g., Big Brother and Big Sister). There is strong evidence that grouping antisocial young people into detention centers, let alone adult prisons, only intensifies antisocial behavior. The skills to earn a living for a decent wage, to relate to prosocial people, to parent, to build constructive relationships in general are lost in prison settings. Since we are all creatures of habit, young people released from such settings tend to drift back to what they know. Generally, the longer the time served in prison, the more dangerous kids become.[28] For the majority who have been grouped from early childhood with children who also have behavioral problems, jail or detention only reinforces their identification with antisocial peers. Most of these children have come from households where parents were too busy or too troubled to focus on raising children. Prison may be their first exposure to the structured learning of everyday skills.

Not only is the incarceration of juveniles expensive—up to $100,000 per year per juvenile and rising—but it is often ineffective at deterring further criminal behavior. Three quarters of the teenagers released from juvenile institutions are soon arrested again.[29] About half wind up continuing the cycle at a cost per year that is often high enough to pay for three children to attend Harvard. Many studies have confirmed a grim picture of delinquent recidivism. One recent study by Dorothy Lewis of a group of ninety-seven formerly incarcerated delinquent boys showed that all but six had adult criminal records, most for violent crimes.[30] While easier for adolescents than for adults, it's hard to change one's sense of self-image, peer identification, and basic living skills and habits from an antisocial to a prosocial orientation. And society doesn't make it easy, even for very young felons. The *New York Times* profiled a boy it called Tony in a series entitled "When Trouble Starts Young."[31] When Tony, age thirteen, tried to return to a junior high school as a condition of his release from detention after a grocery store robbery, he had simply missed too much. Earning a living at minimum wage also had no appeal. In telling the story of Tony, reporter Joseph Treaster wrote:

> Halsey Junior High, where he had last attended class in the eighth grade, did not want to take him back. Gershwin Junior High, nearby, did not seem eager to have him either. But Mr. Gattuso [school staff] made some calls and, after about six weeks, Tony was admitted to Gershwin. "I went like two or three days," Tony said, "and that was it. Every time I went there, they weren't doing anything in class. They were practicing for graduation, and I said, "Why am I practicing for graduation? I wasn't even in school." Tony said Mr. Gattuso had offered to help him find a job. But he wasn't interested. "I figured you work all those hours and just get a little bit of money," he said. "You can rob somebody in five minutes and get more money than you'd make in like a week of working."

A major barrier to the success of the juvenile justice system is the lack of a bridge back into the community—to schools, jobs, and non-delinquent friendships. Even when juvenile systems have succeeded with their goals, because of a lack of resources, few juveniles exiting juvenile justice will successfully be reabsorbed into the community, beginning with school. There are several hurdles, including a dearth of special schools, the need to maintain safety in regular schools, the lack of a system to maintain partial credits for formerly truant students, and the embarrassment of learning disabled and formerly truant students. Many need extra help. Alternative schools designed for delinquent youth typically re-expose returning youth to more "bad kids."

One promising alternative that is receiving increasing attention is "after care" for juveniles who have served time in detention or jail and are now ready to return to their communities. These programs, which vary greatly in their intensity and costs (from $3,000 to $8,000 per youth) assign young people to individual advocates who provide mentoring, regular telephone contact, and weekly meetings with youths and their families to keep them on track. They help children go back to school to find jobs and to integrate into gatherings of prosocial peers. New friendships are built through athletics and recreational activities, in contrast to probation and parole, in which officers rely on weekly or monthly office visits and periodic drug testing to keep tabs on potential recidivists. Case managers in after care programs ideally work with a dozen or fewer youngsters, in contrast to the one hundred or more of the typical parole officer's workload. The effectiveness of the after care program appears to be about as good as the mentor-to-youth ratio is low. Michael Corriero, a New York State Supreme Court judge who deals with the most serious juvenile offenders in Manhattan, says, "We need almost a one-on-one with these kids. We try to have it, but it's not properly funded or supported."[32]

Desperate to place responsibility for children as close as possible to the source of the problem, some communities have tried to hold parents responsible for their children's delinquency. When kids act out in Silverton, Oregon, for example, parents may be brought to court and charged with bad parenting. Ordering parents to attend classes on parenting or drug abuse is an alternative to fines of up to $1,000. But typically parents of delinquent children, many of whom are as young as seven, feel they have little ability to control their children. Skills may help, but the problems are often deeper. With many of the offending children coming from homes in which the parents are also offenders, or mentally ill, or drug abusing, this approach has little hope of measurable impact on the growth of delinquency, unless the concept of parenting is expanded to include not only skills, but also the broader supports essential to constructive parenting, including treatment for the parents' own mental illnesses and drug abuse.

By the teen years, these children are often repeating the cycle of their parents, including early pregnancies, alcohol addiction, and drug use. These are the beginnings of the undoing of yet another generation. Feeding the continuum is the dramatic increase in drug use by young adolescents, which has nearly doubled to 21 percent in 1995 from 11 percent in 1991.[33] Alcohol use in adolescence is also on the rise. Among high school seniors surveyed in 1995, 72 percent reported drinking alcohol; 52 percent said they had been drunk. Forty percent of tenth graders and 20 percent of eighth graders also reported having been drunk.[34] Given the connections between early neurological damage and the use of drugs or alcohol during pregnancy and the potential impact on sperm of these substances, especially during adolescence, we may see a much larger wave of attentional and learning disorders in the next generation.

LAST STOP: SCHOOL

Children appearing in the juvenile justice system are typically students who are well known to school administrators for truancy, skipping classes, poor grades, and learning and emotional disabilities. A surprising number—estimated at 20 percent—have low intelligence from obvious developmental problems such as fetal alcohol syndrome. Many are also conduct-disordered students who have been identified earlier at the grade-school level—long before delinquent behavior comes to light.

Schools—like the juvenile justice system—are caught by changing social factors in a Catch-22. At the center of the dilemma is special education, the federally mandated stream of dollars that exists to make sure that all children, regardless of their handicaps, have access to an education that will meet their needs. Most of the children receiving federal dollars for special education are not deaf, blind, or classified as having an obvious physical disability. The vast majority have specific learning disabilities such as reading and information processing problems. From 1976 to 1994, the number of children with specific learning disabilities requiring special services went from just under 800,000 served annually to nearly 2.4 million, an increase of 1.6 million or 45 percent.[35] In 1993–4, approximately 7.7 percent of all children enrolled in school received special education services compared to 4.5 percent in 1976–7, an increase of about 70 percent.[36] Students with specific learning disabilities (SLD) account for the majority of that increase, comprising more than half of all disabled children served.[37] Five percent of all children enrolled in school require these services, a number which is expected to increase.[38] Teachers typically observe that there are far more children needing these services than children actually receiving them. It is also interesting to note that Ritalin is now being prescribed for 3–5 percent of all children in the United States to control attention disorders. Because most of these children are males, this means that 10–12 percent of all boys in the United States between the ages of six and fourteen are on this medication.[39]

Once students are identified with special needs—physical, emotional, or cognitive—they are entitled to special services. The federal government requires each school district to match federal dollars in providing for such children. Meeting this requirement may consume up to a quarter of the total operating budget for a district. In addition, when children enter kindergarten unprepared to learn—with limited vocabularies, poor emotional regulation, poor social skills, hunger, chronic illness, or other health problems—schools find themselves responsible not only for formal education, but also for the roles of social workers, nurses, mental health counselors, confidants, baby sitters, meal providers, drug and alcohol preventionists, and parents. Teachers may be called upon to teach such diverse skills as manners, sex education, AIDs prevention, and bowel control, all formerly the jurisdiction of parents. And they must be knowledgeable about the signs of child abuse and neglect.

While social services in the schools are crucial, at the same time schools are struggling to teach reading, writing, and math. Among fifteen industrialized nations, thirteen year olds in the United States rank 7th in science achievement and 12th in mathematics achievement—well below competitor nations.[40] Public schools have almost no funding to serve their brightest students, and gifted students from financially impoverished backgrounds are particularly bereft. Public schools in the United States are not functioning effectively as either social service agencies or as educational institutions. For children en route to the criminal justice system, public education currently affords few ameliorating opportunities.

SCHOOL DAYS, SCHOOL DAYS, GOOD OLD GOLDEN RULE DAYS

- Approximately 50 children were killed on school grounds each of the last of three years.
- 3 million felony and misdemeanor crimes are committed at schools each year, with the severity increasing each year.
- 5,000 teachers are attacked or assaulted at schools each month, 1,000 serious enough to require medical attention.
- 1 out of 11 teachers say they have been attacked at school.
- 160,000 students miss school each day because they are afraid.
- 135,000 juveniles carry guns to school daily.[41]

THE EYE OF THE STORM

While children are increasingly perpetrating crime,[42] they are also increasingly likely to be the victims of crime. "The number of children seriously injured by abuse nearly quadrupled between 1986 and 1993.[43] Not only did child abuse reporting increase by 61 percent, but so also did confirmed injuries increase by 36 percent in the same period.[44] According to the annual report of the Children's Defense Fund for 1997, every day 8,523 children are reported abused or neglected, and 3 children die from abuse or neglect."[45] The overwhelming majority of professionals analyzing the data on reported vs. con-

261

firmed cases of abuse believe that the numbers in each category reflect only the most extreme cases—that the problem is much larger than the numbers and is increasing. Tom Morgan, a metropolitan district attorney, is quoted in *Body Count* as saying:

> It is estimated that about 22 percent of children with learning disabilities acquired their disability as a result of severe child abuse and neglect. . . . The National Institute of Justice has reported that being abused or neglected as a child increases the likelihood of arrest as a juvenile by 53 percent, as an adult by 38 percent, and for a violent crime by 38 percent.[46]

Along with the juvenile justice and education systems, the child welfare system is also caught, with an impossible task, between opposing social and political forces: to protect children from their own families. The stories of violent outcomes for children living in chaotic and abusive families become grimly redundant. Stories such as that of the ten-year-old fifth-grade boy in Englewood, Colorado, who sexually abused eighteen-month-old Jazmine Hean in May 1996 and then beat her with a dog chain and stomped on her. With shoe marks on her head and hand, he left her to die in a bed with a dead cat. The boy's family had a long history of both child neglect and family violence. The family had been involved with the county social services since they moved to Englewood in 1977. In 1978 neighbors were reporting that the children were not being fed and that their mother was beating them with her fists. In a report on the mother written five years before the ten-year-old killer was born, the chief domestic relations counselor wrote, "The accounts from a variety of sources regarding her habitual neglect boggle the mind." The report cited several episodes of serious neglect including hospitalization of a son for "failure to thrive," or lack of normal weight gain often associated with child neglect. The report also described the father, Mickey Horton, as a man who "had difficulty controlling his anger." Both parents had been charged with abuse and neglect in the past and had received twenty-three citations for code violations on the family home, mostly for trash, litter, and derelict vehicles. Police were called to the residence forty times in the two years preceding Jazmine's killing, fifteen times at the family's request.

When the police arrived on the scene after Jazmine's murder, they found the house filthy and overcrowded. Much the same, in fact, as it had been in 1982, when an inspection revealed "an accumulation of food and trash in the dining and kitchen areas, clean and soiled clothing scattered throughout the residence, severely soiled carpets, heavy accumulation of debris throughout the residence, heavy accumulation of paper, open cans, rags, and other items in the bedroom . . . cooking facilities were covered with grease and crusted food."[47] Two days after Jazmine's death, Horton was served with a summons detailing 135 code violations, and city workers constructed a chain-link fence around the house and served notice that it would be demolished in sixty days unless he came up with an acceptable plan for its rehabilitation.

The child welfare file on Jeffrey and his siblings, John and Julie, lists regular reports of abuse and neglect, more than half of which were validated. Neighbors called the agency responsible for helping those children, and in some cases services were briefly made available. Jeffrey's mother requested the agency's help voluntarily on more than one occasion prior to Julie's birth when she was overwhelmed by two small children, pregnancy, and her own chronic bouts of depression.

But the children fell through the cracks. In spite of short periods of assistance, no concerted effort was ever in place to deal with the complex combination of factors at play: drugs, mental illness, abuse, neglect, multiple moves, multiple boyfriends, to name only a few. The most frequent response of the agency was to remove the children to foster care, a consequence that deterred Jeffrey's mother from honest disclosure of the help she needed. In the existing system of child protective services, treatment programs carry not only stigma but also the risk of providing agency workers with information that can be used against parents in a battle to retain or regain custody of their children. For Jeffrey and his family, the child welfare system was simply not equipped to assist beyond emergency services or crisis intervention. Had services been offered during Jeffrey's mother's first pregnancy and the months after birth by supportive outreach from the health department or from an early education program to help with mental health problems, substance abuse treatment, employment, housing, and so forth, chronic patterns could have been precluded or interrupted at natural points of access to the family.[48]

Like juvenile officers and teachers, case workers in child protective services are beleaguered by caseloads they can't begin to handle; most are carrying 30 percent to 50 percent more cases than are recommended by national standards. Litigation against child welfare agencies has become a routine form of child advocacy; lawsuits have been filed or threatened in almost every state.[49] At least twenty-one state child welfare agencies are currently under court supervision because they have failed to take proper care of abused and neglected children. One federal court judge told a reporter for the *New York Times* that there were "outrageous deficiencies" in protective services; another judge described the situation as "a bleak and Dickensian picture."[50] Major stories outlining the circumstances of children's wrongful deaths at the hands of parents and noting that child welfare stood by and watched are everyday news. And structural reforms that redistribute authority for child protective services from state to county levels or vice versa have done little to change the picture. Our attempts to reform the child welfare system have created problems of their own. Foster care systems are overrun and underfunded. Infants under the age of one account for a quarter of all children in foster care. An estimated three in five foster children have serious health problems, and a similar proportion are at risk of problems from prenatal drug exposure. Fifty percent of young children in foster care have unidentified or unmet needs for health care. One in eight of those children receive no routine health care; one in three have not received their immunizations.[51]

Countless media reports on juvenile justice, on public schools, and on child welfare systems in the United States confirm major problems with all three systems. All of these systems were created to serve fewer children with less intense needs. The explosion of children in dire circumstances and with increasingly serious problems exceeds the bureaucracies' capacities to keep up with either the quantity or intensity of services required. All of these systems fail for the same reason: they are overwhelmed by complexities they cannot possibly handle thoroughly.

In order for child welfare to have successfully intervened with Jeffrey and his family, three factors would have had to be in place. First, the child welfare system would have had to be able to develop an integrated treatment plan together with other agencies (e.g., alcohol or drug treatment, employment, and mental health). Staff and bureaucracies would have had to work together, preferably under one roof, with common goals and incentives. Second, the agencies would have had to make their services available and accessible so that the family could work and still attend treatment sessions with the help of child care and transportation assistance. And most important, services would have had to be provided early enough in the developmental cycle of the children to support and stimulate their basic potential, and to prevent obvious risks from taking their toll.

The violent children of the future are now babies. If we want to reduce the predictable tide of needful children that will continue to overwhelm existing bureaucracies, we can. But achieving this will require us to create a very different continuum of services, which begins with addressing the needs of parents around us who are now pregnant or parenting babies.

Strong efforts to intervene from the point of conception, gestation, and birth, particularly for children at high risk, are beginning to receive attention. Promising prevention programs such as home visitation of all new babies by a trained public health nurse or trained paraprofessional are increasingly being researched, refined, and implemented on a small scale in several states. Head Start has moved from focusing only on children three to five to create centers for and in-home outreach to families with children from birth to three (Early Head Start).

However, it is still an all but impossible task for parents to find substantive help and intervention for their infants and toddlers in most communities. Witness the story of Karen and Michael. Karen, a fifth-grade teacher, was excited about and well prepared for the birth of her first child, Michael, now twenty months old. She had participated in Lamaze classes with her husband and chose to have a midwife assist her in delivering her baby in a local hospital. Her labor was less than four hours; she used no drugs or anesthesia. While she had worried that Michael was not more active during the last few weeks of pregnancy, he was born easily and seemed healthy. Soon after birth, however, problems began to appear. He had difficulty sucking and didn't take to the breast, even after weeks of assistance from a lactation specialist. He appeared to be irritable and developed reflux, a condition that caused him to spit up frequently and to cry with digestive discomfort. He trembled when he cried, and his movements were jerky. He was extraordinarily stiff, would not mold to his mother's body, and was highly sensitive to light and sound. Michael would waken from sleep right into screaming. He had trouble sleeping and woke up for long periods around the clock. At three and four months of age, he still would not look at a human face but generally preferred inanimate patterned objects such as wallpaper or vertical blinds.

At each well-baby visit, Karen mentioned her growing concerns to her pediatrician, who minimized all of them and told her not to worry. As the weeks passed, Karen became isolated by Michael's tendency to become overstimulated when she ventured out with him. As her loss of sleep and the effects of Michael's irritability mounted, she became more desperate. In tears at a doctor visit scheduled to treat an ear infection when Michael was three months old, she poured out her fear to the pediatrician that something was seriously "wrong" with her baby. The doctor again discounted Michael's symptoms and recommended to Karen that she see a therapist for antidepressants. Fortunately, a family friend of Karen's who was a child therapist corroborated Karen's observations. She knew that Michael's shakiness, refusal of eye contact, stiffness, and poor regulation of states of arousal were clear signals that all was not right. The friend began calling various specialists she knew to decide how to connect Karen with the help she needed for her baby. A call to the local health science center's child development and rehabilitation center referred her to a pediatric neurologist. The neurologist's nurse scolded the friend for inquiring about these symptoms in a three-month-old baby—"too young" was her brusque conclusion. She recommended that Karen or her pediatrician should call the neurologist back if Michael had not outgrown these signs of "immaturity" by six to eight months of age.

Refusing to give up, Karen's friend called a personal friend at the medical school who was a specialist in treating attention deficits. This specialist made a personal call to a friend of his, a developmental pediatrician, who agreed to see Michael. Two weeks after this call and months after Karen first began expressing concerns to her doctor, the developmental pediatrician examined Michael and noted a strong left-sided dominance in motor functions, as well as the stiffness and the trembling. She prescribed a course of physical therapy.

By nine months of age, as Karen worked with Michael under the direction of the physical therapist, many of his symptoms had begun to abate. He outgrew the reflux, began sucking normally, established good eye contact and reciprocal vocalizing. But, although he crawled and was active, Michael could not sit up. He also remained very stiff, and his shakiness continued, intensifying as he grew tired. At ten months, the developmental pediatrician recommended an MRI scan of Michael's brain to acquire further diagnostic information. The results of the MRI showed an old hemorrhage in the temporal occipital region, which the neurologist believes occurred immediately before or just after birth. While the neurologist immediately eliminated trauma or an external blow as the cause of the problem, it took several months to determine the reason for the hemorrhage. Michael had a rare blood disease which caused internal bleeding around the time he was born. As the result, Michael experienced chronic head pain during his first months of life, lowering his ability to tolerate additional frustration or excitement. Michael's symptoms have now mostly disappeared and, at almost two, he appears to be a very normal little boy who has overcome his early losses. He is active, energetic and very well coordinated.

But accessing a diagnosis and treatment during the critical time of his early brain development was extraordinarily difficult. Karen was educated, aggressive, and able to pay for Michael's care outside of her managed-care policy, which was being well guarded by a pediatrician who could not discern Michael's symptoms even when Karen pointed them out. In addition, Karen had personal connections to a route of influence and inside help that would normally only be made available by more "blatant" or "urgent" symptoms of impairment.

Karen's experience is unfortunately typical. Passed off as signs of immature nervous, motoric, or emotional development—or blamed on the mother—early signs of neurological abnormalities in infants are often overlooked. The opportunity for rerouting the damaged neurological circuits during the time Michael's brain was still highly plastic could have been missed, resulting in more profound effects and cumulative damage. The subtleties of early infant physical and emotional behavior, and the hesitant messages from frightened parents, are frequently passed over until preschool or kindergarten, when more obvious symptoms may be caught in federally funded early intervention screenings. Few communities have the trained staff or outreach programs, even in private clinics, to do a good job of screening for early emotional and behavioral problems affecting infants.

No one is more aware of this lack or more knowledgeable about how to meet it than Dr. T. Berry Brazelton, America's favorite pediatrician. Dr. Brazelton's newest effort, being developed in partnership with his colleague Dr. Ed Tronick, is Touchpoints, a program designed to train child-focused professionals in the first three years of emotional and behavioral development.[52] Based on his book by the same title, Touchpoints training prepares professionals to work with parents in a sensitive and strength-based context so that parents are knowledgeable and prepared for the surges and regressions of normal development, including recognition of signs of pathology. By offering parents anticipatory guidance just ahead of their child's behavioral changes, when both parents and children are vulnerable and relationships are challenged, many problems can be prevented.

Another extraordinarily promising training that is gradually penetrating the public health system is NCAST, Nursing Child Assessment Satellite Training, developed by Dr. Kathryn Barnard at the University of Washington. Like Touchpoints, NCAST focuses on outreach to parents of children zero to three. It primarily trains nurses who are meeting with pregnant and new mothers in public and private settings. It's tools include a feeding and a teaching scale, each of which identifies in clear language the specific behaviors that characterize a healthy interaction between a parent and a child engaged in feeding or teaching and learning. Tiny units of behavior: reciprocal eye contact, vocalizations for babies and for mothers, a variety of touches and voice tones—dozens of minute behaviors—are listed on a binary scale. The magic of the NCAST scales lies in their usefulness with young or first-time parents or with parents who themselves were abused or neglected as babies.

Complex positive interactions like emotional regulation are broken down into a series of individual behaviors that can be modeled and taught. The baby's ability to communicate his or her needs clearly and the baby's responsiveness to the parents' behaviors are also scored. NCAST training for parents and the professionals who work with them can help demystify the complexities of healthy early relationships so that positive interactions can be supported or taught in a nonstigmatizing way at the time the interactive patterns between parents and babies are forming. One of its greatest strengths lies in its ability to allow parents to, first of all, see what they are doing right and then to work with them to strengthen that base.[53]

NCAST and Touchpoints can both most effectively be embedded in programs that serve young or first-time parents from pregnancy through the child's third year of life. Several promising programs are now beginning to emerge in many states. These programs share the goal of supporting parents from the earliest possible point in their relationships with their babies rather than allowing those relationships to erode to the point of lost potential and trigger the need for later-stage services. Early Head Start, Healthy Start, which provides home visitors, and the Nurse Home Visitation Program, pioneered by Dr. David Olds, are three examples.

When we think of crime prevention programs, we may think of boot camps, midnight basketball, drug education classes in schools, or organized neighborhood watches. However, an April 1997 report to Congress by a team of criminologists found none of those to be particularly effective.[54] By contrast, the study reported that infant home-visitation programs appear to have lasting effects because problems are dealt with early.

MOTHER HUBBARD'S CUPBOARD

Violent behavior is often linked to poverty or the underclass to the point that some policy analysts cite poverty as the primary cause of violence in our culture. There is no question that poverty is an indirect contributor to violent behavior. Children growing up in significant poverty are measurably more fearful and antisocial than children of affluent peers and often show signs of depression by age five. They have more behavior problems including temper tantrums and show more signs of aggression, a pattern that continues into adolescence. Impoverished parents are more likely to be depressed, show less warmth, and have a more authoritarian discipline style, including yelling and hitting. This style is often attributed to an ongoing fear for their children's safety and the need to maintain immediate physical control in the face of external threats such as driveby shootings.[55]

But while financial poverty is often cited as the root of violence, one has to ask: If we were to eliminate poverty, would we still have violence? The answer is clearly yes. Material poverty certainly contributes to familial stress, to the erosion of health and safety, and to the subsequent depletion of confidence and competence parents need to raise their children. But the problem of crime and violent behavior won't be solved through the now ancient argument that all we really need to do is eliminate poverty. Even if a good case could be made for this argument, voters are unwilling to approach the problem of violence through that door. From both a substantive and a financial perspective, we have to look more deeply and more specifically.

Impoverishment in the families producing violent children often exists at a deeper than material level. When we look closely at the families of violent children across classes and racial differences, we find an impoverishment of human connectedness, trust, support, and emotional nurturing. People feel angry and alienated—often for several generations. There is a sense of separateness; a chronic irritability; an absence of optimism, joy, and knowing how to laugh; and a need to numb against hopelessness. When children are born into such settings, child abuse and neglect are palpable potentials. Nurses in hospitals often say they can identify at birth which babies will soon become known to child welfare agents. The problem isn't so much that we can't see these children coming as that we aren't sure what to do or how much to get involved.

While several promising paths are available to us, there is no single prescription, no silver bullet. Solutions—like the problems—are complex. We have a growing body of scientific research on the human brain and a growing number of programs that have been well enough evaluated to show strong results for both parents and children. In order for these approaches to have any major impact on violence, however, we will have to radically change our nation's operant view of babies. If American child care practices reflect our beliefs about children, then it is clear that most of us view infancy as only a prelude to the really important period of development. We see babyhood as an innocuous time for learning basic muscle control, which we expect to automatically occur as long as basic needs are met. The truth is, in fact, the reverse. Far from a benign state of perpetual malleability, infancy is the period of our most complex and formative learning and of laying the foundation for how we connect with other people, the effects of which can last for a lifetime.

WE KNOW THAT IN AMERICA TODAY:

- More people are incarcerated than in any other Western industrialized country. The number of people in U.S. prisons will soon exceed the number enrolled in colleges and universities.
- Thirty percent of all crime is committed by juveniles.
- Though only 8 percent of the population, juveniles fourteen to twenty-four are responsible for 14 percent of all violent crimes, 50 percent of all murders, 25 percent of all property crimes, and a majority of all arson arrests.
- Children are the fastest-growing segment of the criminal population; every four minutes a child is arrested for a violent crime.

AND WE ALSO KNOW THAT:

- One child is shot to death every ninety minutes.
- Every day 15 children are killed with guns and 30 are wounded.
- Every day 135,000 children take guns to school.
- Every four hours a child commits suicide.

BUT DO WE CONNECT THIS DATA WITH THE FACTS THAT IN THE UNITED STATES:

- Homicide is the leading cause of death for children under 4; every seven hours a child dies at the hands of his caregiver.
- Every day 8,493 children are reported abused or neglected.
- Every day 1,407 babies are born to teen mothers.
- Every day 790 babies are born at low birth weight.
- One quarter of all children under 4 live in poverty.

GENERALLY NOT.[56]

11

And Still We Wait

As time went on, and the months and years came and went, he was never without friends. Fern did not come regularly to the barn any more. She was growing up, and was careful to avoid childish things, like sitting on a milk stool near a pigpen. But Charlotte's children and grandchildren and great grandchildren, year after year, lived in the doorway. Each spring there were new little spiders hatching out to take the place of the old. Most of them sailed away on their balloons. But always two or three stayed and set up housekeeping in the doorway.

Mr. Zuckerman took fine care of Wilbur all the rest of his days, and the pig was often visited by friends and admirers, for nobody ever forgot the year of his triumph and the miracle of the web. Life in the barn was very good—night and day, winter and summer, spring and fall, dull days and bright days. It was the best place to be, thought Wilbur, this warm delicious cellar, with the garrulous geese, the changing seasons, the heat of the sun, the passage of swallows, the nearness of rats, the sameness of sheep, the love of spiders, the smell of manure, and the glory of everything.

—E. B. WHITE
Charlotte' Web

ALL IS SILENT

Nothing but blackness, cold and silent
Assaulting my senses tonight
Except a single lonely star
So tiny, yet so bright.

Like springtime raindrops, tears fall down
Rolling warm upon my face
They fall, turn to ice, and shatter
A prickly design as intricate as lace.

A scream of vengeance rapes the night
Chilling cries of agony and pain
Blaming me for all that's happened to him
Time and time again.

Nothing but blackness, cold and silent
Assaulting my senses tonight
Except a single lonely star
So tiny, yet so bright.

Drenched in perspiration
Drowning in my fears
Choking on my words
And wiping at my tears.

"Hello? Come back, don't leave!
There's much I need to say!
I'll never get to say it
If you forever go away."

I speak back to the night
"Forgive me, I'm sorry I was violent."
Waiting for his voice again
Yet tonight all is silent.

JEFFREY, FEBRUARY 1997

I can't believe he's there. I try not to think that he's there. When he calls me, I try to think that he's at home somewhere or somewhere else. That's what I try to think because there's no explanation for him to be there. Because I know how my little brother—that kid would give you the shirt off his back. I remember times walking home from school and it'd be freezing snow, stuff coming down. Just horrible. Stuff nobody would take their coats off in and he'd take his coat off and give it to my little sister. And, if I was cold, he'd take his shirt off and give it to me. You can't tell me that's a killer. You can't tell me. And there is no way that anybody in this world will ever convince me. Ever. And I know my little brother better than anybody else out there. I slept with this kid for fourteen years of my life. I slept with him in the same bed. We talked about things at night. There was nothing that we didn't talk about. We knew every—each other inside and out. . . . I mean, I don't think that he really knew what he was doing or that he was even there. It must've been like a dream to him. I've tried to put myself in his situation. I've tried to put myself there. 'Cause he's told me the story of what happened, and I'm putting myself in his shoes, where he's going, and he couldn't have been there.

JOHN, AUGUST 1996

From the waters of the womb, to the arms of the caregivers, to the walls of the family home, when the shelters in which we harbor our children are inadequate or destructive, the final shelter our society provides will often be the cement walls of a prison cell. The course of this journey begins with the brain, which is shaping itself in response to the environment from long before birth. Graphic imaging techniques for exploring the frontier encased in our skulls have provided incontrovertible evidence of that which ancient wisdom has told us for centuries: The baby is the father of the man.

This understanding is at the core of a quiet revolution, a revolution as profound as the industrial and technological revolutions that have paved the way. We are now able to turn this advanced technology back on ourselves to further illumine the most complex system of all, that which lies between our ears. The revolution currently taking place is our species' own understanding of ourselves. The baby emerges as the genesis of this understanding.

The strength and the vulnerability of the human brain lie in its ability to shape itself to enable a particular human being to survive its environment. Our experiences, especially our earliest experiences, become biologically rooted in our brain structure and chemistry from the time of our gestation and most profoundly in the first months of life. This knowledge, corroborated by converging lines of research from diverse fields, is nothing short of a revolution in our thinking about brain development, about behavior, and about babies. When we begin to understand that what is happening to us emotionally, socially, and intellectually in our environments is actually being reflected in our physical organism through the brain, we begin to look at many things differently: disease, therapy, education, television, and—most fundamentally—the experiences we allow our children to absorb from the beginning.

Our challenge is to move this information into the cultural mainstream, to create a critical mass of people who know and who care—who will over time enable this information to move from understanding to practice. We are a long way from that goal. Prevention, as opposed to the late-stage treatment of violent behavior, or of any problem, is a difficult concept to sell. In an article called "Treating Violence as an Epidemic," Jane Stevens reflects:

> In fact, resistance to public-health initiatives dates from 1854, when British physician John Snow tried to convince London residents that they could avoid cholera by drinking clean water. During that summer, one of the hottest on record, Snow tramped through the city's steamy, fetid streets to tally some of the hundreds of daily deaths resulting from the devastating plague, and to take copious notes on the habits, homes and recent travels of the dying.

After months of work, he noticed that outbreaks were clustered in areas supplied by a certain water company.

In those days, several companies distributed water in London, some through pipes to homes or to wells from which neighborhoods drew their water. By tracking the water from a well at the Broad Street pump, Snow discovered that people who drank water from it were dying. Still, officials refused to believe his theory that cholera was spread by water. The medical community proposed that bad air or dust spread the disease, but most people believed cholera was something that infected people who were poor and led unkempt lives. More church was the answer.

Snow knew he was right and watched in frustration as people continued to die. One day, out of sheer desperation, he ripped the handle off the Broad Street pump. The effect was nearly immediate. Fewer people in that part of London came down with cholera. Snow, never credited while alive for his work associating the disease with its risk factors, is generally regarded as the father of epidemiology. Today, in the world of public health, "ripping the handle off the Broad Street pump" has become the metaphor for taking action.[1]

When it comes to preventing violence in our nation, there are significant barriers to "ripping the handle off the Broad Street pump." The most profound of these may be deeply personal. In order to wrap one's mind around the reality of the negative, often appalling, conditions affecting increasing numbers of children, we face at least three potential obstacles. The first of these may be grief, anger, or sadness from personal childhood experiences: the feelings evoked of our own pain as children, especially if we have been neglected, abused, or experienced losses very early. It may be hard to put ourselves in a position where we open old wounds and reexperience the pain of early trauma. Many of us will immediately recoil at mention of the topic; others of us, upon further exploration, may choose to distance ourselves or insulate ourselves because it hurts too much to continue.

A second obstacle, related to but not the same as the first, is grief or sadness, not at our own childhood memories, but at those we have created for our own children, most often out of ignorance or lack of opportunity. Steeping oneself in the research summarized in this book holds up a mirror to many of us that produces pain and regret. Who we may have been—or are—for our own children almost always falls short of our hopes and illusions; recognition of ourselves in this material is painful whether as a parent or a child.

A third barrier to acting on this information is to feel overwhelmed by the depth and breadth of the problem. The complexity of under-lying factors together with the realization of how many children are affected results in many of us feeling there is too little we can do to make a difference. These feelings are discomforting, and we think that the only way we can protect ourselves from despair is to turn away. For many of us this may work; we read, we become uncomfortable, we choose to distract ourselves and forget. But for those unable to forget, there are other courses of action that may actually help to heal a source of old pain—and that may replace a sense of impotence with great satisfaction.

Researchers and popular advocates like T. Berry Brazelton and Penelope Leach are themselves frustrated by the chasm that exists between what they know and what they are able to make happen. Dr. Brazelton, who has fought a long battle for social policy change, is encouraged by the recent shift of major corporations toward more "family-centered" policies such as flexible time and on-site child care. Nonetheless, as a veteran of federal and state wars waged against the passage of early preventive practices, he says there are three major biases that stand in the way of Americans supporting family-centered legislation:

> One bias is that families ought to be self-sufficient and, if they're
> not, they'd better pay a price for it. Another is that women ought to
> be home with their kids and, if they are not, why everybody's going
> to suffer, and the third bias is that we don't like failure or lack of

success so we're not really going to back up people who aren't successful. These biases operate because they're unconscious. If they are brought up to the surface, then I don't think people would stand for them.[2]

Dr. Penelope Leach has written a courageous book, *Children First*, which calls for the reformation of social policies to support what we know about children's developmental needs. She is concerned about our inability to shift our thinking about children from a historical model, which assumes that most children are surrounded by intact families and extended family support, to a recognition that a growing percentage have neither.

We still have a sense that children belong to parents. That what happens to children is *only* parents' business. It's very easy to get people whipped up about intervention—by the authorities, by the state—when a child dies. Certainly by social services or whatever. With much of this I'm in sympathy, don't get me wrong. But I do think one of the big changes is that parents, particularly women on their own, are more without support than they have ever been in this journey of maternity. And we are counting children as the private business of institutions that in many cases simply don't exist. In a way, it's a kind of nostalgia which keeps exercising us, which says that this is the way it ought to be. Only this is the way it isn't.

We are living at the first time and place in history when having a child is actually a disadvantage. . . . Children don't just cost parents money. It isn't just that parents have to work the same hours and earn the same money as everyone else, but they also have to spread that time and money over extra people. It's also that it costs parents most of the values that this society holds. Children cost us independence. They cost us gender equality, because that begins to crumble when there is a child on the way. It costs us sexual freedom, because who can keep that going while raising a family. Having a child runs contrary to pretty well everything that people value in our society.

What we have to do is make this vital job not so reliant on kids being an emotional payback. It's our job to nurture them, not the other way around. Parenting is so difficult that children have to bring tremendous emotional rewards for the whole parenting business to balance out. I think that's one of the difficulties. We have very small families, very often single children. And it's up to those children to kind of pay their parents back for all these lost opportunities. . . . We really are asking for something that is close to impossible of today's parents. So no wonder we're getting some pretty close to impossible children coming out of it.[3]

Without exception, experts who are leading the charge for policy change speak of the lag between economic changes and our child care practices. Matthew Melmed, executive director of Zero to Three, which links and trains professionals in earliest development, says that it is hard for us to understand this from the perspective of babies:

The whole world has changed around us in terms of workforce requirements, mothers and fathers in the workforce, divorce, and family makeup. The whole sort of social and economic fabric has changed dramatically in the last thirty to forty years. But the needs of babies haven't.[4]

According to some, fundamental cultural values may underlie this lag. As Dr. Gerald Patterson, director of Oregon's Social Learning Center, says:

It seems to me that in the last decade or two our society has been shifting in very small steps so that it's difficult to label a trajectory. Less and less emphasis is on being good parents and a greater and greater emphasis is on being consumers. I don't mean our society is doing that in any blatant sense. It's very subtly done and it's not the outcome of a conspiracy, of course. It's just economic machinery moving on kind of an international scale in such a way to keep your family going. One person working really isn't enough. Both parents have to work. Otherwise, you're going to be downwardly mobile, so you're not living as well as your parents did.

And the effect of both parents working is that there's more and more large chunks of time for adolescents in our society when they're not under adult supervision. The supervision or the mechanisms that are running those situations are driven by other kids. A lot of the contacts that kids are having as adolescents include contacts with adolescents who are mildly out of control. And some of them not so mildly. The new studies in sociology are showing that the amount of unsupervised time correlates very nicely with how delinquent our kids are. What I'm saying is that economic forces of our society have been moving for some time now so that parents are giving up more and more of their investment in supervising their own kids.[5]

Dr. Charles Golden, a psychologist at Nova Southeastern University in Florida, agrees with Patterson:

> We let children free. It used to be that if you were a child or an adolescent, you were watched by other people. There were others around either in the community or in the home or extended family that watched the child so that the child had chances to do things, but not make really big mistakes. But as our society has become more mobile, as we've moved away from the extended family—my mother, for instance, lives in California three thousand miles away. She can't look at my children. She can't be there to help them. Thirty percent of the people who live here move out every year. So you don't know who's around.[6]

Children left "free" to their own supervision as adolescents too often began as babies whose lives started the same way. Dr. Kathryn

Barnard at the University of Washington points to the fact that this "freedom" characterizes many young lives long before they begin:

> We have to look at the staggering statistics. I think something like 40 percent of babies in our country are unintended, and a great many of these are unwanted. And if you look at a high-risk group like poverty, it jumps to 60 percent to 70 percent of the babies being unintended. As Americans, our society was founded on principles of religious freedom. And we are very much aligned with the idea that freedom and independence are important. But we carry this to the extent that we feel strongly about families and parents having the right to treat or parent their child any way they wish.
>
> I think we have reached the limit of how free and independent we can be. To be responsible citizens we have to understand that how people raise their children is not just a matter for that family but for all of society—and we have to accept some responsibility as a society for how children are raised. We have to deal with this resistance that we have, that children are only the responsibility of their parents, period. And we have to ask communities and individuals in communities to accept the collective need that exists to support parents in their caregiving.[7]

In sizing up the effects of our current cultural attitudes concerning our youngest citizens, Dr. Craig Ramey of the University of Alabama says:

> We are seeing the developing realization accompanied by hard data from multiple sources of the power of early experience to shape brain and behavioral development and the apparent inability to totally rectify long-term early exposure to really poor-quality experiences. I don't want to convey that it's impossible to do it, but the task is much, much, much more difficult and expensive than insuring that we get it right the first time.

I am generally optimistic by nature. But what we have available is a solid, well-established knowledge base from a variety of sources to suggest that we ought to be betting on these early experiences as having measurable and lasting effects. It's a moral issue for our society —that we don't feel compelled to act upon it. It's quite damning for the U.S. by contrast to other developed countries like Japan.

We are de facto writing off children neglected, abused and exposed to devastating environments. It's very peculiar. Our constitution does not say all people, except children, have rights. Why is it that we feel we can tolerate these gross injustices to children who have no ability to fend for themselves? It's every bit as significant a debate as Roe vs. Wade.[8]

In spite of major technological advances, which have resulted in improvements in children's overall mortality, there are few child-focused professionals who believe that the overall quality of children's mental health is improving. It appears quite the opposite—that more children are angry, unmotivated, bored, without purpose and direction than ever before in world history.

The Children's Defense Fund data book for 1997 lists the United States as first in defense spending but eighteenth—the worst of all industrialized nations—in the percentage of children below the poverty level. We are first in military technology and military exports but twelfth in mathematics achievement and seventh in science achievement of thirteen year olds among fifteen industrialized nations, as mentioned previously. While we are the top producers of health technology, we are eighteenth in infant mortality and nineteenth in the percentage of our babies born at low birth weights. Our rates of incarceration and child abuse are unparalleled in the Western world.

Several experts believe that unless these trends are reversed, our future as a nation is in peril. In his treatment of severely abused children, Bruce Perry sees daily evidence of the unraveling of our nation's social fabric. He views the increase in murderous violence by children as a direct result of the diminishment of these children's higher cortical capacities through abuse and neglect. Testimony to the process he calls "devolution," Perry warns that as more and more children are exposed to neglect and abuse, not only are individuals being limited, but society is also cumulatively affected over time by this loss.

In looking at the social implications of our widespread failure to tend adequately to our babies, Ramey says:

> We have outlived the cowboy myth. . . . Civilizations in fact do rise and fall. The American experience doesn't share that cycle yet. We still haven't experienced our Nazism, our Bosnia, or whatever point of reference you might pick. I am struck by how quickly civilizations now come apart. In the early 1980s no one would have predicted that the Soviet Union or Yugoslavia would have come apart so quickly. . . . The idea that the veneer of civilization in very old societies is pretty damn thin has certainly been born out in the last decade. The degree to which people can become cruel, almost inhuman, is breathtaking.[9]

THROUGH A GLASS DARKLY

Current efforts to prevent violence typically consist of generating lists of effective programs and disseminating information on them in an effort to rally public support program by program, a strategy that has proved to be ineffective in the political arena. Even the best of these programs and the sponsors of the most enlightened policies will admit that they are always fighting for their lives. Primary prevention programs all struggle for adequate funds to continue each year. The author of *Within Our Reach: Breaking the Cycle of Disadvantage,* Dr. Lisbeth Schorr, said in a policy speech at Harvard's Kennedy School of Government in the spring of 1993, that just five years after the book was published, over 50 percent of the model programs she had put forward were defunct, primarily due to lack of funding.[10] Policies appear to be similarly vulnerable. Political promises come and go. The Children's Defense Fund has a series of posters that succinctly sums up the fate of babies in the political process. One poster features a photograph of a baby crawling away from the camera. A large target is painted across its diapered bottom. The copy reads: "When it comes to cutting budgets they always go for the easiest target first." Garnering the committed political support necessary to turn the tide for even one generation of our children continues to elude us.

Albert Einstein noted that, "The world that we have made as a result of the level of thinking we have done thus far creates problems that we cannot solve at the same level at which we created them." We know that things are getting worse for our children. Overwhelmed, we still wait for top-down solutions—decisions from the president, or other elected officials, or the heads of agencies like the surgeon general—which we hope will make a difference. But the problems affecting our children, including violence, are getting worse. Top-down solutions from government will not soon be forthcoming. A trite but true fact is that babies don't vote. Until we have an informed public who insist on change and empower politicians accordingly, our children will continue to suffer. Change will come from the bottom up, from everyday people who understand that violence and the entire menu of serious issues affecting us all—hunger, war, deforestation, overpopulation, to name but a few—rely for their management and solutions on raising healthy children who will as adults care and be able to think through complex problems. The hand that rocks the cradle shapes these outcomes. The voice of greatest urgency regarding the issue of violence and children is perhaps that of Dr. Bruce Perry:

> No set of intervention strategies will solve these transgenerational problems. In order to solve the problem of violence, *we need to transform our culture.* We need to change our child-rearing practices, we need to change the malignant and destructive view that children are the property of their biological parents. Human beings evolved not as individuals, but as communities. Despite Western conceptuali-

zations, the smallest functional biological unit of humankind is not the individual—it is the clan. No individual, no single parent-child dyad, no nuclear family could survive alone. We survived and evolved as clans, interdependent—socially, emotionally, and biologically. . . . It is in the nature of humankind to be violent, but it may not be *the* nature of human kind. Without major transformation of our culture, without putting action behind our "love" of children, we may never learn the truth.[11]

The key to the cultural transformation Dr. Perry calls for may in fact be hiding not in the file drawers of policy makers or even in the reports of well-evaluated programs. The core lies much closer to our hearts and hands than we may have believed. As is true with our search for the roots of violence, the understanding we need is found in the nursery. The baby, the unpretentious, naked beginning of human development, embodies processes essential to our continuing evolution.

Dr. Ed Tronick, who studies maternal depression and its effects on children's development, asked about the larger social implications of his work, speaks of the profound importance of the lifelong lessons we each learn in the nursery:

> Humans are designed for communication and sharing meanings. All processes, be they cognitive or emotional processes, are a joint creation of two people and are dependent on social exchange. So the infant comes into the world designed to participate and to appropriate the meaning systems of adults from the caregiver's constant contact. Without this kind of exchange, development goes awry. The emotional exchanges between infants and caregivers function for the brain the way we think of nutrients functioning for the body. Emotional input is the nutrient for structuring the brain, for structuring the child. This emotional communication is the defining characteristic of our species.[12]

HUSH, LITTLE BABY

Imagine for a moment being little—smaller than you can consciously remember being. Imagine you are very new to life, say about three months old. You've been asleep and you are just waking up, lying on a mattress in a crib. You open your eyes and see your short little arms and legs, new little fingers and toes that still seem to have a mind of their own. You have a big heavy head and a short neck, a big round tummy that's feeling very empty. As you come awake, you feel that wet thing around your middle that is beginning to feel heavy and cold. Agitated, you begin to wiggle, move your arms, kick your feet, and you make a few soft sounds. Your eyes feel itchy, and you are getting this feeling in your tummy that you don't like. You begin to rub your eyes and make a few more sounds. To your surprise you hear a loud cry coming out of your mouth and your face is wet and your eyes begin to feel worse. Now you are crying and kicking and breathing hard. But no one comes. You look to see, but no one comes. And you are crying harder and your middle is hurting now with the air you've swallowed and you are hot and wet and screaming. Still no one comes. And the room is still and there's nothing there but the sheet and the slats of your crib. You are scared and your stomach hurts and you are alone. Finally, you hear footsteps. A cold nipple is stuck in your mouth and you see the blurred back of someone leaving and you are sucking and turning to see who is walking away, and the bottle falls over. And your mouth is empty, your eyes are hot and wet, your stomach still hurts. You are screaming for someone to help. You hear footsteps and see the arms sweep down and the hand you hope is reaching for you sticks the nipple in again, but hard so that it hurts and you choke. The footsteps go away and you cry out. Your mouth loses the nipple and your arms are beating and your feet kick the mattress. You are hungry and angry and scared. You are screaming to an empty room.

Your need for food and attention followed by this response or a variation of it happens over and over again several times a day, at least thirty times in the course of a week. Sometimes the wet thing around your middle comes off. Sometimes you are picked up. But the faces are not happy when they see you and the voices are often loud and angry. You spend a lot of time here alone playing with your hands and the sheet, kicking your legs, feeling your body, memorizing the pattern of the crib bars, the blinds, and the wallpaper.

If you are this baby, you will—like all babies—continue to eat, sleep, and, with relatively rare exceptions, grow. Some handling, essential formula, warmth, basic diaper changing is enough for survival. But in the recesses of your brain, connections you were born primed to make are left to wither before you have ever been able to sit up. You cannot seem to make things happen when you need something. No matter what you do no one comes to comfort you and tell you softly that everything is okay. The focused loving attention of the powerful beings in your world is not what you know. You have no reason to believe that comfort and safety will come when you signal distress. The circuitry in your brain that is receptive to these interactions may be impaired or never built at all. And this circuitry connects with all the rest of your body.

Now imagine being another baby waking up, like the first, from a long nap on a mattress in a crib. You open your eyes and feel your body and make a few soft sounds as you begin to look around the room. Familiar faces of colorful smiling nursery characters capture your attention for a few minutes as you focus on the sound of your own voice. Within a few minutes, you hear rhythmic footsteps and a voice you know that sounds happy and soothing. Arms reach down and scoop you up over the shoulder that feels and smells just right. You rub your nose and eyes against a soft neck and feel the pats and cuddles that go with that familiar voice. Soon you are lying down looking into eyes that see only you. That wet thing around your middle goes away and is replaced with something warm and dry. And now you are lying back in those arms with a warm nipple in your mouth, and there is the best face of all singing a sound you love to listen to. You are rocking and your tummy is relaxing with warm milk and you are right with the world.

The experiences of each baby are reflected in the matter being built in their brains and ultimately in the rest of their bodies. But after months of these very different introductions to life, these babies—like their individual experiences—will have little resemblance to each other. In addition to structural differences, the biochemistry in one organism is being set for fear, for sadness, for anger—being overrun by strong negative feelings experienced with little or no ability to modulate their effects. The second infant is learning trust, connection, pleasure, and contentment; the ability to regulate emotions is being learned interactively with another person, and the normal curiosity of the child to learn about the world is emerging inside expectations of confidence in self and others. Here is the foundation for stemming increasing violence and for our future on the planet.

Beyond our understanding of violence, babyhood is central to our understanding of our own needs at their most essential. This is the place we all came from—naked, vulnerable, innocent, hopeful, curious, and dependent for our lives on our ability to connect with another. In spite of elaborate defenses we have wrapped around ourselves to appear otherwise, we still each carry this essence.

While none of us would advocate for endlessly maintaining the dependency and vulnerability of babyhood, there are processes key to our first stages of life that remain essential to our survival, not just as individuals but as a society. This has been an unpopular concept in Western thinking, particularly in America, which began as an adolescent colony breaking from its European parents. From its first battles to establish separation, America has valued self-reliance, independence, and toughness.

But now our preeminence as a world power may in fact be dependent on new ideals and new myths. While our idealization of the rugged individualist and the rags-to-riches success stories may have served us while we established autonomy in our nation's first two centuries, these ideals without balance may actually be our undoing. It appears that while we have put great effort toward protecting ourselves from external dangers, the greater threat is from internal deterioration of the soft tissue at our nation's core.

BABY FACE

At the 1995 annual meeting of the Association for Pre- and Perinatal Psychology and Health, Dr. David Chamberlain in a keynote address pointed out that babies—if we are paying attention—show us very graphically what is happening to them. As a culture Americans don't want this information, at least not on a personal level. We insulate ourselves from this knowledge. What our babies need—rich and poor babies—is costly and frequently inconvenient in terms of our time and pleasure, to say nothing of money. Babies want one person close all the time. They want to eat around the clock continually. They want us there with them when they wake up, including numerous times in the night. They want to be the center of our world.

Dr. James McKenna, a world expert on sudden infant death syndrome, says that we Americans "have a tendency to treat babies as what we want them to become as opposed to who they actually are." He notes that the caregiving patterns favored by cultures change much more quickly than babies' biology. Speaking in San Diego on February 14, 1997 to an audience of psychotherapists, he entitled his talk "The Society Which Mistook Its Children for Bats." He began by showing a slide that illustrated the number of years humans have lived on the planet. He directed his laser pointer to a green line representing 3.6 million years. He said:

> This is the time when man became upright-walking humanoids, culture-bearing, tool-using homo sapiens and/or homo erectus. During this period, our emotional substrats, our parenting systems, our sexual behavior, our psychological dispositions were formulated and were designed and sculpted by natural selection.

He then directed his pointer to a tiny red dot that looked like a period at the end of the green line and said:

> This little red dot represents the industrial revolution, at which time many things changed historically—our conceptions of what behavior is appropriate. Even going back to the agricultural revolution, which is about ten thousand years ago in terms of significant evolutionary change, there hasn't been any at all. We're basically giving birth to stone age babies who are trying to live in the space age world. And there's enormous discrepancy in those two types of worlds. The question I ask is: Is there both a physiological and a psychological consequence when we get too far from the context within which the baby's body was designed and the types of expectations which that baby actually has?

McKenna makes an extraordinarily clear case for rethinking basic child care practices that many of us take for granted, particularly the unquestioned practice of isolating infants in their own beds for sleep. By comparison to other primates, the human baby has a much longer period of dependency on the mother. For the most essential physiological processes the baby's central nervous system remains immature for several months, relying on closeness to the mother's body to set its basic rhythms, including eating, states of sleep, and alertness. This makes constant access to a caregiver and the quality of that access key to the early programming of the baby. "Selecting a pattern of social care for a baby is essentially selecting a pattern of physiological regulation for the baby. They're one and the same thing. There is no distinction." Understanding this fundamental biological programming in infants is crucial to reducing sudden infant death, which McKenna sees as a by-product of the Western world's unique cultural experiment of isolating sleeping infants.

McKenna's videotaped segments of mothers and infants sleeping together show that when the mother moves in her sleep, the baby also moves, their patterns of arousal remaining reciprocal even while asleep. Movements and sounds by one generate movements and sounds by the other. These sequential exchanges, he says, account for the maintenance of the baby in relatively lighter states of sleep that prevent the infant's descent into what he calls stage-five sleep, which can be lethal (SIDS).

Isolating infants for sleep is a very expensive consequence of prioritizing parents' independence and autonomy over the basic biological expectations of the infant. The baby's physiology is unprepared for this cultural reversal. One consequence of this and other practices that confuse "parental best interest" with that of the baby is that the United States has one of the highest rates of mortality for children under age one year of all industrialized nations in the world.[14]

Besides being a strong voice for breastfeeding and for babies sleeping with their parents, McKenna is an advocate for child care practices that are based on an informed understanding of infant biological and emotional needs. "The bottom line is that we have to at least begin to understand these things in terms of the infant and *then* see what we can do about it in terms of the culture."

Like Dr. David Chamberlain, McKenna implores us to begin with babies and the people who nurture them, parents, and everyone. And if he is right in his assertion that babies' biological and emotional needs haven't changed in the short time since the industrial revolution—then it would be reasonable to conclude that adult biological and emotional needs haven't changed either. But our culture, fueled by huge changes in technology and economics, drives us forward at such speed that we adults can hardly keep pace—and some crucial needs of babies and their caregivers may have unwittingly been left alongside the road.

The current economic pressures of our culture are often in direct conflict with essential needs for adults—as well as for babies. Time to "smell the roses," including quiet time with the people we love, is essential to emotional renewal for all of us—and it is often lost in competing pressures for time. The reality is that in spite of great technological advances and appreciable gains in science, health, and communications, most of us still hunger for missing elements of stable

human emotional connections and the belief that sanity and rationality will prevail in our communities. Many are choosing to simplify
their lives by cutting back on material expectations and sacrificing the
"rat race" for time at home with young children—difficult decisions
and seldom without stressors of their own.

Perhaps we *need* a little child to lead us. Perhaps our real challenge is to hold the face and the needs of the baby like a template
over all of the decisions we make. If we superimposed the face and
the needs of the baby over our daily decisions, what would we have
to do differently? What would it mean for our families—immediate
family or extended family? What would it mean for our relationships
with families around us, in the neighborhood, church, or at the next
farm down the road? What would our schools or our stores or banks
or religious institutions have to do differently? What would it mean
for day care centers, for government, for social services, or health care?
If every time we voted or considered a political candidate, we held
the face and needs of a baby at the forefront of our expectations, might
we see a shift in policies? What if we shopped only where stores were
thoughtfully organized and adequate facilities were provided for
people with babies? What if we demanded that babies' emotional, as
well as physical, needs be honored in designing day care, in developing employee benefits, in designing flexible work schedules? What
if public education systems saw each baby at birth as a prospective
student and worked with parents to prepare them for school by
providing a strong emotional and cognitive foundation? Building
communities around babies rather than fitting babies in around the
edges of communities—even if they got only the consideration that
puppies receive in Portland, Oregon—would go a long way toward
the prevention of violence.

"Tomorrow's violent criminals still lie in their cribs today. To prevent one in twenty of today's babies from exchanging the slats of their
cribs for prison bars in their adult lives, babies must be in the forefront of our concern. The focus of political, social, religious, and educational policies and practices." For those who insist that babies are

the private responsibility of their own families—that we are each responsible only for our own—remind them of what Marian Wright Edleman, founder of the Children's Defense Fund, has said, "The future which we hold in trust for our own children will be directly shaped by our fairness to other people's children." The myth of self-reliance—as any baby clearly demonstrates—is just that. A value on self-reliance and independence carried to the point of infant mortality, child abuse, school failure, juvenile delinquency, and adult incarceration is actually a fast course toward self-destruction.

The baby—the image of vulnerability and guilelessness—does in fact bring us back to the best in ourselves. If we were really to focus on the baby as a central concern in our culture, we might recognize that the death of the spirit of the baby in an adult threatens rather than strengthens our society.

NURTURING THE NURTURERS

In spite of our preoccupation with independence, autonomy, and self-reliance, we are born dependent on others, and we continue to need others emotionally at every stage of development. The capacity to maintain our baby desire to communicate who we are emotionally and to read this in other people is essential for healthy adult functioning with families, at school, at work, and at play. Emotional connections between individuals are the linchpin of any community's ability to maintain prosocial behavior, and the growing absence of those connections is reflected in social incompetence, estrangement, mental illness, and violence.

Ironically, this understanding of the emotional foundation for learning, playing, and socializing currently takes a backseat to cognitive approaches to preparing young children for school and life. There is tremendous anxiety among many parents about educating their babies. With the growing understanding of baby brain development have come flash cards and music, math, and reading programs that are being promoted as keys to a baby's success. And while this may be beneficial if certain other pieces are in place, such efforts may also miss the intended mark. The story of David Helfgott portrayed in the award-winning movie *Shine* illustrates the cost of attending lopsidedly to cognitive stimulation without consideration of the emotional foundation. As the movie tells the tale, David's well-meaning but rigidly perfectionistic and domineering father was determined that David would be a successful pianist. Beginning when David was a toddler, his father's efforts were targeted only at David's relationship with the piano. Even though David's musical skills eventually brought him national recognition, his early emotional experiences have reverberated throughout his life and led to his nervous breakdown and ongoing mental problems. His skills, without an adequate sense of self and how to relate to others, were built on sand. Not only his career—but his entire life—has been affected by the lack of sensitive attention to the baby needs in David. To watch him perform at the piano today is to witness the ghost of the baby he once was.

With very different circumstances shaping his life, and behind bars rather than at a piano, is the ghost of the baby who was Jeffrey. His crime, for which he should be held responsible, was nevertheless committed by a person whose emotional competence, judgment, and behavior were substantially and directly affected by his earliest experiences. This offers no excuse for his behavior. However, our prisons are overflowing with the ghosts of babies lost to unseen and often unintended crimes in their cradles. The "feeling" circuitry responsible for trusting, connecting, and empathizing in most violent criminals has been damaged. The "thinking" circuitry responsible for focused attention and complex problem-solving has also typically been impaired. Many, if not most, of these brain-reflected and experience-caused problems may at least be partially reparable through intensive therapy and education. But the cost—to the offenders, their victims, and society—is enormous. With few or none of these services in place, prisons remain a top growth industry in our nation. This is our present reality. The *Titanic* is on its course.

But accompanying the new information on the brain and its development comes a new opportunity to alter this course. If healthy emotional and cognitive development—or its antithesis—is substantially rooted in our experiences during the first months of life, then the adults who guide these experiences merit society's attention. The unfolding research on the brain is unequivocal testimony to the fact that the future of any community literally rests on the laps of those who nurture its youngest members.

It is this group—the nurturers of our children, be they parents, extended family, friends or paid caregivers—who are the key to preventing violence. As they shape our future, they need the tools: the skills, information, and social valuing to adequately do the job. When those caring for children are themselves healthy, have adequate financial and emotional support and are equipped with guidance around what to expect of children, how to discipline constructively and how to manage anger and stress, the children in their care are the beneficiaries, but when such needs are poorly met, it is the children who inevitably absorb the consequences.

If Rachel Carson's image of a spring without songbirds produced enough concern in the 1960s to generate widespread efforts to reduce the poisoning of the natural environment, then perhaps there is hope in the 1990s for preventing the poisoning of the cradle of human community. It is the sweetness and the vulnerability, the curiosity and the playfulness, the hopefulness and the innocence, the trust and the arms outreached purely to embrace or to help that is at stake in our times. We face not only the possibility of a spring without songbirds, but a future without people who care or notice the difference.

A RITUAL TO READ TO EACH OTHER

If you don't know the kind of person I am
and I don't know the kind of person you are
a pattern that others made may prevail in the world
and following the wrong god home we may miss our star.

For there is many a small betrayal in the mind
a shrug that lets the fragile sequence break
sending with shouts the horrible errors of childhood
storming out to play through the broken dike.

And as elephants parade holding each elephant's tail
but if one wanders through the circus won't find the park,
I call it cruel and maybe the root of all cruelty
to know what occurs but not recognize the fact.

And so I appeal to a voice, to something shadowy
a remote important region in all who talk:
though we could fool each other, we should consider—
lest the parade of our mutual life get lost in the dark.

For it is important that awake people be awake,
or a breaking line may discourage them back to sleep,
the signals we give—yes, no, or maybe—
should be clear; the darkness around us is deep.

—William Stafford

Appendix A

Factors Associated with Violent Behavior that can be Modified or Prevented by Early Intervention

Several factors may be related to others in another category. None are in and of themselves considered causal. Most biological factors have been researched in interaction with social factors. For example, delivery complications and maternal rejection at one year have been linked to later violent behavior.

BIOLOGICAL FACTORS

Prenatal (zero to seven months' gestation)
- Teratogens (e.g., drugs, alcohol, nicotine)
- Malnutrition
- Genetic factors
- Chronic maternal stress (including not wanting baby)
- Minor physical anomalies

Perinatal (seven months' gestation to one month after birth)
- Delivery complications, birth trauma, head injury
- Prematurity
- Low birth weight

Postnatal (one month to twenty-four months)
- Accidents, head injuries
- Nutritional deficiencies

GENERAL FACTORS

- Low verbal IQ
- Attention-deficit/hyperactivity disorder
- Post-traumatic stress
- Exposure to toxins (e.g., lead)

FAMILIAL FACTORS

- Parental mental illness
- Criminal father
- Low maternal IQ
- Maternal rejection
- Multiple breaks in caregivers; lack of consistent caregiver in early life
- Maternal depression
- Parental substance abuse
- Child abuse
- Parental discord
- Child neglect
- Ineffective discipline

LARGER ENVIRONMENTAL FACTORS

- Living below community economic norm
- Modeling of violent solutions to problems by key models
- Modeling of weapon use in community; access to weapons
- Unavailability of involved adult who teaches values and values child
- Modeling of alcohol, drug use to deal with problems
- Violence in entertainment: television, video games, movies, music, and toys

Note: Several factors may be related to others in another category. None are in and of themselves considered causal. Most biological factors have been researched in interaction with others from the social continuum, for example, delivery complications and maternal rejection at one year have been linked to later violent behavior.

Appendix B

Myths about the Human Brain

- We can fix any damage done early with love and attention later.
- We aren't that affected by experiences we had as tiny babies because we didn't have language yet, and we can't remember things that happened before we could talk.
- How we develop is mostly determined by the environment.
- How we develop is mostly determined by genetics.

Appendix C

Behavioral Effects Following Prenatal Drug Exposure

EFFECT	ALCOHOL	COCAINE	HEROIN	NICOTINE
Hyperactivity	✓	✓	✓	✓
Attention Deficits	✓	✓	✓	✓
Aggressiveness	✓		✓	
Impulsivity	✓	✓	✓	✓
Cognitive Delays/ Learning Difficulties	✓		✓	✓
Impaired Sleep	✓			
Feeding Difficulties	✓	✓		
Irritability	✓	✓		
Fine and/or Motor Impairment or Delay	✓			
Impaired Ability to Adjust to New Stimuli or Situations	✓	✓	✓	
Retardation	✓			
Physical/Facial Deformities	✓			

Appendix D

The Primary Prevention of Violence:
A Continuum of Programs

• **Pre-Parenting Training in Schools:** These classes have most often focused on high school students and have been elective rather than required courses, typically credited in home economics. The best pre-parent training approaches begin in grade school with decision-making and problem-solving skills. By preadolescence (fifth to sixth grade) children learn anger management, and basic communication skills, including how to put angry or sad feelings into words and how to express these difficult emotions constructively. The opportunity for older children to work with preschoolers in a "practicum" (e.g., day care setting) is an essential component of a strong program to prepare young people for the demands of parenting. Example:

NATIONAL ORGANIZATION ADOLESCENT PARENTING AND
PREGNANCY PREVENTION
1319 F. Street NW, Suite 4Y
Washington, DC 20004
(202) 783-5770

• **Comprehensive Pregnancy Prevention:** In contrast to programs primarily focused on contraception, comprehensive approaches to pregnancy prevention to address the underlying factors that often lead teens to risk taking includes tutoring programs, mental health counseling, college and trade preparation, and employment. An example of such a program is:

CHILDREN'S AID SOCIETY NATIONAL TRAINING CENTER
Michael Carrera
350 E. 88th, 3rd Floor
New York, NY, 10128
(212) 876–9716

• **Comprehensive Prenatal Health Care:** These programs include outreach and incentives to high-risk mothers to involve them. They integrate substance abuse treatment, preparation for parenthood education, and child birth preparation.

HEALTHY START
Gladys Wong, Director
2881 Waimano, Home Road
Pearl City, HI 96782
(808) 453–6020

• **Home Visitation for All Newborns:** In some communities, trained nurses begin as part of the prenatal community health programs to call on high-risk pregnant women in their homes. Equipped with baby clothes, formula, and toys, these interventionists help women stop or curtail smoking, drinking, and drug use. They help with birth plans, teach childbirth preparation, and generally "mother the mothers."[1] Following birth, nurses or trained paraprofessionals meet with women giving birth in hospitals to provide comfort and intervention for mothers and babies who can use some extra help. Feeding and sleep problems can be dealt with before negative patterns become entrenched. Unusual developmental signs can be detected and followed. Signs of substance abuse, domestic violence, or early emotional or physical abuse can be observed and acted upon immediately, referrals made to appropriate help. The strongest of these programs provide home visitors as frequently as once a week for an hour or more, or as often as the mother requests, and may continue through the child's fifth birthday or until a family needing continuing support services enters another wraparound program such as Head Start. Participation in these programs is voluntary and services are made available to all parents—not just those "at risk." An April 1997 report to Congress indicated that little of the $3 billion in grants annually given to states and communities for crime prevention programs (e.g.midnight basketball, drug use prevention in schools, neighborhood watch programs, etc.), actually reduced crime. The study found that programs that work have in common a commitment to a long term approach to fundamentally changing thinking and behavior, rather than just a short term amelioration of or reduction in symptoms. Home visitation was one of only two types of all approaches evaluated that was effective in reducing crime.[2] Examples:

HEALTHY START
Gladys Wong, Director
2881 Waimano Home Road
Pearl City, HI 96782
(808) 453–6020

HOME VISITATION 2000
JoAnn Robinson, Codirector of Research
303 East 17th Avenue, Suite 200
Denver, CO 80203
(303) 861–1715 ext. 254

• **Education for First-Time Parents in Emotional and Behavioral Development:** Many strong programs exist to educate parents, their emphasis ranging from the care of newborns to specific behavior management skills with challenged children (e.g., ADHD). Key to preventing violence are programs which stress the emotional exchanges between parents and children and that focus on normal behavioral and emotional—not just physical—development. How to recognize problems and where to turn for help are critical needs for first-time parents of infants and toddlers. Recently there has been an effort in some states to create tax credits as incentives for parents to attend quality-parent education during pregnancy or through the early years of child rearing. Examples:

PARENTS AS TEACHERS
National Center, Inc.
10176 Corporate Square Drive
St. Louis, MO 63132
(314) 432–4330

AVANCE, INC NATIONAL OFFICE
301 S. Frio St., Suite 380
San Antonio, TX 78207

BIRTH TO THREE
Minalee Saks, Director
3875 Kinkaid, Room 15
Eugene, OR 97405
(541) 454–0471

THE PREVENTIVE OUNCE
Jim Cameron, Executive Director
354 63rd St.
Oakland, CA 94618
(510) 658–8359
www.preventiveoz.org.

MELD
123 N. Third Street, Suite 507
Minneapolis, MN 55401-1664
(612) 332–7563

THE TEMPERAMENT PROGRAM
Barbara Zukin, Director
Center for Human Development, Inc.
1100 K Avenue
LaGrande, OR 97850
(541) 962–8835
www.bzukin@chdinc.org

307

• **Day Care/Preschool Education:** Beginning shortly after birth, excellent alternative care can be an essential source of nurturing for children in homes where parents are unable or unwilling to provide cognitive stimulation and consistent loving emotional, as well as physical, care. Though excellent care is difficult to define and even more difficult to find, there are models that have shown effectiveness in securing children's emotional security as well as cognitive gains.

CIVITAN INTERNATIONAL RESOURCE CENTER
Dr. Craig Ramey
University of Alabama at Birmingham
179 6th Avenue S.
Birmingham, AL 35294
(205) 934–8900

EARLY HEAD START
Rosetta Busby, Director
P.O. Box 6250
Arlington, VA 22206
(703) 979–2400

• **Skill Training for Parents of High-Risk Preschoolers:** A few programs across the country show strong results in helping parents who are concerned about early signs of bullying, aggression, and impulsive behavior in their preschool-aged children. These programs generally work with both school and home, providing consistent rules, rewards, and structure. Examples:

FIRST STEPS
Hill Walker, Codirector
Institute on Violence and Destructive Behavior
College of Education
1265 University of Oregon
Eugene, OR 97403
(541) 346–3591

OREGON SOCIAL LEARNING CENTER
Gerald Patterson, Director
207 E. Fifth Street, Suite 202
Eugene, OR 97401
(541) 485–1136

LANE RELIEF NURSERY
Jean Phelps, Director
1720 W. 25th Street
Eugene, OR 97405
(541) 484–0702

THE PREVENTIVE OUNCE
Jim Cameron, Executive Director
354 63rd St.
Oakland, CA 94618
(510) 658–8359
www.preventiveoz.org.

• **Education for Professionals in Emotional and Behavioral Development:**
Even professionals who work with children, such as pediatricians and psychologists,
typically have not been well trained in children's emotional and behavioral development. Physical and cognitive development have historically been emphasized in
the education of professionals about infant and toddler development. There is a
growing understanding of the importance of providing a healthy emotional foundation for learning. Examples:

TOUCHPOINTS
Ed Tronick
1295 Boylston, Suite 320
Boston, MA 02115
(617) 355–5913

ZERO TO THREE
Matthew Melmud, Director
734 15th Street, Suite 1000
Washington, D.C. 20005
(202) 638–1144

CIVITAS INITIATIVE
Suzanne Muchin, Director
16 East Pearson
Chicago, IL 60611
(312) 915–6484

Appendix E

RESOURCES

FOR DATA ON THE STATUS OF CHILDREN

KIDS COUNT DATA BOOK
The Annie B. Casey Foundation
701 Paul Street
Baltimore, MD 21201
(410) 223–2890

THE FUTURE OF CHILDREN
The David and Lucille Packard Foundation
300 Second Street, Suite 102
Los Altos, CA 94022
(415) 948–3696

THE STATE OF AMERICA'S CHILDREN YEARBOOK
The Children's Defense Fund
25 E Street N.W.
Washington, D.C. 20001
(202) 628–8787

INFORMATION ON PROGRAMS THAT WORK

ANNIE B. CASEY FOUNDATION
701 Paul Street
Baltimore, MD 21201
(410) 223–2890

DAVID AND LUCILLE PACKARD FOUNDATION
300 Second Street, Suite 102
Los Altos, CA 94022
(415) 948-7658

FAMILY WORK INSTITUTE
Ellen Galinsky, Director
330 7th Avenue, 14th Floor
New York, NY 10001
(212) 465-2044

HARRIS FOUNDATION
Phyllis Glink, Program Director
2 N. LaSalle Street
Chicago, IL 60602
(312) 621-0625

HEALTHY START
Gladys Wong, Director
2881 Waimano Home Road
Pearl City, HI 96782
(808) 453-6020

KEMP NATIONAL CENTER FOR PREVENTION
    AND TREATMENT OF CHILD ABUSE
Susan Hiatt, Director
1205 Oneida Street
Denver, CO 80220
(303) 321-3963

NATIONAL COMMITTEE FOR THE PREVENTION OF CHILD ABUSE
Anne Cohn-Donnelly
322 S. Michigan, Suite 1600
Chicago, IL 60604
(312) 663-3520

THE CHILDRENS HEALTH FUND
Irwin Redliner, President
317 E. 64th St.
New York, NY 10021
(212) 535-9400
FAX (212) 535-7488

INFORMATION ON EARLY BRAIN DEVELOPMENT AND COMMUNITY ADVOCACY

BENTON FOUNDATION
Susan Bales
1634 I Street NW, 12th Floor
Washington, DC 20006
(202) 638-5770
http:/www.kidscampaign.org

CARNEGIE CORPORATION
Michael Levine, Program Director
437 Madison Avenue
New York, NY 10022
(212) 371–3200

ZERO TO THREE
Matthew Melmud, Director
734 15th Street, Suite 1000
Washington, DC 20005
(202) 638–1144

INFORMATION ON THE ROLE OF FATHERS IN CHILD DEVELOPMENT

NATIONAL FATHERHOOD
   INITIATIVE
Wade Horn, President
1 Bank Street, Suite 160
Gaithersburg, Md. 20878
(301) 948-0599
www.register.com/father/

AMERICAN COALITION FOR
   FATHERS AND CHILDREN
1718 M.St N.W. Suite 187
Washington, DC 20036
(800) 978-DADS
www.acfc.org/

THE FATHERHOOD PROJECT
Families and Work Institute
307 7th Avenue, Suite 1906
New York, NY 10001
(212) 465–2044
www.fatherhoodproject.org/

THE AMERICAN FATHERS
   COALITION
200 Pennsylvania Ave. N.W. Suite 148
Washington, DC 20006
(202) 328–4377
www.erols.com/afc

THE FATHERS FORUM
Bruce Linton, Founder
1521-A Shattuck Ave. Suite 201
Berkeley, CA 94709
(510) 644–0300
www.parentsplace.com/read-room/fathers/index.htm/

Endnotes

CHAPTER 1

1. *The Oprah Winfrey Show,* "Violent Young Children: Could You Be Their Next Victim?" Part 1, Harpo Productions, Inc., June 28, 1995.
2. Interview with Hill Walker, Institute for Violence and Destructive Behavior, University of Oregon, Eugene, Oregon, February 8, 1996.
3. Bureau of Justice Statistics, "Lifetime Likelihood of Going to State or Federal Prison."
4. Bureau of Justice Statistics, "Crime Data Brief: The Costs of Crimes to Victims."
5. Raspberry, William. *The Oregonian,* September, 13, 1996.
6. Butterfield, "More Blacks in Their 20's Have Trouble with the Law."
7. Raine, *The Psychopathology of Crime;* Mednick; Gabrielli, Jr.; and Hutching; "Genetic Influences in Criminal Convictions."
8. Kotulak, "The Roots of Violence." Some experts also believe that the gene altered by a male's consumption of alcohol may be passed on to his male children. This altered gene may impair the recipient offspring's ability to produce the neuro-chemical serotonin, a condition that predisposes that individual to violent crime, especially if the recipient of the altered gene himself drinks alcohol.
9. Interview with Dr. Allan Schore, January 2, 1997.
10. Lewis, "Neuropsychiatric and Experiential Correlates of Violent Juvenile Delinquency."
11. Taken from videotape in the possession of Dr. Bruce Perry of a speech he gave in Houston.
12. Reported by David Wallechinsky, in *Parade* magazine, April 13, 1997.
13. Carnegie Corporation, *Starting Points,* p. x.

315

14. Premeditated violent behavior, also known as sociopathy or psychopathy, is discussed most fully in chapter 7.
15. Head injury may in rare cases directly result in violent behavior, hence the use of "rarely."

CHAPTER 2

1. The story of Chelsea was originally presented on *Prime Time Live* by Diane Sawyer, aired January 25, 1996, "Your Child's Brain." (Kate Harrington, producer)
2. Kotulak, "The Roots of Violence."
3. Dawson and Fischer, *Human Behavior and the Developing Brain,* pp. 22–23.
4. "High risk children" are defined in Dr. Ramey's studies by the social attributes of the family and the biological condition of the children.
5. Telephone interview with Dr. Craig Ramey, November 4, 1995.
6. Kotulak, "Unlocking the Mind".
7. Ibid.
8. Diane Sawyer, "Your Childs Brain" January 25, 1996.
9. Perry, "Incubated in Terror."
10. Goleman, *Emotional Intelligence,* p. 16.
11. For more in-depth information on Dr. Perry's concept of "traits to states," see chapter 7.
12. The information from Dr. Allan Schore is drawn from his written work cited in the bibliography and from both phone and personal interviews.
13. Interview with Dr. Allan Schore, March 7, 1997.
14. Gladwell, "Damaged."
15. LeDoux, "Emotional Memory Systems in the Brain."
16. Engel, Ruschman, and Harnay, *Parental Influences.*
17. Goldberg, "Babies Are Smarter than You Think."
18. Chamberlain, "The Cognitive Newborn," p. 62.
19. This story and the information on the research is drawn from Ron Kotulak's article, "How Brain's Chemistry Unleashes Aggression," published in the special section, "The Roots of Violence."
20. Ibid.
21. Perry, "Incubated in Terror."
22. Ibid.
23. Kotulak, "The Roots of Violence."

CHAPTER 3

1. Restak, *The Infant Mind,* p. 56.
2. The descriptions of sensual development are in part adapted from Share, *If Someone Speaks It Gets Lighter,* pp. 108–11.

316

3. Verny and Kelly, *The Secret Life of the Unborn Child*.
4. Chamberlain, "The Cognitive Newborn."
5. Interview with Dr. T. Berry Brazelton, February 2, 1997.
6. Verny and Kelly, *The Secret Life of the Unborn Child*.
7. Chamberlain, "What Babies Are Teaching Us About Violence."
8. Verny and Kelly, *Secret Life of the Unborn Child*.
9. Chamberlain, "What Babies Are Teaching Us About Violence."
10. Share, *If Someone Speaks It Gets Lighter*, p. 110.
11. Chamberlain, *"What Babies Are Teaching Us."*
12. Chamberlain, "The Cognitive Newborn."
13. Restak, *The Infant Mind*, p. 37.
14. Frishman, "The Lost Boys," p. 76.
15. Norton, "Toxic Responses."
16. Graham, "Congenital Abnormalities."
17. Restak, *The Infant Mind*, p. 51.
18. Day and Richardson, "Comparative Teratogenicity."
19. Ibid., p. 42.
20. Ibid.
21. Rich and Dean, "A Previously Unexamined Source of Delinquency."
22. Jacobson & Jacobson, "Prenatal Alcohol Exposure."
23. National Institute on Alcohol Abuse and Alcoholism, Alcohol Alert #13, p. 2.
24. Coles, "Critical Periods for Prenatal Alcohol Exposure.
25. Ibid.
26. Reported by Tara Meyer, "Expectant Mothers Drinking More," *Oregonian*, April 25, 1997, based on a 1995 telephone survey done by the National Center for Disease Control and Prevention.
27. Interview with Dr. Mary Schneider, October 16, 1996.
28. Dorozyaski, "Grapes of Wrath."
29. Phelps, "Psycho-Educational Outcomes of Fetal Alcohol Syndrome." Much of the data in this section is drawn from this review of the literature on the long-term impact of FAS.
30. Cicero, "Effects of Paternal Alcohol."
31. Ibid.
32. Brown, et al., "Effects of Prenatal Alcohol Exposure at School Age."
33. Bloss, "The Economic Cost of FAS."
34. Streissguth, "A Long-Term Perspective of Fetal Alcohol Syndrome."
35. Ibid.
36. Dorris, *The Broken Cord*, pp. 74–75.
37. Ibid.
38. Ibid., pp. xvii-xix.
39. National Institutes of Health, "Respiratory Health Effects of Passive Smoking."
40. Day & Richardson, "Comparative Teratogenicity."

41. All data from Day and Richardson, "Comparative Teratogenicity," p. 42.
42. Ibid.
43. Ibid.
44. Ibid.
45. Olds, D.L., Henderson, C.R. & Tatelbaum, R. (1994), "Intellectual impairment in children of women who smoke cigarettes during pregnancy, *Pediatrics,* vol. 93 pp. 221–27.
46. The *Oregonian,* October 20, 1996, quoted Bud Wand of the Environmental Health Center for the National Safety Council, Washington, D.C.
47. Coles, et al., "Effects of Cocaine and Alcohol Use in Pregnancy."
48. Chassnoff, "Cocaine: Effects in Pregnancy and the Neonate."
49. Mayes, et al., "Impaired Regulation of Arousal."
50. Ibid.
51. Interview with Dr. Linda Mayes, January 31, 1997.
52. For more detailed information on the impact of drug abuse on parenting, see chapter 8.
53. Interview with Dr. Linda Mayes, January 31, 1997.
54. Ibid.
55. Day and Richardson, "Comparative Teratogenicity."
56. Ornay, Michailevskaya, and Lukashov, "The Developmental Outcome."
57. Ibid.
58. Ibid.
59. Mayes, "Substance Abuse and Parenting."
60. Brackbill, McManus, and Woodward, "Medication in Maternity."
61. Jacobson, et al., "Opiate Addiction."
62. Barrett and Frank, *The Effects of Undernutrition,* p. 117.
63. Levine, Carey, & Crocker, *Developmental Behavioral Pediatrics,* chapter 29.
64. Dodge, "Social Cognition and Children's Aggressive Behavior"; Scerbo and Raine, "Neurotransmitters and Antisocial Behavior."
65. Barrett and Frank, *The Effects of Undernutrition.*
66. Ibid., pp. 177–78.
67. Levine, Carey, and Crocker, *Developmental Behavioral Pediatrics,* p. 179.
68. Barrett and Frank, *The Behavioral Effects of Undernutrition,* p. 175.
69. *Focus on Children: The Beat of the Future,* Columbia University Graduate School of Journalism Conference on Children in the News, p. 78.
70. Raine, *The Psychopathology of Crime.*
71. Clarke, et al., "Evidence for Heritability."
72. Ibid.
73. Ibid.
74. For further information on this point see chapter 2.
75. McGue, Bacon, and Lyken, "Personality Stability and Change."
76. Raine, *The Psychopathology of Crime,* pp. 198–200.
77. Ibid., p. 198.

CHAPTER 4

1. Restak, R. *The Infant Mind*. p. 181.
2. The account of Dr. Watson and the quotation are taken from Hardyment, *Dream Babies.*
3. Chamberlain, "What Babies Are Teaching Us."
4. Ibid.
5. Raine, Brennan, and Mednick, "Birth Complications."
6. Kandel and Mednick, "Perinatal Complications."
7. For an in-depth discussion of attachment and the effects of disruption to this process, see chapter 8.
8. Bowlby, *Forty-four Juvenile Thieves;* Rutter, *Maternal Deprivation Reassessed.*
9. Chamberlain, "What Babies Are Teaching Us."
10. Clarke and Schneider, "Prenatal Stress Has Long-Term Effects"; Clarke and Schneider, "Prenatal Stress Alters Social and Adaptive Behaviors in Adolescent Rhesus Monkeys."
11. Dr. Bruce McEwen, presentation at National Institute of Mental Health, Advancing Research on Developmental Plasticity: Integrating the Behavioral Science and Neuroscience of Mental Health, Chantilly, Virginia, May 1996.
12. Ibid.
13. Ikeda, "Prenatal Stress Increases Adult Aggressive Behavior."; Schenider, et al., "Timing of Prenatal Stress."
14. Powell and Emory, "Birthweight and Gestational Age Outcomes."
15. From personal interview with Drs. Kraemer, Clarke and Schneider at University of Wisconsin, Madison, October 8, 1996.
16. Chamberlain, "What Babies Are Teaching Us."
17. Janus, *Echoes from the Womb,* p. 102.
18. David, et al., *Born Unwanted.*
19. Janus, *Echoes from the Womb,* p. 102.
20. Bustan and Coker, "Maternal Attitude toward Pregnancy."
21. Janus, *Echoes from the Womb.*

CHAPTER 5

1. Barkley, *Attention Deficit Hyperactivity Disorder,* p. 175.
2. Ibid., p. 178.
3. Loeber, et al. "Which Boys Will Fare Worse," p. 500.
4. Ibid., p. 507.
5. Ibid., p. 507.
6. Barkley, *Attention Deficit Hyperactivity Disorder,* pp. 93, 168.
7. Haapasalo and Tremblay, "Physically Aggressive Boys From Ages 6 to 12," p. 1050.
8. Meyers, et al., "Psychopathology, Biosocial Factors, Crime Characteristics," p. 1485.

9. Loeber, "Antisocial Behavior," pp. 499–509.
10. Barkley, *Attention Deficit Hyperactivity Disorder,* p. 63.
11. Ibid., p. 77.
12. Ibid., p. 79.
13. Satterfield, et al., "Prediction of Antisocial Behavior."
14. Interview with Breena Satterfield, September 13, 1996.
15. Ibid.
16. Loeber, et al., "Developmental Sequences"; Loeber, et al., "Developmental Pathways."
17. Cicchetti and Toth, Eds., "Internalizing and Externalizing Expressions of Dysfunction;" Loeber, et al., "Which Boys Will Fare Worse;" Halperin, et al., "Impulsivity."
18. Rutter, *Studies of Psychosocial Risk.*
19. Loeber, "Antisocial Behavior."
20. Zametkin, "An Overview of Clinical Issues in ADHD"; Barkley, *The ADHD Report,* p. 5.
21. Day and Richardson, "Comparative Teratogenicity," p. 46.
22. Cicero, "Effects of Paternal Exposure to Alcohol."
23. Hartsough and Lambert, "Medical Factors in Hyperactive and Normal Children."
24. Barkley, *Attention Deficit Hyperactivity Disorder,* p. 105.
25. Benes, "Development of the Corticolimbic System"; Dawson, "Developing Brain Behavior Relations," in *Human Behavior and the Developing Brain,* pp. 199–214 and 378.
26. Gianino and Tronick, "The Mutual Regulation Model."
27. Field, et al., "Infants of Depressed Mothers Show Depressed Behavior."
28. Edelmen, *Neural Darwinism.*
29. Perry, "Incubated in Terror." The impact of early abuse on brain development is explored in detail in chapter 7.
30. Haapasalo, and Tremblay, "Physically Aggressive Boys From Ages 6 to 12"; Tremblay, et al., "A Bimodal Preventive Intervention."
31. Meyers, et al., "Psychopathology, Biopsychosocial Factors, Crime Characteristics, and Classification."
32. Conference, "The Cutting Edge: Critical Issues in Child and Adolescent Mental Health," Children's Hospital and Health Center, San Diego, and Division of Child and Adolescent Psychiatry, Department of Psychiatry, University of California, San Diego School of Medicine, February 1997, in San Diego, California.
33. Tremblay, et al., "A Bimodal Preventive Intervention."
34. Haapasalo and Tremblay, "Physically Aggressive Boys"; Moffitt, "Adolescence-Limited and Life-Course Persistent Antisocial Behavior."
35. Ibid.
36. Zoccolillo, et al., "The Outcome of Childhood Conduct Disorder," p. 982.

37. Barkley, *Attention Deficit Hyperactivity Disorder,* p. 178.
38. Dr. Gerald Patterson's comments were made in a letter sent to the authors February 12, 1997, in response to his review of the chapter manuscript.
39. Children's Defense Fund, *The State of America's Children* Yearbook 1997 pp. 56, 68.

CHAPTER 6

1. Accounts of the history of the study of temperament theory are taken from *Galen's Prophecy* by Dr. Jerome Kagan.
2. Interview with Dr. Stella Chess, October 14, 1995.
3. Chess and Thomas, "Dynamics of Individual Behavioral Development."
4. Interview with Dr. Stella Chess, October 14, 1995.
5. Kagan, *Galen's Prophecy.*
6. Ibid.
7. For further information on the influence of caretaking on the development of temperament see chapter 8.
8. Summarized by Dr. Jerome Kagan in *Galen's Prophecy.*
9. Gallagher, "How We Become What We Are," reported on the research of Steven Suomi of the National Institute of Child Health and Human Development, p. 44.
10. Rothbart, "Measurement of Temperament in Infancy."
11. An "inborn" characteristic may or may not be heritable. Temperament characteristics may be inherited, or they may be created by experiences in the environment of the womb or by conditions such as prematurity or birth trauma (for example, lack of oxygen).
12. Van Den Broom, "The Influence of Temperament and Mothering."
13. Ibid.
14. Dawson and Fischer, *Human Behavior and the Developing Brain,* p. 360.
15. Goleman, *Emotional Intelligence,* p. 227. For additional information, see chapter 7.
16. Ibid.
17. Ibid.
18. Kochanska, "Socialization and Temperament."
19. Scerbo and Kolko, "Child Physical Abuse and Aggression."
20. Kagan, *Galen's Prophecy,* p. 149.
21. The implication of the temperament information is not that all is lost by negative early caregiving patterns resulting in internalizing or externalizing behaviors. The key in the preschool years (2 to 4) is to begin to teach children how to put strong negative feelings into words and to learn rudimentary problem solving. For example, Johnny snatches the red truck that Billy is playing with.

Billy howls and tries to pull it back. This leads to a series of blows. An adult intervenes to help both boys name their feelings and come up with a fair solution. "I know you are mad at Johnny, Billy, and you want the truck back. But hitting hurts Johnny, and when he hits you back, you hurt, too. Let's sit down and talk about it. Johnny, when you wanted the red truck, what else could you have done? . . ." Regardless of the temperament of the child or an existing diagnosis of ADHD, this teaching is essential—and is an example of how constructive preschool experiences can be therapeutic interventions for high-risk children.

22. Tremblay, et al., "A Preventive Intervention for Disruptive Kindergarten Boys."
23. Brain chemistry is again accountable for wide differences in inhibited children. Children who are inhibited—but who also have high serotonin levels, are sociable and reach out to other people—while cautious and sensitive, may not be shy.
24. Kagan, *Galen's Prophecy*, p. 534. For a more detailed discussion of limbic activity, see chapter 2.
25. Dawson and Fischer, *Human Behavior and the Developing Brain*, p. 347.
26. Goleman, *Emotional Intelligence*, p. 221.
27. Ibid., p. 220.
28. This research, combining behavior disorders and temperament dimensions, raises new questions about the assumption that the element of impulsivity is the underlying trait linking the three behavior disorders.
29. Halperin, et al., "Impulsivity and the Initiation of Fighting."
30. Farrington, "Are There Any Successful Men from Crimnogenetic Backgrounds?"
31. Rothbart, et al., "Temperament and Social Behavior in Childhood."
32. Kochanska, "Socialization and Temperament."
33. Warner and Smith, *Vulnerable, but Invincible.*
34. Brennan, et al., *"Psychophysiological Protective Factors for Crime,"* p. 5.
35. Smith and Prior, "Temperament and Stress Resilience," p. 168.

CHAPTER 7

1. The story of the ordeal of the Chowchilla children was adapted from Dr. Lenore Terr's account in *Too Scared to Cry.*
2. The story of Yummy is drawn from several sources: *Toronto Star,* "'I Am Very Sick,' slain boy said: A Portrait of a Troubled Child," by George Pappajohn, September 3, 1994; *San Diego Union-Tribune,* "A Killer at 11: How Society Has Failed Our Children," by Robert Caldwell, September 11, 1994; *Chicago Sun Times,* "Close Escape Routes for Violent Children," editorial, December 11, 1994; *Oregonian,* "Boy 11 Sought in Shootings Found Dead," September 2, 1994.
3. Perry, Pollard, and Blakely, "Childhood Trauma."

4. For further information, see chapter 2.

5. Perry, Pollard, and Blakely, "Childhood Trauma."

6. This chapter on the links between early abuse and neglect and violence draws on the pioneering work of Dr. Bruce Perry at the Baylor College of Medicine in Houston, including personal interviews, published articles, and unpublished materials. Dr. Perry's theories will be set forth in detail in a book scheduled for release in the summer of 1998, *Maltreated Children: Experience, Brain Development, and the Next Generation*. Norton, New York.

7. Perry, "Incubated in Terror."

8. Perry, et al., "Childhood Trauma."

9. Loeber, et al., "Developmental Pathways;" Lewis, Mallouh and Webb, "Child Abuse, Delinquency, and Violent Criminality."

10. Widom, "Does Violence Beget Violence?"

11. Lewis, "From Abuse to Violence." In 1979, 79 percent of the violent children Lewis studied reported witnessing extreme violence between their parents compared with only 20 percent of nonviolent offending children.

12. The artificial separation of mind and body was set in Western thinking by the work of Descartes. The repudiation of this philosophical construct is the topic of an excellent book by Dr. Antonio Demasio, *Descartes' Error,* which is listed in the bibliography.

13. Cannon, *Bodily Changes in Pain, Hunger, Fear, and Rage*. New York, Appleton, 1929.

14. Cicchetti, Toth, and Hennessey, "Research on the Consequences."

15. Carlson, et al., "Disorganized/Disoriented Attachment Relationships," p. 525.

16. Beeghly and Cicchetti, "Child Maltreatment, Attachment, and the Self System," p. 6.

17. Cicchetti, Toth, and Hennessey, "Research on the Consequences," p. 43.

18. Weiss, et al., "Some Consequences of Early Harsh Discipline."

19. Cole, et al., "Predicting Early Adolescent Disorder."

20. Perry, "The Vortex of Violence" from *Maltreated Children.*

21. Interview with Dr. Bruce Perry, August 18, 1996.

22. Ibid.

23. Interview with Dr. Allan Schore, March 10, 1997.

24. Eth and Pynoos, "Developmental Perspective on Psychic Trauma in Childhood.

25. Reported by Ron Kotulak on the work of Dr. Robert Cairns, University of North Carolina in Chapel Hill, *Chicago Tribune,* December 14, 1993.

26. Perry, "Incubated in Terror."

27. Kotulak, "The Roots of Violence."

28. Elliott, "Violence: The Neurologic Contribution."

29. Lewis, et al., "Psychiatric, Neurological, and Psycho-Educational Characteristics."

30. Lewis, et al., "Neuropsychiatric, Psycho-Education, and Family Characteristics."

31. Rosenbaum and Hodge, "Head Injury and Marital Aggression," reported that

52 percent of the wife batterers in the study had a history of head injury, compared to 22 percent of nonbatterers; Rosenbaum, "The Neuropsychology of Marital Aggression," reported that 92 percent of battering males had a history of head injury that preceded domestic violence.

32. Raine, *The Psychopathology of Crime,* p. 195.
33. Milner and McCanne, "Neuropsychological Correlates of Physical Child Abuse."
34. Raine, *The Psychopathology of Crime,* p. 195.
35. Golden, et al., "Neuropsychological Correlates of Violence and Aggression," p. 5.
36. Ibid.
37. Ibid., p. 7. This syndrome may also result from some forms of epilepsy, which may be subtle and difficult to detect. It may also be greatly exacerbated in certain individuals by consumption of alcohol and drugs.
38. Ibid., p. 19.
39. In some cases of head injury, nurturing alone will not be enough to reduce the negative impact. Education and specialized skills may be essential to providing adequate support for seriously injured children.

CHAPTER 8

1. Drawn from stories published in the *Oregonian,* July 3 and July 4, 1996 and June 13, 1997, August 10, 1997 and August 21, 1997. It is interesting to note that in a front page story in *The Oregonian* published a year after the fire on August 10, 1997, reporters Holly Dansk and Alex Pulaski attributed Ray's violent behavior to "critical events beginning in infancy." This is the first newspaper story the authors found in over five years of research to do so.
2. *Oregonian,* July 4, 1996.
3. Lewis, et al., "Biosocial Characteristics of Children Who Later Murder"; Meyers, et al., "Psychopathology, Biopsychosocial Factors, Crime Characteristics and Classification"; Lewis, et al., Neuropsychiatric Psycoeducational and Family Characteristics."
4. Meyers, et al., "Psychopathology, Biopsychosocial Factors, Crime Characteristics and Classification."
5. Perry, "Incubated in Terror."
6. Scerbo, "Aggression in Physically Abused Children; Scerbo and Kolko, "Emotional Regulation as a Protective Factor in Childhood Aggression.
7. Brennan, et al., "Psychophysiological Protective Factors for Males."
8. Scerbo and Kolko, "Emotion Regulation as a Protective Factor in Childhood Aggression;" Scerbo, "Aggression in Physically Abused Children."
9. Brennan, et al., "Psychophysiological Protective Factors for Males."

10. Bowlby, *A Secure Base.*
11. Both a psychological and a brain-based biological template are, in fact, developing. The development of the biological template is described in the work of Dr. Allan Schore, UCLA Department of Medicine. See, A.N. Schore, *Affect Regulation and the Origin of the Self: The Neurobiology of Emotional Development.*
12. In a follow-up news story on Tray and Kiana in March of 1997, the *Oregonian* reported that Tray, now three, continues to take care of his little sister. Tray's father told the reporter, "He's learned to count, so he's always making sure she has an equal amount." Tray's father is in college, studying to become a social worker. Both children attend group therapy for children who have lost a parent. Their father works with the children, helping to keep their mother's memory alive by visiting her favorite place at the beach, playing games she used to play with them, and talking about her often. Tray's father tells him his mother is in heaven. When Tray expresses frustration at not knowing how to get there, his father says, "You'll go there when you get older. For now, just dream and think about her when you go to sleep and that way you can see her and keep a picture of her in your head."
13. Eisenberg, *The Caring Child.*
14. Alper, "Is Empathy Innate?"
15. Kochanska, "Socialization and Temperament."
16. Bowlby was the first to recognize the impact of early maternal separation on infant development. After World War II, in a report to the World Health Organization, he warned of the risks of separating children from their mothers, even neglectful mothers. He warned that separated children were at increased risk of mental illness and delinquency.
17. Weiss, et al., "Some Consequences of Early Harsh Discipline."
18. These type D babies as assessed in the Strange situation are also likely to be rated by their parents on a temperament questionnaire as having "difficult" temperaments. They also typically score higher on instruments rating risk factors.
19. Interview with Dr. Allan Schore, March 10, 1997. Schore's reference to a "good enough mother" alludes to a phrase coined by D. W. Winnicutt. The term expresses the idea that no mother can or should be perfect. Even with the best of mothers, there is a natural struggle between the meeting of her own needs and those of her infant.
20. Schore, "The Experience-Dependent Maturation of a Regulatory System," p. 73.
21. Demasio, *Descartes' Error.*
22. Perry, "Incubated in Terror."
23. Interview with Dr. Allan Schore, January 24, 1997.
24. Scerbo and Kolko, "Emotional Regulation as a Protective Factor in Childhood Aggression."

25. Emde, Robinson, and Nikkari, "Reactions to Restraint and Anger."
26. Olds, et al., "The Potential for Reducing Antisocial Behavior."
27. Tremblay, et al., "A Bimodal Preventive Intervention."
28. For more information on this subject see chapter 5.
29. Eisenberg and Mussen, *The Role of Prosocial Behavior in Children*.
30. Brennan, et al., "Psychophysiological Protective Factors for Males."
31. Kraemer, "Social Attachment, Brain Function, Aggression and Violence."
32. Ibid.
33. Cicchetti, Toth and Hennessey, "Research on the Consequences."
34. Greenspan and Cunningham, "Where Do Violent Kids Come From?"
35. Meyers, et al., Psychopathology, Biopsychosocial Factors, Crime Characteristics and Classification."
36. Zero to Three, *Heart Start*.
37. Erickson and Pianta, "New Lunchbox, Old Feelings," p. 37.
38. Ibid., p. 36.
39. "Turning Point," ABC Television, January, 1997. The film footage of the Romanian children provokes our shock and sympathy when we see the tragic faces of so many children severely neglected from conception. We wonder what kind of country would allow 100,000 or more of their babies to live in such appalling circumstances. But many children in our own country are also gestating in despair and fear and are being born into circumstances of chronic neglect and abuse in numbers which are steadily increasing. Last year alone, 3,111,000 American children were reported abused or neglected. While our nation's maltreatment of so many babies may not be as clearly visible or as acutely inhumane as Romania's, it is nontheless devastating to millions of American children.
40. Ibid.
41. Dixon and Stein, *Encounters with Children,* pp. 247–57.
42. Tamis-LaMonda and Bornstein, "Is There a 'Sensitive Period' in Human Development?"
43. Ibid., p. 88.
44. Ibid., pp. 93–94.
45. Low socioeconomic status tends to compound the impact of anxious attachment.
46. Erickson and Pianta, "New Lunchbox, Old Feelings," p. 40.
47. Ibid.
48. Ibid.
49. Ibid., p. 43.
50. Ibid.
51. Ibid.
52. Hofer, "Hidden Regulators."
53. Dr. James McKenna of Pomona College asserts that in our culture, where ba-

bies typically sleep in isolation from their mothers, it is the interruption of this symbiotic system that results in sudden infant death.

54. Hofer, "Hidden Regulators," p. 221.
55. Ibid.
56. Ibid, p. 227.
57. Kraemer, "Social Attachment, Brain Function, Aggression, and Violence."
58. Ibid.
59. Interview with Dr. Gary Kraemer, October 7, 1996.
60. Dawson, Hessel, and Frey, "Social Influences."
61. Carlson, et al., "Disorganized/Disoriented Attachment Relationships," p. 529.
62. Dawson, Hessel, and Frey, "Social Influences."
63. Interview with Dr. Geraldine Dawson, January 19, 1996.
64. Dawson, "Development of Emotional Expression and Emotional Regulation in Infancy."
65. Field, "Infants of Depressed Mothers."
66. Tronick and Gianino, "The Transmission of Maternal Disturbance."
67. Field, "Infants of Depressed Mothers."
68. Interview with Dr. Geraldine Dawson, January 19, 1996.
69. Dawson, Hessel and Frey, "Social Influences," pp. 760–61.
70. Ibid., p. 763.
71. This is very similar to the "inhibited/uninhibited" and "bold/timid" characterizations studied by the temperament theorists.
72. Dawson, Hessel, and Frey, "Social Influences," p. 763.
73. Dawson, "Development and Psychopathology," p. 769.
74. Ibid., p. 767.
75. Ibid., p. 769.
76. Ibid., p. 770.
77. Ibid., p. 771.
78. Field, "Infants of Depressed Mothers," pp. 1–13.
79. Ibid., p. 8.
80. Ibid., p. 9.
81. Ibid., p. 11.
82. Kochanska, "Socialization and Temperament."
83. Advertisement in the *New York Times* for *Newsweek,* special edition on birth to age three, April 22, 1997.

CHAPTER 9

1. Wade Horn, "Come Home Missing Fathers."
2. Phares, "Where's Poppa?"
3. Phares and Compas, "The Role of Fathers."
4. Thomas, "A Father's Role."

5. Ibid., p. 5.
6. Ibid., p. 6.
7. Ibid.
8. For further information on this topic, see chapter 3.
9. Cicero, "Effects of Paternal Alcohol," p. 37.
10. Ibid., p 38.
11. Ibid.
12. Ibid.
13. Ibid, p. 40.
14. Ibid, p. 39.
15. Ibid, p. 40.
16. Ibid.
17. Kotulak, "The Roots of Violence."
18. Phares, and Compas, "The Role of Fathers," p. 388.
19. National Commission on Children, "Just the Facts."
20. Gottman, "The Dissolution of the American Family," p. 103.
21. Phares, "Where's Poppa?"
22. Ibid.
23. National Center for Health Statistics in the *HHS News,* June 1996, reported a slight decrease in the overall birth rate to unmarried women from 32.6 percent to 32 percent.
24. Furstenberg and Cherlin, "Divided Families."
25. Phares, "Where's Poppa?"
26. Furstenberg and Nord, "Parenting Apart."
27. Furstenberg and Cherlin, "Divided Families."
28. Bennett, DiIulio, and Walters, *Body Count,* p. 45. This type of data sometimes triggers a simplistic "crime gene" analysis which looks to race as a factor in violent crime. But, as reported in earlier chapters, there is no genetic explanation for violence that implicates one race over another (see chapter 1). The number of African-Americans under the jurisdiction of the criminal justice system is appalling evidence of the disproportionate number of African-American children who experience the negative social factors reported in earlier chapters. The prenatal, perinatal, and the first two years' experiences of many African-American babies have been disproportionately affected by the effects of poverty, including parental drug use, domestic violence, single and teen parenthood, lack of prenatal care, inadequate housing, child neglect, and lack of adequate child care and education.
29. Interview with Dr. Penelope Leach, January 15, 1997.
30. Phares, "Where's Poppa?" p. 656
31. Data provided by Wade Horn in written comments on the chapter manuscript, sent to authors on January 15, 1997.
32. Horn, "Come Home Missing Fathers."

33. Thomas, "A Father's Role," p. 5.
34. Minnerbrook, "Lives Without Fathers."
35. Raine, *The Psychopathology of Crime,* p. 256.
36. Ibid., p. 245.
37. Ibid., p. 253.
38. Ibid., p. 254.
39. Ibid.
40. Office of Juvenile Justice and Delinquency Prevention, "Violent Families and Violent Youth."
41. Raine, *The Psychopathology of Crime,* p. 254.
42. Ibid.
43. Ibid, p. 255.
44. Ibid.
45. Interview with Dr. T. Berry Brazelton, March 16, 1995.
46. Sacks, "Children Need Both Mom and Dad to Thrive."
47. Interview with Wade Horn, December, 1996.
48. Ibid.
49. Yogman, Kindlon, and Earls, "Father Involvement," p. 58.
50. Kromelow, Harding, and Touris, "The Role of the Father," p. 521.
51. Ibid., p. 522.
52. Yogman, Kindlon, and Earls, "Father Involvement," p. 59.
53. Ibid.
54. Ibid.
55. Ibid.
56. Ibid., p. 63.
57. Given similar styles of parenting between the parents, infants show very similar patterns of attachment to both mothers and fathers. Paternal warmth has positive effects on child development that are similar to those of maternal warmth such as success in achievement, psych-social adjustment, and sex role development. (Phares, "Where's Poppa?" p. 657.)
58. Kromelow, Harding, and Touris, "The Role of the Father."
59. Ibid., p. 522.
60. Ibid., p. 527.
61. Heatherington and Parke, *Child Psychology: A Contemporary Viewpoint.*
62. Bennett, DiIulio, and Walters, *Body Count,* p. 196.

CHAPTER 10

1. The story of James was reported by Nena Baker in the *Oregonian,* October 7, 1994.
2. From television documentary "Kids Behind Bars," *A&E Investigative Reports,* 6/16/97 featuring Dr. Arthur Miller, Harvard Law School.

3. Personal inverview with Dr. Ron David, June 9, 1995.
4. Bennett, DiIulio, and Walters, *Body Count,* p. 18.
5. Ibid.
6. U.S. Department of Justice, Office of Justice Programs, Bureau of Justice Statistics, "Crime Data Brief: The Costs of Crime to Victims, February 1994.
7. Ibid.
8. DiIulio, "Stop Crime Where It Starts."
9. Carvajal, "Records as Long as 7-Year-Old Arm."
10. DiIulio and Mitchell, "Who Really Goes to Prison in Wisconsin?"
11. Ostrow, "Number of Juvenile Murders Is Soaring."
12. Bennett, DiIulio, Walters *Body Count* Simon & Schuster N.Y. 1996 p. 26.
13. Richard Lacayo "When Kids Go Bad" *Time* Magazine September 19, 1994.
14. Data on Girls from Juvenile Offenders and Victims: 1996 Update on Violence, The U.S. Dept. of Justice, Office of Juvenile Justice and Delinquency Prevention, p. 11.
15. Bennett, DiIulio and Walters, *Body Count.*
16. Butterfield, "Juvenile Crime Will Keep on Rising."
17. Bureau of Justice Statistics, "Crime Data Brief."
18. Epstein, "Children Make Up the Majority of Firebugs."
19. Hernandez, "Young Blood: Violence by Teens Isn't New."
20. *Newsweek,* "Gangstas' in the Ranks."
21. Butterfield, "More in the U.S."
22. Ibid.
23. Butterfield, "More Blacks."
24. Manzano, "Prisons Become Growth Industry."
25. "Beyond Probation," Joseph B. Thaster, *The New York Times,* 12/29/94.
26. Greenwood, et al., "Diverting Children from a Life of Crime."
27. Hughes, "NYS Leads Nation in Violent Youth Crime."
28. Purnick, "Youth Crime: Should Laws Be Tougher?"
29. Lewis, et al., "A Clinical Follow-up of Delinquent Males."
30. Ibid.
31. Treaster, "When Trouble Starts Young."
32. Ibid.
33. Kolata, "Experts Are at Odds on How Best to Tackle Rise in Teenagers' Drug Use."
34. Wren, "Adolescent Drug Use Continues to Rise."
35. The Future of Children: Special Education for Children with Disabilities, Vol. 6:1, spring 1996, David and Lucille Packard Foundation, Los Altos, California.
36. Ibid.
37. Ibid.
38. Ibid.

39. Crossette, "Agency Sees Risk in Drug to Temper Child Behavior."
40. Children's Defense Fund (1996) *The State of America's Children*, p. xx.
41. All data in this section "School Days" from Applebome, "For the Ultimate Safe School, Eyes Turn to Dallas."
42. In spite of a slight recent reduction in juvenile arrests for violent crime, the overall rate of juvenile arrests has continued to increase, according to the 1996 data from the FBI.
43. Childrens Defense Fund (1996) *The State of America's Children*.
44. Ibid.
45. Ibid.
46. Bennett, DiIulio, and Walters, *Body Count*, p. 76.
47. A series of articles on the Horton family ran in May of 1996 in the *Denver Post* and the *Rocky Mountain News*.
48. Examples of such programs are Minnesota's Parents as Teachers and Hawaii's Healthy Start.
49. Pear, "Many States Fail to Meet Mandates on Child Welfare."
50. Ibid.
51. The data on foster care was taken from Children's Defense Fund (1996), *The State of America's Children*.
52. Brazelton, *Touchpoints*.
53. A list of program resources can be found in appendix D.
54. Congress hired a team of experts at the University of Maryland to determine the effectiveness of the $3 billion worth of expenditures made by the Department of Justice to help local law enforcement and community groups prevent crime.
55. Goleman, *Emotional Intelligence*, p. 256.
56. All data are from Children's Defense Fund, *The State of America's Children*, 1996 and 1997.

CHAPTER 11

1. Stevens, "Treating Violence as an Epidemic," p. 23.
2. Interview with Dr. T. Berry Brazelton, January 8, 1997.
3. Interview with Dr. Penelope Leach, January 15, 1997.
4. Interview with Matthew Melmed, January 30, 1997.
5. Interview with Dr. Gerald Patterson, January 9, 1997.
6. Interview with Dr. Charles Golden, January 12, 1997.
7. Interview with Dr. Kathryn Barnard, January 9, 1997.
8. Interview with Dr. Craig Ramey, January 24, 1997.
9. Ibid.
10. A resource list of effective program models and agencies that can provide further information can be found in Appendix D and E.

11. Perry, "Incubated in Terror."
12. Interview with Dr. Ed Tronick, October 20, 1996.
13. Conference of the American Psychological Association Division 39: "The Cutting Edge" February 14, 1997, San Diego.
14. In their 1997 edition of *The State of America's Children,* the Children's Defense Fund reported that if American babies had the same mortality rate as Japanese babies, over 15,000 more U.S. babies would have survived in 1994 alone.

APPENDIX D

1. The phrase "mother the mothers" was coined by JoAnn Robinson, codirector of research with David Olds at the University of Colorado Health Sciences Center.
2. The other approach the study identified as successful in reducing crime was police programs which target high-crime areas and, in addition to vigorous enforcement against serious crimes, vigorously enforce penalties against anti-social misdemeanors (e.g., urinating in public) and petty vandalism.

Bibliography

Alper, J. (May 19, 1995), "Is Empathy Innate?" *San Francisco Chronicle,* Sunday Section: This World, p. 14.

Applebome, P. (September 20, 1995), "For the Ultimate Safe School, Eyes Turn to Dallas," *New York Times.*

Barkley, R.A. (1990), *Attention Deficit Hyperactivity Disorder: A Handbook for Diagnosis and Treatment,* Guilford Press, New York.

Barkley, R., et al. (February 1996), *ADHD Report* 4(1).

Barrett D., and Frank, D. (1987), *The Effects of Undernutrition on Children's Behavior,* Gordan and Breach Science Publishers, New York.

Bates, J.E., and Wachs, T.D. (1994), *Temperament: Individual Differences at the Interface of Biology and Behavior,* American Psychological Association, Washington, D.C.

Beeghly, M., and Cicchetti, D. (1993), "Toward an Ecological/Transactional Model of Community Violence and Child Maltreatment: Consequences for Children's Development, *Psychiatry* 56:96–118.

Bennett, W.J.; DiIulio, J.J., Jr.; and Walters, J.P. (1996), *Body Count: Moral Poverty . . . and How to Win America's War Against Crime and Drugs,* Simon & Schuster, New York.

Besharov, D.J. (1989), "The Children of Crack: Will We Protect Them?" *Public Welfare* 47:6–11.

Bloss, G. (1994), "The Economic Cost of FAS," *Alcohol Health and Research World,* National Institute on Alcohol Abuse and Alcoholism, 18(1):53–54.

Bornstein, M.H. ed. (1987), *Sensitive Periods in Development: Interdisciplinary Perspectives,* Lawrence Erlbaum and Associates, Hillsdale, New Jersey.

Bowlby, J. (1946), *Forty-four Juvenile Thieves: Their Characters and Home Life,* Baillere, Tindall and Cox, London.

333

Bowlby, J. (1988), *A Secure Base: Parent-Child Attachment and Healthy Human Development*, Basic Books, New York.

Brackbill, Y.; McManus, K.; and Woodward, L. (1985), *Medication in Maternity: Infant Exposure and Maternal Information*, Monograph Series #2, University of Michigan Press, Ann Arbor.

Brazelton, T.B. (1992), *Touchpoints: Your Child's Emotional and Behavioral Development*, Addison-Wesley Publishing, Reading, Massachusetts.

Brennan, P.A.; Raine, A.; Schulsinger, F.; Mednick, S.A.; Kirkegaard-Sorenson, L.; Knop, J.; Hutchings, B.; and Rosenberg, R. (1997), "Psychophysiological Protective Factors for Male Subjects at High Risk of Criminal Behavior," *American Journal of Psychiatry* 154:853–855.

Brennan, P.A., and Mednick, S.A. (in press), "Perinatal and Medical Histories of Antisocial Individuals," in *Handbook of Antisocial Behavior*, Stoff, D.; Breiling, J.; and Maser, D., eds.

Brown, R.; Coles, C.D.; Smith, I.E.; Platzman, K.A.; Silverstein, J.; Erickson, S.; and Falek, A. (1991), "Effects of Prenatal Alcohol Exposure at School Age," *Neurotoxicology and Teratology* 13:369–376.

Bureau of Justice Statistics (February 1994), "Crime Data Brief: The Costs of Crime to Victims," NJC—145865.

Bureau of Justice Statistics (March 1997), "Lifetime Likelihood of Going to State or Federal Prison," U.S. Department of Justice Special Report, Washington, D.C.

Bureau of Justice Statistics Bulletin (January 1997), "Prison and Jail Inmates at Midyear 1996," U.S. Department of Justice, Washington, DC.

Bustan, M.N., and Coker, A.L. (1994), "Maternal Attitude Toward Pregnancy and the Risk of Neonatal Death," *American Journal of Public Health*, 84(3):411–414.

Butterfield, F. (October 5, 1995), "More Blacks in Their 20's Have Trouble with the Law," *New York Times*.

Butterfield, F. (August 9, 1996), "More in U.S. Are in Prisons, Report Says," *New York Times*.

Cannon, W.B. (1929), *Bodily Changes in Pain, Hunger, Fear and Rage*, Appleton, New York.

Caravajal, D. (March 9, 1995), "Records as Long as a 7-Year-Old Arm," *New York Times*.

Carlson, V.; Cicchetti, D.; Barnett, D.; and Braunwald, K. (1989), "Disorganized/Disoriented Attachment Relationships in Maltreated Infants," *Developmental Psychology* 25(4): 525–531.

Carnegie Corporation (1994), *Starting Points: Meeting the Needs of Our Youngest Children*, New York.

Carson, R. (1962), *Silent Spring*, Houghton Mifflin, Boston.

Center for the Future of Children (Spring 1996), *The Future of Children: Special*

Education for Students with Disabilities, David and Lucille Packard Foundation, Palo Alto, California.

Chamberlain, D. (1987), "The Cognitive Newborn: A Scientific Update," *British Journal of Psychotherapy* 4:30–71.

Chamberlain, D. (September 1995), "What Babies Are Teaching Us About Violence." Pre- and Perinatal Psychology Journal 10(2):51–74.

Chassnoff, I., ed. (1988), "Cocaine Effects in Pregnancy and the Neonate," *Drugs, Alcohol, Pregnancy and Parenting,* Kluwer Academic Press, Boston.

Chess, S., and Thomas, A. (1992), "Dynamics of Individual Behavioral Development," *Developmental-Behavioral Pediatrics,* 2nd edition, Levine, M.D.; Carey, W.B.; and Crocker, A.C., eds., W.B. Saunders Company, Philadelphia.

Children's Defense Fund (1996), *The State of America's Children,* Washington, D.C.

Children's Defense Fund (1997), *The State of America's Children,* Washington, D.C.

Chugani, H.T. (1994), "Development of Regional Brain Glucose Metabolism in Relation to Behavior and Plasticity," in *Human Behavior and the Developing Brain,* Dawson, G., and Fischer, K.W., eds., Guilford Press, New York.

Cicchetti, D., and Beeghly M. (1994), "Child Maltreatment, Attachment, and the Self System: Emergence of an Internal State Lexicon in Toddlers at High Social Risk," *Development and Psychopathology* 6:5–30.

Cicchetti, D., and Lynch, M. (1993), "Toward an Ecological/Transactional Model of Community Violence and Child Maltreatment: Consequences for Children's Development," *Psychiatry* 56: 96–118.

Cicchetti, D., and Toth, S.L., eds. (1991), *Internalizing and Externalizing Expressions of Dysfunction: Rochester Symposium on Developmental Psychopathology,* volume 2, Lawrence Erlbaum and Associates, Hillsdale, New Jersey.

Cicchetti, D.; Toth, S.L.; and Hennessy, K. (1989), "Research on the Consequences of Child Maltreatment and Its Application to Educational Settings," *Topics in Early Childhood Special Education* 9(2):33–53.

Cicero, T.J. (January 1994), "Effects of Paternal Alcohol on Offspring Development," *Alcohol Health and Research World,* National Institute on Alcohol Abuse and Alcoholism, 18(1): 37–41.

Clarke, A.S.; Kammerer, C.; and George, K. (1995), "Evidence of Heritability of Neopinephrine, HVA, and 5-HIAA Values in Cerebrospinal Fluid of Rhesus Monkeys," *Biological Psychiatry* 38(9):572–577.

Clarke, A.S., and Schneider, M.L. (May 1996), "Prenatal Stress Alters Social and Adaptive Behaviors in Adolescent Rhesus Monkeys," Poster #5 presented at National Institute of Mental Health Conference, "Advancing Research on Developmental Plasticity: Integrating the Behavioral Science and the Neuroscience of Mental Health," Chantilly, Virginia.

Clarke, A.S., and Schneider, M.L. (1993), "Prenatal Stress Has Long-Term Effects on Behavioral Responses to Stress in Juvenile Rhesus Monkeys," *Developmental Psychobiology* 26(5):293–304.

Cole, J.D.; Lochman, J.E.; Terry, R.; and Hyman, C. (1992), "Predicting Early Adolescent Disorder from Childhood Aggression and Peer Rejection," *Journal of Consulting and Clinical Psychology* 60:783–792.

Coles, C.D.; Platzman, K.A.; Smith, I.E.; James, M.; and Falek, A. (1992), "Effects of Cocaine and Alcohol in Pregnancy on Neonatal Growth and Neurobehavioral Status," *Neurotoxicology and Teratology* 14:23–33

Columbia University Graduate School of Journalism (1992), *Focus on Children: The Beat of the Future,* Report on Media Conference, New York.

David, H.P.; Dytrych, Z.; Matejcek, Z.; and Schuller, V. (1988), *Born Unwanted: Developmental Effects of Denied Abortion,* Springer, New York.

Dawson, G., and Fischer, K.W., eds. (1994), "Development of Emotional Expression and Emotional Regulation in Infancy: Contributions of the Frontal Lobe," *Human Behavior and the Developing Brain,* Guilford Press, New York.

Dawson, G., and Fischer, K.W., eds. (1995), *Human Behavior and the Developing Brain,* Guilford Press, New York.

Dawson, G.; Hessel, D.; and Frey, K. (1994) "Social Influences on Early Developing Biological and Behavioral Systems Related to Risk for Affective Disorder," *Development and Psychopathology* 6:759–799.

Dawson, G.; Panagiotides, H.; Klinger, L.G.; and Hill, D. (1992), "The Role of Frontal Lobe Functioning in the Development of Infant Self-Regulating Behavior," *Brain and Cognition* 20:152–175.

Day, N., and Richardson, G. (January 1, 1994) "Comparative Teratogenicity of Alcohol and Other Drugs," *Alcohol Health and Research World,* National Institute of Alcohol Abuse and Alcoholism, 18(1):42–48.

Demasio, A. (1994), *Descartes Error: Emotion and the Human Brain,* G. Putnam, New York.

DiIulio, J. (July 31, 1996), "Stop Crime Where It Starts," *New York Times,* New York.

DiIulio, J. Jr., and Mitchell, W. "Who Really Goes to Prison in Wisconsin?" Wisconsin Policy Research Institute, p.#19.

Dixon, S., and Stein, M. (1992), *Encounters with Children: Pediatric Behavior and Development,* Mosby Books, Boston.

Dodge, K.A. (1980), "Social Cognition and Children's Aggressive Behavior," *Child Development* 51:162–170.

Dorozyaski, A. (January 1, 1993), "Grapes of Wrath," *Psychology Today* 26:18–25.

Dorris, M. (1989), *The Broken Cord,* Harper Perennial, New York.

Edelman, G. (1987), *Neural Darwinism,* Basic Books, New York.

Eisenberg, N. (1992), *The Caring Child,* Harvard University Press, Cambridge, Massachusetts.

336

Eisenberg, N., and Mussen, P.H. (1989), *The Roots of Prosocial Behavior in Children,* Cambridge University Press, Cambridge, England.

Elkington, J. (1985), *The Poisoned Womb,* Penguin, Hammondsworth, Middlesex, England.

Elliot, F.A. (1992), "Violence: The Neurologic Contribution: An Overview," *Archives of Neurology* 49:595–603.

Emde, R.N.; Robinson, J.; Nikkari, D., "Reactions to Restraint and Anger Related to Expressions," manuscript in preparation.

Engel, G.; Ruschman, F.; Harnay, V.; and Wilson, D. (1985) *Parental Influences in Health and Disease,* Little Brown, Boston.

Epstein, R. (January 20, 1997), "Children Make up the Majority of Firebugs," *Oregonian.*

Erickson, M.F., and Pianta, R.C. (1989) "New Lunchbox, Old Feelings: What Kids Bring to School," *Early Education and Development* 1(1):35–47.

Eth, S., and Pynoos, R.R. (1985), "Development Perspective on Psychic Trauma in Childhood," *Trauma and Its Wake,* Figley, C.R., ed., Bruner/Mazel, New York.

Farrington, D.P. (1988), "Are There Any Successful Men from Crimnogenetic Backgrounds?" *Psychiatry* 51:116–130.

Field, T. (1995), "Infants of Depressed Mothers," *Infant Behavior and Development* 18:1–13.

Field, T.; Healy, B.; Goldstein, S.; Perry, S.; Bendall, D.; Schanberg, S.; Zimmerman, E.; and Kuhn, C. (1988), "Infants of Depressed Mothers Show Depressed Behavior Even with Non-Depressed Adults," *Child Development* 59:1569–1579.

Fontana, V.J., and Moolman, V. (1991), *Save the Family, Save the Child: What We Can Do to Help Children at Risk,* Dutton, New York.

Fox, N., (October 1996), Oral presentation to the Eleventh Occasional Temperament Conference, University of Oregon, Eugene.

Frishman, R. (January 1, 1995), "Little Lost Boys," *Ladies' Home Journal* 62:76.

Furstenberg, F.F., Jr., and Cherlin, A.J. (1991), *Divided Families: What Happens to Children When Parents Part,* Harvard University Press, Cambridge, Massachusetts.

Furstenberg, F.F., and Nord, C.W. (November 1995), "Parenting Apart: Patterns of Child Rearing after Marital Disruption," *Journal of Marriage and the Family.*

Gallagher, W. (September 1994), "How We Become What We Are," *Atlantic Monthly.*

Gandelman, R. (1992), *Psychobiology of Behavioral Development,* Oxford University Press, New York.

Gazzaniga, M.S. (1992), *Nature's Mind: The Biological Roots of Thinking, Emotions, Sexuality, Language, and Intelligence,* Basic Books, New York.

Gianino, A., and Tronick, E.Z. (1988), "The Mutual Regulation Model: The Infant's Self and Interactive Regulation, Coping and Defense," *Stress and*

Coping, Field, T.; McCabe, P.; and Schneiderman, N., eds., Lawrence Erlbaum and Associates, Hillsdale, New Jersey.

Gladwell, M. (March 3, 1997), "Damaged," *The New Yorker.*

Goldberg, J. (July 1993), "The Amazing Minds of Infants," *Life,* Special Issue: "Babies Are Smarter than You Think."

Golden, C.J.; Jackson, M.L.; Peterson-Rohne, A.; and Gontkovsky, S.T. (1996), "Neuropsychological Correlates of Violence and Aggression: A Review of the Clinical Literature," *Aggression and Violent Behavior* 1:3–25.

Goleman, D. (1995), *Emotional Intelligence: Why It Matters More than IQ,* Bantam, New York.

Gottman, J. (1995), "The Dissolution of the American Family," in *Family: The First Imperative,* O'Neill, J., ed, The William and Dorothy K. O'Neill Foundation, Cleveland, Ohio.

Graham, J.M. (1992), "Congenital Anomalies," *Developmental-Behavioral Pediatrics,* 2nd edition, Levine, M.D.; Carey, W.B., and Crocker, A.C., eds., W.B. Saunders, New York, pp. 229–243.

Greenspan, S., and Cunningham, A. (August 22, 1993), "Where Do Violent Kids Come From?" *Charlotte Observer,* reprinted in the *Washington Post.*

Greenwood, P.W.; Model, K.E.; Rydell, C.P.; and Chiesa, J. (April 1996), *Diverting Children from a Life of Crime: Measuring Costs and Benefits,* Rand Criminal Justice Program, prepared for the University of California at Berkeley, James Irvine Foundation.

Haapasalo, J., and Tremblay, R.E. (1994) "Physically Aggressive Boys from Ages 6 to 12: Family Background, Parenting Behavior, and Prediction of Delinquency," *Journal of Consulting and Clinical Psychology* 62(5):1044–1052.

Halperin, J.M.; Newcorn, J.J.; Matier, K.; Dedi, G.; Hall, S.; and Vanshdeep, S. (1995), "Impulsivity and the Initiation of Fights in Children with Disruptive Behavior Disorders," *Journal of Child Psychology and Psychiatry* 36(7):1199–1211.

Hardyment, C. (1983), *Dream Babies: Three Centuries of Good Advice on Child Care,* Harper and Row, New York.

Hartsough, C., and Lambert, N. (1985), "Medical Factors in Hyperactive and Normal Children: Prenatal, Developmental and Health History Findings," *American Journal of Orthopsychiatry* 55:190–210.

Healy, J.M. (1987), *Your Child's Growing Mind: A Guide to Learning and Brain Development from Birth to Adolescence,* Doubleday, New York.

Heatherington, E.M., and Parke, R.D. (1986), *Child Psychology: A Contemporary Viewpoint,* McGraw-Hill, New York.

Herman, J.L. (1992), *Trauma and Recovery: The Aftermath of Violence–from Domestic Abuse to Political Terror,* Basic Books, New York.

Hernandez, R. (February 11, 1996), "Young Blood: Violence by Children and Teens Isn't New," *Oregonian.*

Hessel, C.; Dawson, G.; Frey, K.; Panagiotides, H.; Self, J.; Yamada, E.; and Osterling, J. (May 1996), "A Longitudinal Study of Children of Depressed Mothers: Psychobiological Findings Related to Stress," Poster #14 presented at National Institute of Mental Health Conference, "Advancing Research on Developmental Plasticity: Integrating the Behavioral Science and the Neuroscience of Mental Health," Chantilly, Virginia.

Hewlett, S.A. (1991), *When the Bough Breaks: The Cost of Neglecting Our Children,* Basic Books, New York.

Hofer, M.A. (1995), "Hidden Regulators: Implications for a New Understanding of Attachment, Separation, and Loss," *Attachment Theory: Social, Developmental, and Clinical Perspectives,* Goldberg, S.; Muir, R.; and Kerr, J., eds., Analytic Press, Hillsdale, New Jersey.

Horn, W.F. (June 16, 1996), "Come Home, Missing Fathers," *Houston Chronicle,* Section: Outlook.

Hughes, K. (August 1994), "NYS Leads Nation in Violent Youth Crime," *Gannett News Service.*

Ikeda, S.C.; Hood, K.E.; Granger, D.A.; and Gottlieb, B. (May 1996), "Prenatal Stress Increases Adult Aggressive Behavior and Adrenocortical Reactivity in Mice," Poster # 15 presented at National Institute of Mental Health Conference, "Advancing Research on Developmental Plasticity: Integrating the Behavioral Science and the Neuroscience of Mental Health," Chantilly, Virginia.

Institute of Medicine (1985), *Preventing Low Birthweight,* National Academy Press, Washington, D.C.

Institute of Medicine (1989), *Research on Children and Adolescents with Mental, Behavioral and Developmental Disorders,* National Academy Press, Washington, D.C.

Jacobson, B.; Nyberg, K.; Grongladh, L.; Eklund, B.; Bygdeman, M.; and Rydberg, U. (1990), "Opiate Addiction in Adult Offspring through Possible Imprinting after Obstetric Treatment," *British Medical Journal* 301:677–682.

Jacobson, J.L., and Jacobson, S.W. (January 1, 1994), "Prenatal Alcohol Exposure and Neurobehavioral Development," *Alcohol Health and Research World,* National Institute on Alcohol Abuse and Alcoholism 18(1):30–36.

Janus, L. (1997), *Echoes from the Womb,* Jason Aronson, Livingston, New York.

Kagan, J. (1994), *Galen's Prophecy,* Basic Books, New York.

Kandel, E., and Mednick, S. (1991), "Perinatal Complications Predict Violent Offending," *Criminology* 29(3):519–529.

Kaplan, L.J. (1978), *Oneness and Separateness: From Infant to Individual,* Touchstone, New York.

Karen, R. (1994), *Becoming Attached: Unfolding the Mystery of the Infant-Mother Bond and Its Impact on Later Life,* Warner Books, New York.

Kochanska, G. (1991), "Socialization and Temperament in the Development of Guilt and Conscience," *Child Development* 62:1379–1392.

Kolata, G. (September 18, 1996), "Experts Are at Odds on How Best to Tackle Rise in Teen-Agers' Drug Use," *New York Times.*

Kotulak, R. (1993), *Chicago Tribune,* Series: "Unlocking the Mind," April 11–15, and special section: "The Roots of Violence: Tracking Down Monsters within Us," December 12–15.

Kraemer, G.W. (in press), "Social Attachment, Brain Function, Aggression and Violence," *Unlocking Crime: The Biosocial Key,* Raine, A.; Farrington, D.; Brennan, P.; and Mednick, S., eds.

Kraemer, G.W.; Ebert, M.H.; Schmidt, D.E.; and McKinney, W.T. (1989), "A Longitudinal Study of the Effects of Different Social Rearing Conditions on Cerebrospinal Fluid, Norepinephrine and Bigenic Amine Metabolites in Rhesus Monkeys," *Neuropsychopharmacology* 2(3):175–189.

Kromelow, S.; Harding, C.; and Touris, M. (1990), "The Role of the Father in the Development of Stranger Sociability during the Second Year," *American Journal of Orthopsychiatry* 60(4):521–530.

Lamb, M.E., ed. (1997), *The Role of the Father in Child Development,* 3rd edition, John Wiley, New York.

Landesman-Dweyer, S., and Emanuel, I. (1982), "Smoking during Pregnancy," *The Beginnings of Infancy,* Belsky, J., ed., Columbia University Press, New York.

Leach, P. (1994), *Children First,* Knopf, New York.

LeCroy, C.W. (1988) "Parent-Adolescent Intimacy: Impact on Adolescent Functioning," *Adolescence* 23(89):137–147.

LeDoux, J. (1993), "Emotional Memory Systems in the Brain," *Behavioral and Brain Research* 58.

Lenman, R., and Doms, T. (1993), *Young Fathers: Changing Roles and Emerging Policies,* Temple, Philadelphia.

Levine, M.D.; Carey, W.B.; and Crocker, A.C. (1992), *Developmental Behavioral Pediatrics,* 2nd edition, W.B. Saunders, Philadelphia.

Lewis, D.O. (1992), "From Abuse to Violence: Psychophysiological Consequences of Maltreatment," *Journal of American Academy of Child and Adolescent Psychiatry* 31(3).

Lewis, D.O. (1990), "Neuropsychiatric and Experiential Correlates of Violent Juvenile Delinquency," *Neuropsychology Review* 1(2).

Lewis, D.O.; Mallouh, C.; and Webb, V. (1989), "Child Abuse, Delinquency, and Violent Criminality," *Child Maltreatment Theory and Research on the Causes and Consequences of Child Abuse and Neglect,* Cicchetti, D., and Carlson, V., eds., Cambridge University Press, Cambridge, England.

Lewis, D.O.; Moy, E.; Jackson, L.D.; Aaronson, R.; Restifo, N.; Serra, S.; and Simos, A. (1985), "Biopsychological Characteristics of Children Who Later Murder: A Prospective Study," *American Journal of Psychiatry* 14(10):1161–1167.

Lewis, D.O.; Pincus, J.H.; Bard, B.; Richardson, E.; Prichep, L.S.; Feldman, M.; and Yeager, C. (1986), "Psychiatric, Neurological, and Psycho-Educational

Characteristics of 15 Death Row Inmates in the United States," *American Journal of Psychiatry* 143:838–845.

Lewis, D.O.; Pincus, J.H.; Bard, B.; Richardson, E.; Prichep, L.S.; Feldman, M.; and Yeager, C. (1988), "Neuropsychiatric, Psycho-educational, and Family Characteristics of 14 Juveniles Condemned to Death Row in the United States," *American Journal of Psychiatry* 145(5):584–589.

Lewis, D.O.; Yeager, C.A.; Lovely, R.; Stein, A.; and Cobham-Portorreal, C.S. (1994), "A Clinical Follow-Up of Delinquent Males: Ignored Vulnerabilities, Unmet Needs, and the Perpetuation of Violence, *Journal of American Academy of Child and Adolescent Psychiatry* 33(4):518–529.

Loeber, R. (May 1991), "Antisocial Behavior: More Enduring than Changeable?" *Journal of American Academy of Child and Adolescent Psychiatry* 30:393–397.

Loeber, R.; Green, M.S.; Keenan, K.; and Lahey, B. (April 1995), "Which Boys Will Fare Worse? Early Predictors of the Onset of Conduct Disorder in a Six-Year Longitudinal Study," *Journal of American Academy of Child and Adolescent Psychiatry* 34(4):499–509.

Loeber, R.; Green, M.S.; Lahey, B.B.; Christ, M.A.; and Frick, P.J. (1992), "Developmental Sequences in the Age of Onset of Disruptive Child Behaviors," *Journal of Child and Family Studies* 1:21–51.

Loeber R.; Wung, P.; Keenan, K.; Giroux, B.; Stouthamer-Loeber, M.; Van Kammen, W.B.; and Maughan, B. (1993), "Developmental Pathways in Disruptive Child Behavior," *Development and Psychopathology* 5:103–133.

Lou, H.; Hendriksen, L.; Bruhn, P.; Bonner, H.; and Nielsen, J. (1989), "Striatal Dysfunction in Attention Deficit and Hyperactivity Disorder," *Archives of Neurology* 46:48–52.

Magid, K. (1988), *High Risk: Children Without a Conscience,* Bantam, New York.

Magid, K. (in press), *Innocence to Violence,* KM Productions, Denver.

Mahler, M.S.; Pine, F.; and Bergman, A. (1975), *The Psychological Birth of the Human Infant: Symbiosis and Individuation,* Basic Books, New York.

Manzano, P. (June 20, 1996), "Prisoners Become Growth Industry in Oregon," *Oregonian.*

Mayes, L.; Bornstein, M.H.; Chawarska, K.; and Granger, R. (1995), "Information Processing and Developmental Assessments in 3-Month-Old Infants Exposed Prenatally to Cocaine," *Pediatrics* 95(4).

Mayes, L.; Bornstein, M.H.; Chawarska, K.; Haynes, M.O.; and Granger, R. (1996), "Impaired Regulation of Arousal in 3-Month-Old Infants Exposed Prenatally to Cocaine and Other Drugs," *Development and Psychopathology* 8:29–42.

Mednick, S.; Gabrielli, W., Jr.; Hutching, B. (May 25, 1984), Genetic Influences in Criminal Convictions: Evidence From an Adoption Cohort," *Science* 224: 891–894.

Meyer, T. (April 25, 1987), "Expectant Mothers Drinking More," *Oregonian.*

Meyers, W.C.; Scott, K.; Burgess, A.W.; and Burgess, A.G. (November 1995),

"Psychopathology, Biopsychosocial Factors, Crime Characteristics and Classification of 25 Homicidal Youths," *Journal of American Academy of Child and Adolescent Psychiatry* 34(11):1483–1489.

Milner, J.S. (1991) *Neuropsychology of Agression,* Kluwer Academic Press, Boston.

Milner, J.S., and McCanne, T.R. (1991). "Neuropsychological Correlates of Physical Child Abuse," in *Neuropsychology of Aggression,* Milner, J.S., ed., Kluwer Academic Press, Boston.

Minnerbrook, S. (February 27, 1995), "Lives without Father," *U.S. News & World Report.*

Moffitt, T.E. (1993) "Adolescence-Limited and Life-Course Persistent Antisocial Behavior: A Developmental Taxonomy," *Psychiatric Review* 100:674–701.

National Center for Health Statistics (June 1996), "HHS News," U.S. Department of Health and Human Services, Washington, DC.

National Commission on Children (1991), *Beyond Rhetoric: A New American Agenda for Children and Families,* Final Report of the National Commission on Children, Superintendent of Documents, U.W. Printing Office, Washington, D.C.

National Commission on Children (1993), *Just The Facts: A Summary of Children and Their Families,* Washington, DC.

National Institute on Alcohol Abuse and Alcoholism (July 1993), "Alcohol Alert #13, National Institute of Mental Health, U.S. Department of Health and Human Services, Washington, D.C.

National Institute on Alcohol Abuse and Alcoholism (January 1, 1994), "Special Focus: Alcohol-Related Birth Defects," *Alcohol Health and Research World,* National Institute of Mental Health, Department of Health and Human Services, Washington, D.C.

National Institutes of Health (1993), "Respiratory Health Effects of Passive Smoking: Cancer and Other Disorders," The Report of the U.S. Environmental Protection Agency, U.S. Department of Health and Human Services, Washington, D.C.

National Institute of Justice (1996), "Research Preview: The Cycle of Violence Revisited," *Research on Progress Seminar Series,* Washington, D.C.

Newsweek, "Gangstas' in the Ranks," July 24, 1995, p. 48.

New York Times (1993), "When Trouble Starts Young, special series, May 15–18; December 12–14, 25–26, 28–30.

Noble, E. (1993), *Primal Connections: How Our Experiences from Conception to Birth Influence Our Emotions, Behavior, and Health,* Fireside, New York.

Norton, S. (1985), "Toxic Responses of the Central Nervous System," in *Toxicology: The Basic Science of Poisons,* 3rd edition, Klassen, C.D.; Amdur, M.O.; and Doull, J., eds., Macmillan, New York, pp. 229–243.

Office of Juvenile Justice and Delinquency Prevention (1995), *Juvenile Offenders and Victims: A National Report,* U.S. Department of Justice, Washington, D.C.

Office of Juvenile Justice and Delinquency Prevention (1996), "Juvenile Offenders and Victims: 1996 Update on Violence," Fact Sheet #21, U.S. Department of Justice, Washington, D.C.

Office of Juvenile Justice and Delinquency Prevention (December 1994), "Violent Families and Youth Violence," U.S. Department of Justice, Washington, D.C.

Olds, D.; Pettit, L.M.; Robinson, J.; Eckenrode, J.; Kitzman, H.; Cole, R.; and Powers, J. (in press), "The Potential for Reducing Antisocial Behavior with a Program of Prenatal and Early Childhood Home Visitation," *Journal of Community Psychology.*

Ornay, A.; Michailevskaya, V.; and Lukashov, I. (1996), "The Developmental Outcome of Children Born to Heroin-Dependent Mothers, Raised at Home or Adopted," *Child Abuse and Neglect* 20(5):385–396.

Ornstein, R. (1993), *The Roots of the Self: Unraveling the Mystery of Who We Are*, HarperCollins, San Francisco.

Ostrow, R.J. (March 3, 1996), "Number of Juvenile Murders Is Soaring," *Los Angeles Times.*

Pear, R. (March 17, 1996), "Many States Fail to Meet Mandates on Child Welfare," *New York Times.*

Perry, B. (1997), "Incubated in Terror: Neurodevelopmental Factors in the Cycle of Violence," *Children in a Violent Society*, Osofsky, J.D. (ed.), Guilford Press, New York, pp. 124–149.

Perry, B. (in press), *Maltreated Children: Experience, Brain Development, and the Next Generation*, W. Norton, New York.

Perry, B. (1996), "Neurodevelopmental Adaptations to Violence: How Children Survive the Intragenerational Vortex of Violence," *Violence and Childhood Trauma: Understanding and Responding to the Effects of Violence on Young Children*, Gund Foundation, Cleveland.

Perry, B. (Spring 1993), "Neurodevelopment and the Neurophysiology of Trauma: Conceptual Considerations for Clinical Work with Maltreated Children," *The Advisor*, American Professional Society on the Abuse of Children, 6:1.

Perry, B. (in press), "Neurodevelopmental Aspects of Childhood Anxiety Disorders: Neurobiological Responses to Threat," *Textbook of Pediatric Neuropsychiatry*, Coffey, C.C., and Brumback, R.A., eds., American Psychiatric Press, Washington, D.C.

Perry, B.; Pollard, R.; Blakely, T.; Baker, W.; and Vigilante, D. (1995), "Childhood Trauma, the Neurobiology of Adaptation, and 'Use-Dependent' Development of the Brain: How 'States Become Traits,'" (Civitas Child Trauma Programs), *Infant Mental Health Journal* 16(4).

Phares, V. (May 1992), "Where's Poppa? The Relative Lack of Attention to the Role of Fathers in Child and Adolescent Psychopathology, *American Psychologist.*

Phares, V., and Compas, B.E. (1992), "The Role of Fathers in Child and Adolescent Psychopathology: Make Room for Daddy," *Psychological Bulletin* 111(3): 387–412.

Phelps, L. (January 1, 1995), "Psycho-Educational Outcomes of Fetal Alcohol Syndrome," *School Psychology Review*.

Powell, R., and Emory, E.K. (May 1996), "Birthweight and Gestational Age Outcomes from Antepartum Nonstress Test," Poster #25 presented at National Institute of Mental Health Conference, "Advancing Research on Developmental Plasticity: Integrating the Behavioral Science and the Neuroscience of Mental Health," Chantilly, Virginia.

Prager, K.; Malin, H.; Graves, C.; Speigler, D.; Richards, L.; and Placek, P. (1983), "Maternal Smoking and Drinking Behavior Before and During Pregnancy," *Health, United States,* U.S. Department of Health and Human Services, Washington, D.C.

Prothrow-Stith, D. (1991), *Deadly Consequences: How Violence Is Destroying Our Teenage Population and a Plan to Begin Solving the Problem,* HarperCollins, New York.

Purnick, J. (May 9, 1996), "Youth Crime: Should Laws Be Tougher?" *New York Times*.

Raine, A. (1993), *The Psychopathology of Crime: Criminal Behavior as a Clinical Disorder,* Academic Press, New York.

Raine, A.; Brennan, P.; Mednick, S. (1994), "Birth Complications Combined with Early Maternal Rejection at Age 1 Year Predispose to Violent Crime at Age 18 Years," *Archives of General Psychiatry* (American Medical Association) 51.

Restak, R. (1986), *The Infant Mind,* Doubleday, Garden City, New York.

Rich, S., and Dean, C.W. (1996), "A Previously Unexamined Source of Delinquency: Fetal Alcohol Effects: An Emerging Paradigm," presented to the Academy of Criminal Justice Sciences Conference, Las Vegas, Nevada.

Rosenbaum, A., and Hodge, S.K. (1989), "Head Injury and Marital Aggression," *American Journal of Psychiatry* 46:1048–1051.

Rothbart, M.K. (1981) "Measurement of Temperament in Infancy," *Child Development* 52:569–578.

Rothbart, M.K.; Attadi, S.A.; and Hershey, K.L. (1994), "Temperament and Social Behavior in Childhood," *Merill-Palmer Quarterly* 40:21–39.

Rutter, M. (1982), *Maternal Deprivation Reassessed,* 2nd edition, Penguin, Hammondsworth, England.

Rutter, M. (1988), *Studies of Psychosocial Risk: The Paper of Longitudinal Data,* Cambridge University Press, New York.

Rutter, M., and Rutter, M. (1993), *Developing Minds: Challenge and Continuity across the Life Span,* Basic Books, New York.

Sacks, M. (November 23, 1995), "Children Need Both Mom and Dad to Thrive, Studies Suggest," *The Seattle Times*.

Satterfield, J.; Swanson, J.; Schell, A.; and Lee, F. (1994), "Prediction of Antisocial Behavior in Attention-Deficit Hyperactivity Disorder Boys from Aggression/Defiance Scores," *Journal of American Academy of Child and Adolescent Psychiatry* 33(2):185–190.

Scerbo, A.S. (May 1996), "Aggression in Physically Abused Children: The Interactive Role of Emotion Regulation," paper presented at the NATO Advanced Study Institute conference, "Biosocial Bases of Violence: Theory and Research," Rhodes, Greece.

Scerbo, A.S., and Kolko, D.J. (1995), "Child Physical Abuse and Aggression: Preliminary Findings on the Role of Internalizing Problems," *Journal of American Academy of Child and Adolescent Psychiatry* 34(8):1060.

Scerbo, A.S., and Kolko, D.J. (1995), "Emotion Regulation as a Protective Factor in Childhood Aggression," paper presented at the 75th Annual Meeting of the Western Psychological Association, Los Angeles.

Scerbo, A.S., and Raine, A. (1992), *Neurotransmitters and Antisocial Behavior: a Meta-Analysis,* under review (cited in Raine, A. *Psychopathology of Crime* p. 345).

Schneider, M.L.; Roughton, E.C.; Moore, C.F.; and Clarke, A.S. (May 1996), "Timing of Prenatal Stress Affects Neurobehavioral and Endocrine Responses in Rhesus Monkey Offspring," Poster #28 presented at National Institute for Mental Health Conference, "Advancing Research on Plasticity: Integrating the Behavioral Science and the Neuroscience of Mental Health, Chantilly, Virginia.

Schore, A.N. (1994), *Affect Regulation and the Origin of the Self: The Neurobiology of Emotional Development,* Lawrence Erlbaum and Associates, Hillsdale, New Jersey.

Schore, A.N. (1996), "The Experience-Dependent Maturation of a Regulatory System in the Orbital Prefontral Cortex and the Origin of Developmental Psychopathology," *Development and Psychopathology* 8: 59–87.

Schorr L.B., and Schorr, D. (1988), *Within Our Reach: Breaking the Cycle of Disadvantage,* Doubleday, New York.

Share, L. (1994), *When Someone Speaks It Gets Lighter: Dreams and the Reconstruction of Infant Trauma,* Analytic Press, New Jersey.

Smith, J., and Prior, M. (1995), "Temperament and Stress Resilience in School Age Children: A Within Families Study, *Journal of American Academy of Child and Adolescent Psychiatry* 34(2):168.

Stevens, J. (August 1994), "Treating Violence as an Epidemic," *Technology Review* 97:23.

Streissguth, A.D. (1994), "A Long-Term Perspective of FAS," *Alcohol Health and Research World,* National Institute on Alcohol Abuse and Alcoholism, 18(1): 74–81.

Streissguth, A.D. (1982), "Maternal Alcoholism and the Outcome of Pregnancy," in *In the Beginning: Readings on Infancy,* Belsky, J., ed., Columbia University, New York.

Tamis-LeMonda, C., and Bornstein, M.H. (1987), "Is There a Sensitive Period in Human Mental Development?" in *Sensitive Periods in Development: Interdisciplinary Perspectives,* Bornstein, M.H., ed., Lawrence Erlbaum and Associates, Hillsdale, New Jersey.

Terr, L. (1990), *Too Scared to Cry: How Trauma Affects Our Children . . . and Ultimately Us All,* Basic Books, New York.

Terr, L. (1994), *Unchained Memories: True Stories of Traumatic Memories Lost and Found,* Basic Books, New York.

Thomas, P. (October 1, 1992), "A Father's Role," *Harvard Health Letter,* Harvard University, Cambridge, Massachusetts.

Thornberry, T. P. (1994), "Violent Families and Youth Violence" U.S. Dept. of Justice, Office of Juvenile Justice and Delinquency Prevention Fact Sheet #21.

Tremblay, R.E.; Pagani-Kurtz, L.; Masse, L.C.; Vitaro, F.; and Pihl, R.O. (1995), "A Bimodal Preventive Intervention for Disruptive Kindergarten Boys: Its Impact through Mid-Adolescence," *Journal of Consulting and Clinical Psychology* 63(4): 560–568.

Tronick, E., and Gianino, A.F., Jr. (1986), "The Transmission of Maternal Disturbance to the Infant," in *Maternal Depression and Infant Disturbance,* Tronick, E., and Field, T., eds., Jossey Bass, New York.

U.S. Department of Justice (September 17, 1996), "Victims Report 9% Fewer Crimes Last Year," Press Release, Washington, DC.

Van den Broom, D.C. (1994), "The Influence of Temperament and Mothering in Attachment and Exploration: An Experimental Manipulation of Sensitive Responses among Lower-Class Mothers with Irritable Infants," *Child Development* 65:1457–1477.

Verny, T., and Kelly, J. (1981), *The Secret Life of the Unborn Child,* Delta, New York.

Warner, E.E., and Smith, R.S. (1982), *Vulnerable, but Invincible: A Longitudinal Study of Resilient Children and Youth,* McGraw-Hill, New York.

Waters, E.; Vaughn, B.E.; Posada, G.; Kondo-Ikemura, K., eds. (1995), *Cultural and Cognitive Perspectives on Secure-Base Behavior and Working Models: New Growing Points Attachment Theory and Research,* Monographs of the Society for Research in Child Development, Serial 244, vol. 60, nos. 2–3.

Weiss, B.; Dodge, K.A.; Bales, J.E.; and Pettit, C.S. (1992), "Some Consequences of Early Harsh Discipline: Child Aggression and a Maladaptive Social Information Processing Style," *Child Development* 63:1321–1335.

Wellington, N., and Rieder, M.J. (1993), "Attitudes and Practices Regarding Analgesia or Newborn Circumcision," *Pediatrics* 94(4):541–543.

Widom, C.S. (1989), "Does Violence Beget Violence?" *APA Psychological Bulletin* 104(1):3–28.

Wren, C. (December 20, 1996), "Adolescent Drug Use Continues to Rise," *New York Times.*

Yogman, M.W.; Kindlon, D.; Earls, F. (1995), "Father Involvement and Cognitive/Behavioral Outcomes of Preterm Infants," *Journal of American Academy of Child and Adolescent Psychiatry* 34(1):58–66.

Zametkin, A.J. (February 1996), "An Overview of Clinical Issues in ADHD," *ADHD Report,* 4(1):5–18.

Zero to Three (1992), *Heartstart: The Emotional Foundations of School Readiness,* National Center for Clinical Infant Programs, Arlington, Virginia.

Zigler, E.F., and Lang, M.E. (1991), *Child Care Choices: Balancing the Needs of Children, Families, and Society,* Free Press, New York.

Zoccolillo, M.; Pickles, A.; Quinton, O.; and Rutter, M. (1992), "The Outcome of Childhood Conduct Disorder; Implications for Defining Adult Personality Disorder and Conduct Disorder," *Psychological Medicine* 22:971–986.

Zuckerman, B. (1989), "Effects of Marijuana and Cocaine Use on Fetal Growth," *New England Journal of Medicine* 320:762–768.

Index

364